D1446963

Distributed Computing Systems
Synchronization, Control and Communication

Distributed Computing Systems
Synchronization, Control and Communication

Edited by

Y. PAKER

Mathematics and Computing Division
Polytechnic of Central London, London, UK

J.-P. VERJUS

IRISA-INRIA, Campus Universitaire
de Beaulieu, Rennes, France

1983

ACADEMIC PRESS
A Subsidiary of Harcourt Brace Jovanovich, Publishers
London   New York
Paris   San Diego   San Francisco   São Paulo
Sydney   Tokyo   Toronto

ACADEMIC PRESS INC. (LONDON) LTD.
24/28 Oval Road
London NW1

United States Edition published by
ACADEMIC PRESS INC.
111 Fifth Avenue
New York, New York 10003

British Library Cataloguing in Publication Data
Distributed computing systems.
 1. Electronic data processing   Congresses
 I. Paker, Y.   II. Verjus, J.P.
 001.64   QA76.9.D5

 ISBN 0-12-543970-9

 LCCCN 83-70947

Printed in Great Britain by
Whitstable Litho Ltd, Whitstable, Kent
from camera-ready copy supplied by
Publication Preparation Service,
Penicuik, Scotland

CONTRIBUTORS

ABRAMSKY, S. *Computer Systems Laboratory, Queen Mary College, Mile End Road, London E1 4NS, UK.*

BANATRE, J.-P. *IRISA-INRIA, Campus Universitaire de Beaulieu, Avenue du Général Leclerc, 35042 Rennes - Cédex, France.*

BANINO, J.-S. *INRIA, Rocquencourt B.P. 105, 78150 Le Chesnay, France.*

BORNAT, R. *Computer Systems Laboratory, Queen Mary College, Mile End Road, London E1 4NS, UK.*

BOZYIGIT, M. *Polytechnic of Central London, 115 New Cavendish Street, London W1R 8AL, UK.*

CAMPBELL, R.H. *Department of Computer Science, University of Illinois at Champaign-Urbana, Urbana, Illinois 61801, USA.*

CARVALHO, O.S.F. *Institut de Programmation, Université Pierre et Marie Curie - Paris VI, 4 Place Jussieu, 75230 Paris, Cédex 05, France.*

DANG, M. *Laboratoire IMAG, B.P. 68, 38402 Saint Martin d'Hères, Cédex, France.*

ENGLISH, H. *Polytechnic of Central London, 115 New Cavendish Street, London W1R 8AL, UK.*

HERMAN, D. *IRISA-INSA, Campus Universitaire de Beaulieu, Avenue du Général Leclerc, 35042 Rennes - Cédex, France.*

JACKSON, K. *System Designers Ltd, Systems House, 1 Pembroke Broadway, Camberley, Surrey GU15 3XH, UK.*

JENSEN, E.D. *Department of Computer Science/Electrical Engineering, Carnegie-Mellon University, Pittsburgh, PA 15213, USA.*

LAUER, P.E. *Computing Laboratory, The University of Newcastle-upon-Tyne, Claremont Tower, Claremont Road, Newcastle-upon-Tyne NE1 7RU, UK.*

MAZARE, G. *Laboratoire IMAG, B.P. 53X, 38041 Grenoble, Cédex, France.*

MICHEL, G. *CNET/CNS B.P. 42, 38240 Meylan, France.*

MORGAN, C. *Programming Research Group, Oxford University Computing Laboratory, 45 Banbury Road, Oxford OX2 6PE, UK.*

NORTHCUTT, J.D. *Department of Computer Science/Electrical Engineering, Carnegie-Mellon University, Pittsburgh, PA 15213, USA.*

PAKER, Y. *Polytechnic of Central London, 115 New Cavendish Street, London W1R 8AL, UK.*

RASHID, R.F. *Department of Computer Science/Electrical Engineering, Carnegie-Mellon University, Pittsburgh, PA 15213, USA.*

ROUCAIROL, G. *Institut de Programmation, Université Pierre et Marie Curie — Paris VI, 4 Place Jussieu, 75230 Paris, Cédex 05, France.*

SHA, L. *Department of Computer Science/Electrical Engineering, Carnegie-Mellon University, Pittsburgh, PA 15213, USA.*

VERJUS, J.-P. *IRISA-INRIA, Campus Universitaire de Beaulieu, Avenue du Général Leclerc, 35042 Rennes — Cédex, France.*

This text is the outcome of an International Seminar held at
the Polytechnic of Central London (PCL), London, UK, 20-24th
September 1982, organized jointly by the Institut National de
Recherche en Informatique et Automatique (INRIA) and the
Polytechnic. A similar advanced course was held the previous
year at the Institut de Recherche pour Informatique et Systèmes Aléatoires (IRISA), Rennes, France by INRIA for French
participants. Out of 22 papers presented to the International
Seminar, these proceedings include 13, many revised and re-
edited. This book is aimed at both researchers and prac-
titioners.

The technological trends of the last decade or so have
made the building of distributed computer systems more attractive and their usage more widespread. Therefore, we observe
much interest in the formal, conceptual aspects and also in
the methodology for building and understanding such systems.
The Distributed Computer Systems Programme launched by the
Science and Engineering Research Council in the UK in 1979 is
a case in point to demonstrate the interest and importance
attached to this field. Similarly, in France there is a co-
ordinated research programme covering the same field supported
by the Centre National de la Recherche Scientifique (CNRS).

It is hoped that this book will serve a useful purpose in
the understanding of distributed computer systems and the
underlying parallelism. The collection of papers included
reflects some of the current work going on in several research
centres. No claim is made, however, that the text is comprehensive, nor that it covers all the topics with sufficient
breadth or depth. Indeed, considering the vastness of the
topic, this would be an impossible task within the bounds of
a single book.

To narrow the scope of the subject, a distributed computer
system is defined as consisting of a number of nodes interconnected by communication lines, hence there is no memory
sharing. Furthermore, delay times due to communications are
significant with respect to processing times. In order to

treat the theoretical and practical problems of synchronization and control in distributed computer systems, the papers
in the text are presented in three groups.
    The first group includes articles to cover experiences,
specification and analysis of parallelism in distributed computer systems. In the first paper, J.-P. Verjus introduces the
concept of synchronization between concurrent or co-operating
processes by means of a resource allocation example. This
illustrates the three different approaches to solving the
distributed synchronization problem by distributing, splitting
or duplicating state variables. The next paper by L. Sha *et
al.* introduces a new relational model of data consistency to
deal with operating system situations where the serialization
model is not always applicable. This is done in the context
of the Archons project global operating system replicated at
separate nodes of a loosely coupled multi-computer. D. Herman
treats the control of synchronization by first using a high
level language which is independent of location of processes.
This then leads to the installation of a local process controller at each site which co-operates by managing approximate
representation of the state of the system. The paper of O.S.
F. Carvalho and G. Roucairol follows a similar line and introduces a systematic mechanism localized at each node to define
protocols that ensure correctness of distributed algorithms.
C. Morgan introduces a formal specification language using
mainly the mathematical set theory notation. A communication
system is presented as a vehicle to introduce the language
formalism and the notation. P. Lauer presents a conceptual
apparatus called COSY to formulate the analysis of those
aspects of systems arising from their concurrency and yet
capable of being readily translated into practical terms. The
text is written using a new construct called "dossier" which
also includes its own definition. J.-P. Banatre's paper is
concerned with the presentation of some co-operation schemes
and of their use in the construction of parallel programs.
    The second group of papers covers the issues related to
programming languages and their extensions. S. Abramsky and
R. Bornat's paper presents a dialect of Pascal, called Pascal-
m, designed to facilitate type-secure programming of systems
of communicating processes, based on mailboxes. R. Campbell's
paper describes another extension to Pascal where the previously introduced Path expressions are extended by features
for distributed programming. MASCOT described by K. Jackson
is a formalism based on network diagrams used to express
software structure of a real-time parallel processing system.
This leads to the extended Pascal notation PACE.
    The third group of papers addresses itself to more practi-
cal aspects and implementations. The CHORUS project described

by J.-S. Banino introduces the concept of "actors" for message
passing to support execution of distributed applications. A
local area network designed for real-time industrial applications is described in the paper of M. Dang, G. Mazaré and
G. Michel. The final paper covers the MICROSS system used for
interactive graphic modelling and performance evaluation of
distributed computer structures developed by Y. Paker,
M. Bozyigit and H. English.
   We wish to acknowledge the support received from the
sponsors of the International Seminar, namely the PCL and
INRIA, and the help received from the US Army European Office
and the SERC Distributed Systems Programme.

Editors

London, UK
Rennes, France
September 1983

CONTENTS

Contributors   v

Preface   vii

PART 1

Expression, Specification and Analysis of Synchronization of
    Distributed Processes

Synchronization in Distributed Systems:
    An Informal Introduction
    J.-P. Verjus   3

Distributed Co-operating Processes and Transactions
    L. Sha, E.D. Jensen, R.F. Rashid and J.D. Northcutt   23

Towards a Systematic Approach to Implement Distributed
    Control of Synchronization
    D. Herman   51

Assertion, Decomposition and Partial Correctness of
    Distributed Control Algorithms
    O.S.F. Carvalho and G. Roucairol   67

Specification of a Communication System
    C. Morgan   93

Computer System Dossiers
    P.E. Lauer   109

Co-operation Schemes for Parallel Programming
    J.-P. Banatre   149

PART 2

Programming Languages for Distributed Processes

Pascal-m: a Language for Loosely Coupled
    Distributed Systems
    S. Abramsky and R. Bornat   163

Distributed Path Pascal
    R.H. Campbell   191

MASCOT and Multiprocessor Systems
  K. Jackson   225

PART 3

Local Area Networks and Distributed Systems

Architecture of the CHORUS Distributed System
  J.-S. Banino   251

Local Area Networks for Distributed Process
  Control Systems
  M. Dang, G. Mazaré and G. Michel   265

MICROSS: Graphics Aided Simulation of Distributed
  Computer Systems
  M. Bozyigit, H. English and Y. Paker   285

Subject Index   303

Part 1

Expression, Specification and Analysis of Synchronization of Distributed Processes

Synchronization in Distributed Systems: an Informal Introduction

Jean-Pierre Verjus

1. INTRODUCTION

In a distributed information system, there are two principal reasons for providing synchronization tools: concurrency or co-operation between processes. These interactions require the exchange of data which are regulated by means of mutual exclusion to shared variables in a centralized system, but are made through communication channels in a distributed system. In this presentation, we introduce the synchronization problem by means of a resource allocation example. We examine the three approaches to solving the problems of distributed control by (1) distributing, (2) splitting, or (3) duplicating the variables associated with the constraints of synchronization.

A distributed system is a set of separate sites. Each site has its own memory and there is no common memory among the sites. The sites are interconnected by communication channels. The following discussion is based on the following three assumptions:

(H1)   When messages are sent (through a communication channel) they are neither altered nor lost.

(H2)   For any two sites i and j, the order in which i sends messages to j is identical to the order in which j receives them from i.

(H3)   The failure (or withdrawal) of a site is detected and signalled to all sites which attempt to communicate with that site.

In a distributed information system there are two principal

reasons for providing synchronization tools:

1) Concurrency - Individual processes, even those that
    belong to independent applications, may need to enter a
    state of concurrency either to share access to system
    resources (of a limited number of types) or just as im-
    portantly, to control access to shared data.

2) Co-operation - Processes that belong to the same appli-
    cation can co-operate for proper execution of the appli-
    cation.

3) (Concurrency and co-operation between several processes
require the exchange of data.) In centralized systems such
exchanges are regulated by means of mutual exclusion to
shared (critical) variables in common memory. (In a distributed
system, these exchanges are made through communication channels.)

1.1. Definition and Example

Consider a system of processes to be synchronized. The processes are considered to proceed in discrete steps, each step
producing an event. The event can be local to the process and
imperceptible to the rest of the system, or on the contrary
it may involve the problem of synchronization just posed. The
latter is termed an observable event or a synchronization
point. In consideration of such events, the following definition is offered:

> Synchronization is the regulation of the evolution of
> concurrent processes, and subsequently of the occur-
> rence of observable events, as a function of the his-
> tory of events in the system of processes.

For our abstract model, we only consider those systems in
which the duration between two events can be ignored. Each
process is represented by a succession of events. The logical
synchronization (as opposed to real-time synchronization) of
a set of processes, each of which has reached some synchronization point, consists of bringing the processes into con-
cordance with the rules governing the behaviour of the particular system. The role of the synchronization monitor is to
order the set of events produced by the concurrent processes,
that is to schedule and regulate the steps of the different
processes with respect to:

1) sequentiality within each process, and
2) the constraints (rules) of synchronization among processes.

The synchronization monitor under consideration here is an
abstraction which functions as an ideal observer. We can

assume that the events observed and regulated by the monitor
are of null duration. The ordering which is created by the
monitor can be represented as a simple sequence of synchronization points. This sequence will be referred to as an event
trace.

For example, consider the following system based on the
actions at a parking lot. The cars are the processes that
compete to occupy parking spaces. Each of these processes can
be represented by the following sequence of events:

e - Entry.   A car gains entry into the lot.
p - Parking.   A car parks in an empty space.
d - Departure. A car leaves the lot.

Only e and d are externally observable events. For a parking lot with N spaces, a legal event trace is a sequence of
e's and d's such that in any prefix of the sequence:

1) the number of e's is necessarily greater than or equal to
    the number of d's, by virtue of the model, and
2) the number of e's must be kept less than or equal to the
    number of d's plus N, in order not to overfill the lot.

For example, of the following event traces, allowing $N = 3$,
" $e\ e\ d\ e\ e\ d$ " is legal, but
" $e\ e\ e\ e\ d$ " is illegal.

1.2. The Synchronization Monitor

Let us consider an actual monitor which implements the abstract expressions of synchronization constraints, such as
those posed in the parking lot example. The monitor oversees
the occurrence of observable events, and is empowered to stop
and restart processes when they reach synchronization points,
so as to guarantee that at any time the effective event trace
remains legal. Thus in the above example, if the monitor has
produced the legal event trace

" $e\ e\ e$ "

then it must block any process which attempts to cross synchronization point e, since there is no space left in the
lot. It continues blocking this synchronization request until
one of the three processes which has crossed point e requests
to cross synchronization point d, i.e. until a space becomes
available.

The synchronization monitor distinguishes among three
classes of actions:

1) Request for synchronization - When a process arrives at a
    point in its execution where it requires synchronization
    with the other processes in the system (i.e. it reaches

an observable event) it issues a request to the monitor.
The monitor stores these requests (see 3 immediately
below).

2) Authorization - The monitor authorizes blocked processes
   to continue execution, and only then does the process
   officially cross the synchronization point at which it
   had been blocked.

3) Bookkeeping - The monitor performs a limited number of
   actions to keep internal records which represent the history and current state of the set of processes it oversees. This bookkeeping can be accomplished either before
   or after the monitor grants authorization.

Thus it is the authorizations which will be represented in
the event trace, and which will delimit the occurrences of
observable events.

In our example, the monitor corresponds in reality to the
attendant who guards the sole outlet of the lot (or perhaps
to a micro-processor controlled barrier). The attendant keeps
a record of all arrivals and departures, and can thereby
effectively implement the synchronization of these events in
accordance with the constraints of the system.

1.3. Problem of Perceiving and Scheduling Events

The perception of requests by the monitor, and the perception
of authorizations by the processes, can be delayed from the
actual occurrence of the observable event. This can result
from propagation delays inherent in information systems (especially distributed ones) and/or from the existence of some
intermediate communication medium).

In the simple example above, this delay can be illustrated
as follows: even if there is only one outlet and one attendant, the latter has only partial knowledge of the state of
the system. He can think that the lot is full and refuse
entry to waiting cars, when in reality there may be some cars
which have left their spaces on the way out, but have not
reached the outlet. There is thus a time lag between the
actual state of events in the system and the perception of
the state.

If the monitor is centralized on a single processor, it is
possible to construct a definitive event trace of authorizations. On the contrary, if the monitor is distributed over
several processors without a common clock, one must prove
that the combination of event traces on the individual processors will appear to the outside observer as identical to
his perception of the single overall event trace.

Thus if there are several outlets and attendants for the
parking lots, each attendant becomes aware of the actions of

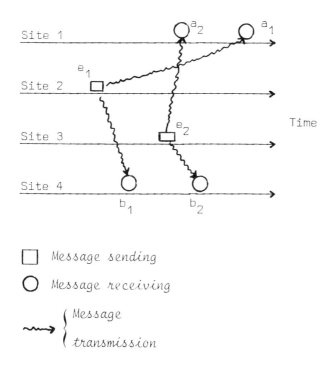

FIG. 1 *Effect of delays in the message transmission in a distributed system.*

the others only after some delay. This introduces a second kind of uncertainty due to the multiplicity of decision-making centres. An attendant can think that no more spaces remain when another attendant has just logged the departure of a car but has not yet notified the other attendants of the availability of the space. Similarly, several attendants might allocate the same space to cars waiting at their respective outlets if they have not properly co-ordinated the exchange of information among themselves.

In the latter case, one can imagine a solution in which the attendants are linked by a telephone system. But this does not conform to the characteristics of the communication channels in a distributed system. Indeed, the delay in the transmission of a message in a distributed system is:

1) greater than the time which separates two observable events of the same process,
2) variable, depending on the moment under consideration, with a potentially significant range of values, and

3) variable from one pair of machines to another pair (where
   a pair consists of a sender and a receiver).

   Two important conclusions are drawn from the above:

(C1) At any given time, a process occurring at one site can
     have only approximate knowledge of the state of any
     other site.

(C2) Even in consideration of H2 above, any two observable
     events in a system can be perceived as occurring in a
     different order by different sites. Referring to Fig. 1,
     at site 1 the event trace $a2$ $a1$ represents the perceived
     order of observable events $e1$ $e2$, whereas the perception
     at site 2 produces there the event trace $b1$ $b2$. Without
     an adequate tool which can guarantee a consistent order-
     ing among the sites, it will be difficult to reconstruct
     the true and legal trace of events in a distributed
     system.

1.4. Consistency, Deadlock, Fairness and Priority

Finally, in order to resolve the problems of synchronization
among processes, very often two complementary objectives must
be guaranteed:

1) that the system will function consistently (e.g. legal
   usage of resources: in the example, no car is allowed
   into the lot if there is no space available), and that
   the system will prevent deadlock;
2) that the system will either treat processes with equality,
   i.e. fairness (not to allow a car to wait for entrance
   while more recent arrivals are granted entry), or on the
   other hand that the system will establish privileges,
   i.e. priority (to allow a higher priority vehicle to enter
   ahead of other vehicles, regardless of the order of arrival at the inlets).

   The rules of synchronization which ensure the first objective do not usually require that the identity of the blocked
processes be known to the monitor. However in the second objective, the rules do function according to either the ident-
ities of the processes themselves, or at least the categories
of the processes (ordinary vs high priority vehicle).

   In the following sections, we shall briefly present the
main mechanisms which have been designed to resolve the problems just presented.

2. EXPRESSION OF A PROBLEM OF RESOURCE ALLOCATION

The example of control of the arrivals and departures in a
parking lot with N spaces is very representative of resource

allocation problems frequently encountered in information
systems. For the sake of unity, we will simply deal with this
one type of problem, considering it to be a good illustration
of a whole class of related problems in distributed systems.

Consider the processes which must cross synchronization
points e and d (analogous to the acquisition and release of
a resource).

Given the following definitions:

$\#e$: the number of times synchronization point e has been
crossed by the processes in the system,

$\#d$: the number of times synchronization point d has been
crossed by the processes,

an abstract expression of the constraints of synchronization
is

$$\#e - \#d \leq N \qquad (1)$$

Note that the expression

$$\#e \geq \#d \qquad (2)$$

is always true by virtue of the model, and thus no constraint
need be established to ensure that it remains true.

To implement (1), events e and d are counted in variables
E and D. The monitor must then execute the sequences (ε) or
(δ), whenever a process reaches synchronization point e or d:

$(\varepsilon):$ *wait* $E - D < N$; $E := E + 1$
$(\delta):$ $D := D + 1$

For example, if several processes arrive simultaneously at
d, the monitor must guarantee the consistency of operations
δ, by executing each operation δ in mutual exclusion (we say
also that these operations are serialized). For the same
reasons, the processes must be serialized, when reaching point
e. However, the operations ε and δ are independent and need
not be mutually exclusive (serialized) with respect to each
other. This is no longer the case if we adopt a single variable scheme, letting Y represent the number of free spaces:

$$Y = N - E + D \qquad (3)$$

Then, both operations of the monitor update the same
variable:

$(\varepsilon'):$ *wait* $Y > 0$; $Y := Y - 1$
$(\delta'):$ $Y := Y + 1$

In this case, all the operations of the monitor, both of
ε' and δ', must be serialized and executed in mutual exclusion.

We observe that a monitor implementing the operations ε'/δ',
can be represented by a single process which is invoked by
automobile processes reaching synchronization point e and

point d, one event at a time. On the other hand, a monitor
implementing ε/δ can be split into two independent monitor
processes: one to serialize and perform (ε) operations, and
another to serialize and perform (δ) operations. These two
processes co-operate insofar as they share variable S, according to the current model of the producer-consumer problem.

In a centralized system (one outlet in our example) events
e and d can be registered separately in variables E and D, or
together in a single variable Y. The monitor must then employ
a mutual exclusion mechanism for the critical variables, i.e.
one for E and one for D or else just one for Y.

If the system is distributed, the events e and d are not
necessarily observable on the same sites. To implement the
constraint of abstract expression (1), two solutions can be
put forward.

Centralized Control – This trivial solution consists in
grouping on a single site the variables and instructions
necessary for synchronization. The co-ordinated execution (of
concurrent processes) is realized by using a single synchronization monitor process. Other processes located on the various sites send messages to this monitor process. This is
exactly the same situation as in the centralized system (very
little parallelism, and the central site must be inherently
reliable).

Distributed Control – Distributing control over P sites
is equivalent to having p monitor processes. We will examine
here three approaches to solving the problems of distributed
control. They differ from each other in the representation of
the variables associated with the abstract expressions (the
constraints of synchronization). The approaches are, in a
nutshell:

1)   distribute the variables among the monitors,
2)   split each of the variables into p components, or
3)   duplicate the variables into p instances, distribute the
     copies, and ensure their consistency.

3. DISTRIBUTION OF SYNCHRONIZATION VARIABLES

Suppose the parking lot has an inlet and an outlet. In other
words, a monitor process (the attendant) keeps a record of
the entries, $E = \#e$, at Site 1, and another monitor records
the departures, $D = \#d$, at Site 2. Before a car is permitted
to enter (i.e. a process allowed to pass synchronization point
e), the Site 1 monitor must first impose the precondition:

$$(E - D) < N \qquad (4)$$

The site 1 attendant knows precisely the value of E. The Site
2 monitor knows the exact value of D, and can transmit this

value to the first attendant. Considering the transmission delays, the first attendant's value for D lags behind the actual value of D. This lagging representation of D will be referred to as D', such that at all times, $D' \leq D$. If the entrance attendant verifies at Site 1 the precondition

$$(E - D') < N \tag{5}$$

for all cars seeking entry, then condition (4) is automatically satisfied, and the invariant (1) cannot be rendered false.

The preceding example shows that for some cases, it is possible to distribute the variables. In order to enable the monitors to take action, some of the variables may be duplicated. An approximate but controlled consistency between two instances of a variable must be ensured.

Consider instances of the abstract expression

$$\sum C_i \, X_i < K \tag{6}$$

where the C_i and K are constant, and the X_i are monotonically increasing (event counter), as a function of events over time.

Given that for each X_i there exists a site, the site of origin, where the value of that X_i is known exactly, we seek to install the X_i counters in the other sites as X'_i counters, such that the following property P is assured:

P: Replacing the X_i counters with their X'_i images in evaluating the abstract expression always yields a more stringent constraint than evaluating the expression using the original X_i counters. The new condition includes the condition (6).

A more stringent constraint, when satisfied, guarantees that the original constraint is satisfied. This stronger constraint for our example is detailed below.

3.1. Delayed Updating

The technique of delayed updating corresponds to the example informally developed above. The sites of origin send messages to signal their incrementations of their X_i counters. The images of the counters, written as $m(X_i)$, are updated after a certain delay, so that the equation

$$m(X_i) \leq X_i$$

is always true.

The X_i counters with negative coefficients C_i can be replaced in any evaluation of an abstract expression by their corresponding images $m(X_i)$. Since the $m(X_i)$ images are always less than or equal to their X_i originals, a stronger or equivalent constraint is obtained.

3.2. Anticipatory Updating

The X_i counters with positive coefficients C_i can be replaced
by their $M(X_i)$ images if the latter are greater than or equal
to the exact values of their corresponding X_i variables. By
analogy to the management of the $m(X_i)$ images, one can imagine
a procedure for anticipatory updating. Each site of origin
managing an X_i variable can send messages in anticipation of
K incrementations of X_i. These messages take the form –
"Request of Credit: K units".

On receiving such a message, a site which manages an image
of X_i must perform as soon as possible the update action

$$M(X_i) := M(X_i) + K$$

As soon as this update is accomplished (which should be signalled back to the site of origin), the X_i variable can be
incremented K times (of 1) before it is necessary to send out
another set of "Request of Credit" messages. Clearly, the
condition

$$M(X_i) \geq X_i$$

is always true, ensuring that property $P1$ is satisfied for
the X_i with positive coefficients.

Remarks:

1) The management of monotonically decreasing counters
    follows directly analogous rules.
2) To limit the growth of counters E and D, their incremen-
    tation is accomplished modulo K, where K is sufficiently
    large. In our example, it will suffice for K to equal $2N$.
    Constraint (2) then becomes either

$$0 \leq (E - D) < N \quad or \quad N < (D - E)$$

3) In the case of delayed updating, hypothesis H2 is not
    indispensable.
4) The technique of anticipatory updating can introduce
    deadlock, as is the case for example with the expression

$$a + b \leq 1$$

    where a and b are respectively the observable events on
    two separate sites. Deadlock can be avoided thanks to a
    technique of management of demands of credit given in D.
    Herman's paper.

3.3. Bibliographic Comment

It was Bochman [1] who introduced the notion of regular

expressions in the context of delayed updating of synchronization counters. Herman, in his paper included in this text,
has studied the management of approximate representations in
anticipatory updating considering the existence of possible
site failures. The general aspects of distributing synchronization expressions have been developed by André, Herman and
Verjus [2]. Finally, Carvalho and Roucairol [3] have proposed
a systematic procedure for transforming a global assertion
into a protocol among communicating sites.

4. SPLITTING THE SYNCHRONIZATION VARIABLES

Assume in the example of the parking lot that there are p
outlets, each functioning as both an entrance and exit. This
results in

$$E = E0 + E1 + \ldots + Ep\text{-}1$$
$$D = D0 + D1 + \ldots + Dp\text{-}1$$

Let E_i and D_i represent the number of entries and departures
which are recorded by attendant i at site i. The methods developed above can help to build techniques for managing the
$2p$ variables, however, these techniques spawn complex algorithms and a heavy volume of message traffic.

  Another procedure is to distribute the parking spaces among
the p monitors (attendants). Each monitor i has Y_i places at
his disposal for allotting credits of free space. In the course
of events the initial distribution of free spaces will change,
so some monitors may refuse entry to their outlets even though
other monitors have free spaces available under their control.
A partial remedy of this situation is to periodically modify
the distribution of credits.

  Initially we have

$$Y = \sum_{i=0}^{p-1} Y_i = N$$

  Let R_i represent the number of credits which attendant i
periodically relinquishes to attendant $i+1$ mod p. The number
of free spaces at any given time is given by

$$Y = N + D - E = \sum_{i=0}^{p-1} (Y_i + R_i)$$

When the message R_i reaches attendant j ($j = i+1$ mod p),
this attendant adds to his allotment of credits:

$$Y_j := Y_j + R_i$$

On sending the message R_i, attendant i subtracts from his

14   J.-P. VERJUS

allotment of credits:

$$Y_i := Y_i - R_i$$

When a car attempts to enter outlet i, the attendant allows
it to pass if $Y_i > 0$; otherwise the attendant blocks the car
and waits for one of two events to occur:

1) the departure of a car from his outlet, resulting in
   $Y_i := Y_i + 1$, or
2) the arrival of a redistribution message from his neighbouring attendant h $(h = i - 1 \bmod p)$, which message when
   received results in $Y_i := Y_i + R_h$.

This example exhibits the possible decomposition of a
variable into the local variables in each of the monitor processes, and the variables used in redistribution messages
which circulate among monitor processes.

This procedure is analogous to the "isarithmic" control
proposed by Price [4] for controlling the admittance of messages into a computer network. This protocol poses a problem
of equity among the requesting processes when the number of
available places becomes small.

This technique of exploding a variable utilizes the mechanisms of distribution of the variables of an expression
(see Section 3 above) with the difference that the initial
expression was not defined in terms of a single abstract
global variable, but in terms of n variables chosen to be
distributed. The bibliographic references for this subject
are the same as for the preceding paragraph.

5. MAINTAINING CONSISTENCY OF A VARIABLE SHARED BY P PROCESSES

As before, we refer to the parking lot example with p outlets.
One possible mode of co-operation among attendants is to implement exclusive use of the variable Y, the number of free
spaces. One simple solution is to organize the outlets in a
virtual ring such that each outlet i is tied to a predecessor
outlet from which it receives messages, and to a successor
outlet, to which it sends messages (see Fig. 2). We refer to
the ring as virtual in order to denote that the relationship
between two outlets is logical, and can be physically implemented using any type of communication channel (from a single
wire to a general network).

A first solution is to have p attendants, one at each outlet, and a traffic director. The traffic director moves from
attendant to attendant along the ring and maintains the value
of Y. When this director arrives at an outlet where a car is
waiting, and the value of Y is positive, the car can be authorized to enter. Then Y must be decremented by 1. Ideally,

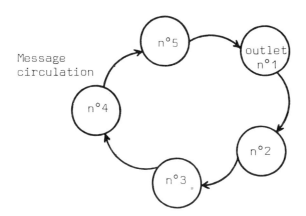

Message circulation

FIG. 2   *Virtual Ring*

the departures should only occur when the traffic director is present with variable Y (in order that Y may be incremented). But in practice, the attendant can allow cars to exit if he remembers the number of departures which occur between appearances of the traffic director.

With this solution only one outlet serves at any given moment as an entrance (the outlet where the director currently resides). The rate of arrivals is determined by the speed with which the traffic director circulates around the ring. It might be faster to make all the cars enter through a single outlet, except of course that this outlet might become inoperative. In this solution the trade-off between performance and reliability must be analysed with respect to the demands of each particular system.

In the above solution the traffic director determines the order in which the cars enter. This is different from the order in which the cars arrive at the outlets. Furthermore, there is no guarantee that a car waiting at outlet i will gain entrance. This problem would arise if every time the director reached a given entrance the value of Y happened to be zero. This situation is called infinite wait or starvation. It is therefore necessary to build a more equitable solution which ensures a fair and ordered service to the outlets.

In a centralized system, this ordered service is achieved either by means of the mechanism of mutual exclusion on a critical variable (Y in the example), the existence of a unique waiting list, or by having a single common system clock. In a distributed system, no single timing source can be postulated; thus, it is necessary to impose a strict and total order in the system. We will study this approach in

Section 6.

When such an order exists, each car is assigned an order
number when it arrives at an outlet (entrance or exit). Thus
it is only necessary to circulate a single instance of Y to
assure consistency. In effect, it is the strict and total
order which assures mutual exclusion for access to Y. Of
course, the mechanism of strict and total ordering requires
a communication protocol among the attendants, in order that
the attendant with order number $i+1$ can know when order number
i has finished its operations. The use of this protocol can
also be used to communicate value of Y. As will be seen, such
a protocol can be based on the principle of broadcasting. An
instance of variable Y is maintained at each site. As soon as
an attendant grants entrance or exit to a car, he broadcasts
to all the other attendants the order number of the car and
the type of operation performed. This broadcast message in-
sures that variable Y can be updated by the other attendants.
The attendant who has the next order number, following the
strict and total order, is the one who is allowed to perform
the next operation.

Evidently, in this example, the departure operations do
not necessarily have to be ordered. At each request for departure, an attendant can let the car go immediately and
broadcast the transaction to the other attendants. Let this
broadcast operation for incrementing Y be denoted: " +1 ".

In this case, the instances of variable Y are not strictly
identical, but remain consistent. If attendant i has just
allowed a car to enter (because it was his turn for an entrance), he will have performed the following operation on
$Y(i)$, his copy of Y.

Decrement $Y(i)$ by 1
Broadcast " -1, Order-Number"

Simultaneously, attendant j may have let a car exit and
performed the operation

Increment $Y(j)$ by 1
Broadcast " +1 "

In this case, $Y(i)$ will have been first decremented then
incremented. For $Y(j)$, it is just the opposite order of
operations. As for the other instances of Y, they may undergo
either order of operations, according to propagations delays.
The order of these two operations are not crucial because the
operations are commutative. This is not always the case, as
we shall see in the next example.

Assume the parking lot has four attendants, A, B, C and D,
such that at time zero, there are 100 free spaces in the lot.
Let three of these attendants make space allocations and

Order of arrival	Request	Value	Request	Value	Request	Value	Request	Value
0		100		100		100		100
1	M1	120	M1	120	M3	90	M2	90
2	M3	108	M2	110	M1	110	M3	81
3	M2	98	M3	99	M2	100	M1	101

FIG. 3 *Example of inconsistent evolution of initially consistent copies.*

communicate with each other by means of the three messages:

M1:   20 more spaces are free
M2:   10 more spaces are occupied
M3:   10% of the available spaces are now unavailable so that
        parking lot cleaning can be done on them.

Figure 3 shows that if the constraint for a strict and total
ordering of the arrival of messages is not met, the resulting
copies of Y at A, B, C and D will be inconsistent. If each
attendant maintains an instance variable representing the
current state of space allocation, then in order for these instances to remain consistent, all the attendants must execute
the update sequences in exactly the same order.

The protocols which assure consistent management of the
state of a system of communicating processes have been described by Herman and Verjus [5] as a system which manages
multiple copies of data, and by Ricart and Agrawala [6] as
well as Kessels [7] as a system of arbitration (or mutual
exclusion) among processes.

6. TOTAL ORDERING OF EVENTS

A strict and total order can be assured by using a single
monitor which assigns a unique number to each incoming request
for an operation. The monitor sends this number to the site
making the request. This solution is not sufficiently robust
to account for the withdrawal of the privileged site (where
the monitor process resides). Furthermore, the system is inefficient since the monitor is a bottle neck. Thus it is
necessary to ensure the order by the co-operation of the

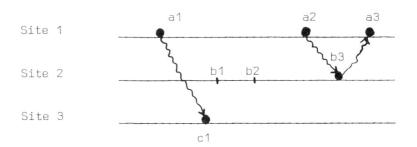

FIG. 4 *Event ordering between the events of a distributed system.*

various processes involved.

This strict and total order must encompass two notions of precedence:

1) precedence between any two events in the same process (implicit in the specification of a process)
2) precedence of the message-sending event of a process with respect to the message-receiving event of another process. (This is necessary because, otherwise, by transitivity, the first rule of precedence would be violated).

At each site, synchronization is realized by assuring the construction of a definite order, for example, in Fig. 4,

$$a1 \ b1 \ a2 \ b2 \ c1 \ b3 \ a3 \ ...$$

This order is eventually different from the absolute temporal order that an external observer would oversee on the set of three sites. However, this order complies with the precedence rules.

Two techniques for ordering are summarized here:

1) Token: A special token message is circulated around the ring. The token contains the current order-number in the total order.
2) Logical Clock (Time Stamp): A logical clock (time stamp) is maintained at each site. The logical clock provides the current order-number.

6.1 Circulation of a Token in a Virtual Ring

It is first necessary to fix the itinerary of the token being passed among the sites. To accomplish this, the sites are arranged in a unidirectional communication ring. Each site can only communicate with its two immediate neighbours (one as a sender, the other as a receiver).

The mechanisms for token circulation are based on the following principle: the token is established with a given configuration of critical state variables, and is passed along the virtual ring. A good set of algorithms which are robust in terms of the withdrawal or breakdown of a site are described by Mossière, Tchuente and Verjus [8], Le Lann [9], Cornafion [10].

6.2. Management of Logical Clocks

At each site a copy of a unique hypothetical clock is maintained, starting from an initial value of zero. Each time a site Si registers the value of its clock Hi (representing one step in the total order), it performs two operations:

1) Register (Hi)
   Increment Hi by 1 and return the new value.
2) Broadcast an incrementation message to all the other sites so that they will increment their clocks. The effect of the message is $Hj := Hj + 1, \forall j \neq i$.

It is clear that all the instances of the logical clock will converge to the same value. (In the absence of any breakdowns, each Hi receives the same number of incrementation messages). However, it is necessary to be able to discriminate among certain identical values. The strict and total order is thus defined by ordered pairs of the form:

$$(Hi, i)$$

where i is the site number:

$$(Hi, i) < (Hj, j) \text{ if } Hi < Hj \text{ or }$$
$$Hi = Hj \text{ and } i < j$$

A simpler method is to reset the clocks only at the time of necessary exchanges between sites. Site Si increments its clock Hi between two successive local events. Furthermore, when Si sends a message, it stamps the message with the value (time) of its clock, Hi. Upon receiving a message, a destination site resets its own clock if it is behind the time indicated by the time stamp on the message. The destination site just increments its clock, and then proceeds to evaluate the message.

Figure 5 gives an example of the way this algorithm functions. As can be seen in Fig. 5, the perceived order of events is different from the absolute chronological order:

1) $a1$, $b1$, and $c1$ are chronologically synchronous, but are serialized by this ordering.
2) $c2$, although it occurs after $b2$, precedes $b2$ in the resulting order.

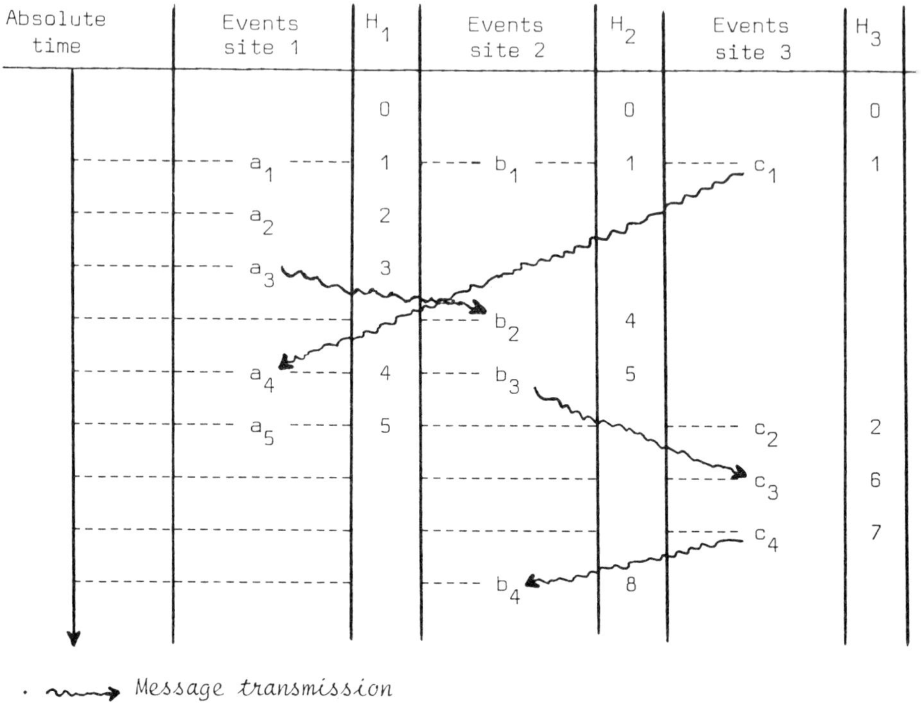

- ~~→ Message transmission

- The resulting total order is :

$$a_1 \; b_1 \; c_1 \; a_2 \; c_2 \; a_3 \; a_4 \; b_2 \; a_5 \; b_3 \; c_3 \; c_4 \; b_4$$

FIG. 5 *Management of the logical clock.*

This method of strict and total ordering proposed by Lamport [11] has some variations, such as that of Kaneko [12]. Note that it has occasionally been proposed to utilize various properties of the communication medium to render this problem trivial, as shown by Banino, Kaiser and Zimmerman [13], and also to use these properties to simplify the required mechanism as proposed by Banatre and Lapalme [14].

7. CONCLUSION

The state of the components of a distributed system can only be known approximately because of 1) the variability of transmission delays along communication channels, 2) the multiplicity of decision-making centres, and 3) the ever-present possibility of site failures. This implies that some form of serial ordering must be constructed and imposed on the sequence of significant events.

We have presented here some techniques to accommodate these problems when one is trying to monitor and synchronize interprocess communications. The impact of site failures has not been fully explored here. A more thorough study and a good bibliography on the subject are to be found both in Cornafion [10], Kohler [15] and Schneider [16].

ACKNOWLEDGMENTS

The author wishes to thank C. Pinkard for the translation of this paper from an original French version.

REFERENCES

1. Bochman, G.V. (1979). Towards an understanding of distributed and parallel systems. P.I. #317, University of Montreal, Montreal, Canada.
2. André, F., Herman, D. and Verjus, J.-P. (1983). "Contrôle du Parallèlisme et de la Répartition", 3ème édition. Rennes. Monographie de l'AFCET. (In press.)
3. Carvalho, O.S.F. and Roucairol, G. (1982). On the distribution of an assertion. *In* "Proc. ACM-SIGACT-SIGOPS Symposium on Principles of Distributed Computing". Ottawa, Canada.
4. Price, W.L. (1974). Simulation studies of an isarithmically controlled store and forward data communication network. *In* "Proc. IFIP Congress", pp.151-154. North Holland, Netherlands.
5. Herman, D. and Verjus, J.-P. (1979). An algorithm for maintaining the consistency of multiple copies. *In* "Proc. First Int. Conf. on Distributed Computing Systems". Huntsville.
6. Ricart, G. and Agrawala, A. (1981). An optimal algorithm for mutual exclusion in computer networks. *Comm. ACM* 24, 1.
7. Kessels, J.L.W. (1982). Arbitration without common modifiable variables. *Acta Information* 17, 135-141.
8. Mossiere, J. Tchente, M. and Verjus, J.-P. (1977). Sur l'exclusion mutuelle dans les réseaux informatiques. IRISA Publ.75. Rennes, France.
9. Le Lann, G. (1978). Algorithms for distributed data-sharing systems which use tickets. *In* "Proc. 3rd Workshop on Distributed Data Management and Computer Networks". Berkeley, California.
10. Cornafion (1981). "Systèmes Informatiques Répartis - Concepts et Techniques". DUNOD Informatique.

√11. Lamport, L. (1978). Time, clocks, and the ordering of
     events in a distributed system. *Comm. ACM* 21, 7.
 12. Kaneko, A., Nishihara, Y., Tsurvoka, K. and Hattori, M.
     (1979). Logical clock synchronization method for dupli-
     cated data base control. *In* "Proc. First Int. Conf. on
     Distributed Computing Systems". Huntsville.
 13. Banino, J.S., Kaiser, C. and Zimmerman, H. (1979). Syn-
     chronization for distributed systems using a single
     broadcast channel. *In* "Proc. First Int. Conf. on Distrib-
     uted Computing Systems". Huntsville.
 14. Banatre, M. and Lapalme, G. (1982). Enchère: A distributed
     auction bidding system. *In* "Proc. 3rd Int. Conf. on Dis-
     tributed Computing Systems". Miami, USA.
√15. Kohler, W.H. (1981). A survey of techniques for synchroni-
     zation and recovery in decentralized computer systems.
     Comp. Surv. 13, 149-184.
 16. Schneider, F.B. (1982). Synchronization in distributed
     programs. *ACM TOPLAC* 4, 125-148.

Distributed Co-operating Processes and Transactions

Lui Sha, E. Douglas Jensen, Richard F. Rashid and J. Duane Northcutt

1. INTRODUCTION

In the Archons project, a "decentralized computer" has a global operating system largely replicated at separate nodes of a loosely coupled multi-computer. The need for failure atomicity in a physically dispersed operating system leads to providing a transaction facility in the operating system kernel. However, conventional transactions are inappropriate here for several reasons. Among them is their basis on the serialization model of data consistency. There are many situations in an operating system where correct concurrent operations are not serializable, yet concurrency is desirable. Thus we propose to solve this problem with a new relational model of data consistency.

Compared with other current work on non-serializable trans-actions, such as using semantic knowledge, an important fea-ture of our approach is that it naturally accommodates an inherent characteristic of distributed systems that infor-mation about remote states is often inaccurate and imcomplete, resulting in probabilistic behavior. Based on our model, we reformulate the notion of co-operating processes and intro-duce the idea of co-operating transactions. This report pro-vides an initial informal snapshot of work in progress on a broad range of issues. In depth treatment of each topic will appear in subsequent publications.

Distributed Computing Systems
ISBN 0-12-543970-9

24   L. SHA *et al.*

2. THE RELATIONAL MODEL OF DATA CONSISTENCY

2.1. Inadequacy of the Serialization Model

Most of the work on synchronization methods for distributed
systems has been done in the context of distributed database
systems, and is based on the serialization model of data
consistency [1]. The basic concept of the serialization model
is that if each transaction executing alone maintains the
consistency of the data objects, then executing transactions
serially and in any order of execution will also be correct,
i.e., maintain the consistency constraints. Therefore, a set
of sufficient conditions for the correct concurrent execution
of transactions is one which can be proven equivalent to a
serial order of execution. One well-known form of these conditions is [2]:

1) Total Ordering: There exists a total ordering of the set
    of transactions.
2) Relative Ordering: For every pair of operations that con-
    flict (i.e., at least one operation is a write), their
    relative order on a shared data object must be identical
    to that of their corresponding transactions in the total
    ordering of transactions.

    Although the serialization model is very general, in the
sense that the consistency constraints can be preserved with
knowledge of conflicts being the only semantic information
about the transactions [3], it is inadequate with respect to
the needs of distributed operating systems. The reasons are
as follows:

1) The serialization model limits concurrency. Kung and
    Papadimitriou [3] show that it uses only syntactic (and
    conflict) information about transactions, and that it is
    possible to formulate more efficient non-serializable
    transactions by using information about data objects or
    additional semantic information about transactions. For
    example, the work of Lamport [4], Kung and Lehman [5],
    Schwarz and Spector [6], Garcia-Molina [7] and Allchin
    and McKendry [8] all further demonstrate this point. Con-
    currency is a critical issue in operating systems and the
    information needed to improve it is often available
    (neither of which may be as much the case at the appli-
    cations level, e.g., in database systems).
2) The serialization model suffers synchronization-induced
    deadlock and rollback problems [1]. Synchronization
    methods based on the serialization model can be classified
    into two basic approaches – two-phase locking and time
    stamps. The two-phase lock approach can lead to deadlock,

while the time stamp approach is prone to problems caused
by rollback.

3) The serialization model precludes a distributed (e.g.,
   either decentralized or network) operating system kernel
   from using atomic transactions for communication and co-
   operation [4]. When a pair of transactions exchange messages in the course of an interaction, their operations
   (i.e., the two way communications) might be interleaved
   so as to violate the relative ordering condition (i.e.,
   2 above) required by the serialization model.
4) The serialization model does not support the synchronization of co-operating processes. Co-operating processes
   must be permitted to change their states autonomously,
   and in any relative ordering, as long as they are not in
   those states that are governed by the specified rules of
   co-operation. However, the serialization model does not
   permit this; its conditions must hold at all times, turn-
   ing the power of its generality against its use for interprocess co-operation.

To remedy these disabilities, we have supplanted the
serialization model with our own model based on relationships
among the data objects. We share the premise that each transaction executing alone preserves the consistency constraints
of the data objects. But we further assume that the relationships affecting synchronization among the data objects are
known. We believe this is a justifiable assumption in our
context of distributed operating systems.

In database systems based on the serialization model,
serializability is taken as the consistency constraint, i.e.,
the correctness criterion. In several current efforts on non-
serializable transactions, serializability is viewed as a
"strong form" of the correctness criteria needed by certain
applications and not by others [6,7,8]. In our approach to
the correctness issue, consistency constraints are modeled as
relations among data objects, and are partitioned into a part
called data invariants and a part called action invariants.
Data invariants must be obeyed by all transactions, whereas
action invariants are additional constraints that are enforced
by individual transactions. Action invariants must not violate
data invariants. The execution of concurrent processes or
transactions is defined to be correct if it satisfies both
the data and action invariants, independent of whether the
processes or transactions are serializable. This is because
serializability is not a relation among data objects and
therefore not a consistency constraint. In our view, serializability is only a set of sufficient conditions to maintain
consistency constraints.

2.2. Classification of Relations

Our relational model of data consistency classifies the possible relationships among data objects as autonomous, dependent, or partially dependent.

1) Autonomous: The relation is defined as the set of the cartesian products of the domains of the data objects. From a synchronization point of view, the implication of an autonomous relationship is that object A can take on any value that is in its domain, regardless of the value of B (i.e., A and B can be updated separately).

   An autonomous relation will be called probabilistic if a joint probability distribution is defined upon the set of cartesian products. The concept of probabilistic relations is important to our discussion in the section on co-operating processes.

2) Dependent: The relation is defined by a proper subset of the cartesian products of the domains of the data objects. In this case, the value taken by a data object, A, is constrained by the value taken by another data object, B, and vice versa. The implication of this type relationship is that when there are dependency relationships among data objects, these data objects can no longer be updated independently.

3) Partially dependent: The relation is defined as a proper subset of the cartesian products of data object domains, a part of which takes the form of cartesian products of subsets of the domains. For example, if the domains of A and B are both {0, 1, 2} with the data invariant "if $A = 2$ then $A = B$", then the partially dependent relation is the set consisting of the tuple <2,2> concatenated with the set of cartesian products {0, 1} x {0, 1, 2}. The notion of partially dependent relationships allows us to view process synchronization as the act of maintaining the data invariants among distributed state variables. Suppose A and B are state variables of processes P_1 and P_2 respectively. We can interpret the example above as "process P_2 must enter state two if process P_1 enters state two, otherwise processes P_1 and P_2 can change their states autonomously."

2.3. Definitions

We now proceed to make the following definitions:

1) Data objects: the user defined, smallest unit of data items that can be synchronized (e.g., locked).

2) Data invariants: the mathematical representation of the dependency relationships among data objects (e.g."$A = B$").

Data invariants must be preserved by all processes or transactions.

3) Atomic data sets: user defined disjoint sets of data objects, each of which is constrained by a user-specified set of data invariants. For example, one set has data objects A and B with invariant "A = B", and another set has data objects C and D with invariant "C > D". Atomic data sets are our model for the modular decomposition of operating system data objects.

4) Action invariants: consistency constraints enforced by individual transactions in addition to data invariants. Action invariants must not violate data invariants. For example, let the data invariant of an atomic data set with two data objects be "A $\geq$ B". Transactions T_1 and T_2 can have their own different actions invariants, "set A equal to the current value of B" and "set A to be (B + 10)". These action invariants must hold at the end of their transactions, but need not hold at other times.

   Since data objects belonging to different atomic data sets are autonomous, when a transaction accesses data objects belonging to different atomic data sets, it needs only to satisfy its own action invariants and data invariants on a set by set basis. For example, let the data invariants of two independent and replicated bank accounts be "A_1 = A_2 $\geq$ 0" and "B_1 = B_2 $\geq$ 0". A fund transfer transaction between A and B must satisfy three conditions: "both accounts after fund transfer must be positive", "the replicated copies must be identical", and "both the debit and the credit must be done". If any of these conditions fail to hold, the transaction must be aborted. Note that the first two conditions are just the data invariants. But the last condition is an action invariant that governs the relation between data objects belonging to two different atomic data sets, specifically $A_1 + B_1$ = ($A_1 + B_1$ at the start of the transaction). It must hold at the end of the transaction, but not necessarily at other times, because the sum of these two accounts must be permitted to change independently at all other times.

5) Conformity: a concurrent access to shared data objects which preserves all of the data invariants and satisfies all action invariants. Note that conformal transactions may or may not be serializable.

2.4. Representations of Data Objects and Data Invariants

Each data object is internally represented by triplets, <name, value, version number>. When a data object is created, its initial value is assigned to version zero of this data object, such as "A[0] := 1".

When the data object is to be updated, a new version of
the object is created and the transaction works on this new
version. For example, the code "A: = A + 1" in an update
transaction corresponds to the following steps:

A[v+1] := A[v];   {v is the version number}
A[v+1] := A[v+1] + 1; {A := A+1}
v := v+1;   {if the transaction commits}

If this transaction successfully commits, the new version
becomes permanent. Old versions can be kept in the log file
as back-ups or discarded. The importance of this representation to us is that it provides a concrete representation of
the data invariants. For example, the data invariant "A = B"
could be represented as A[v] = B[v], v = 0, 1, 2, 3, ...
When a transaction updates an object (or objects) in an atomic
data set, it must produce a new version of the entire atomic
data set. Since data invariants are defined upon data objects
with identical version numbers, a version of an atomic data
set exists at a particular time if and only if that version
of all its objects exists at that time.

2.5. Issues in Maintaining Data Consistency

One of our goals in developing our relational model of data
consistency is to provide a means of maintaining the consistency of distributed data objects and state variables with a
higher degree of concurrency than permitted by the serialization model, without synchronization induced deadlock and
rollback problems. In this work, we will present a simple condition that is sufficient to maintain the data consistency
without deadlock or rollback problems and provides a higher
degree of concurrency than possible with the serialization
model. The following discussion is presented here in an intuitive fashion, but will appear in a more formal manner in
Sha's thesis [9]. The general implications of including the
use of semantic knowledge in this model will be discussed in
[10].

The key to maintaining the consistency of data objects is
the serialization of conflicting operations on the shared objects. A general distributed database system has to be in-
sensitive to the changes in application programs. A commonly
accepted solution is to use only syntactic information about
transactions in the process of maintaining consistency, which
leads to the serialization model. As a result of the lack of
semantic information about data objects and transactions, it
is impossible for a system to decide the appropriate points
at which to enforce serialization. This requires that

serialization must be applied to all transactions, and that
transactions are used as the basic unit of operation in synchronization.

In the context of centralized operating systems, semaphores
were developed for the purpose of providing the serialization
of operations through mutual exclusion. The use of semaphores,
however, requires detailed knowledge of the code in which they
are found, and the possible interactions among operations on
the shared data objects. In general, these requirements make
programs using semaphores difficult to write and understand.
Monitors were developed later, and fulfilled the need to provide the serialization of conflicting operations by encapsulating subsets of a system's shared data structures and
serializing requests to perform operations on these data
structures. As compared with semaphores, monitors are generally used where coarser granularity of synchronization is
needed. Although monitors often provide less concurrency than
semaphores, the modularity improvement is considered to be
worth the price.

We believe that, with respect to synchronization, the
distributed operating system environment lies somewhere in
between that of distributed database systems and centralized
operating systems. The serialization of conflicting operations
on shared data objects should be done when appropriate, not
indiscriminately, nor with such a fine degree of granularity
as with semaphores. The decision of when it is appropriate to
perform serialization of operations should result from analysis of the dependency relations among the distributed data
objects. If a dependency is deterministic and must be maintained with respect to all accesses, the objects should be
grouped together in an atomic data set, which serves as a unit
of synchronization. In this regard, an atomic data set is
similar to the encapsulated data structures in a monitor. However, there are two important differences between atomic data
sets and the data structures in monitors. First, we permit
concurrent serializable operations within an atomic data set,
whereas monitors permit only one procedure at a time to access
a shared data structure. Second, if the relations of an atomic
data set are partial dependencies, then the serialization
occurs only when the co-operating processes (or transactions)
are in the dependent phase. In short, we replace the global
serialization required by the serialization model with set-
wise serialization enforced only when it is necessary. It
should be noted that, the relations among any two data objects
belonging to different atomic data sets are autonomous, therefore operations upon them need not be serialized - i.e.,
relative orderings can be arbitrary.

To understand the deadlock problem in synchronization

methods based on the serialization model, one must analyze the
various dependency relations among data objects. For example,
suppose the relation between the values A and B is A = f(B).
Any transaction that updates one object, must update the other
in order to maintain the dependency relation. However, a system based on the serialization model does not have knowledge
of this dependency relation, and thus cannot ensure that all
transactions either acquire write-locks on both A and B, or
neither of them. Consequently, if one transaction acquires a
write-lock on A simultaneously with another transaction ac-
quiring a write-lock on B, deadlock becomes inevitable. In
fact, the detection of deadlock here and the subsequent abortion of transactions serves the purpose of preventing the
violation of dependency relations. Although it is possible to
avoid this type of deadlock without requiring that the dependency relationships be known (e.g., by allowing a transaction
to acquire all of its write-locks prior to execution, or
ordering all execution with respect to the data objects), it
often results in an unacceptable loss of concurrency. The
concept of an atomic data set helps in solving the problem
deadlock by grouping data objects according to their dependency relations, and thereby grouping their locks accordingly.

The cause of synchronization induced rollback in time-
stamping synchronization approaches is similar to that which
causes deadlock, i.e., the lack of knowledge concerning the
dependency relationships among the system's data objects. Data
objects (as A and B in the above example) should not accept a
request until having processed all those with earlier timestamps. For example, if a transaction with a time-stamp of 3
is accepted at A, while a transaction with a time-stamp of 5
is accepted at B, transaction 5 must be aborted when the trans
action with a time-stamp of 3 arrives at B. Without knowledge
of the data object's dependency relations, it is all but impossible to avoid such synchronization-induced rollback without seriously sacrificing concurrency.

2.5.1. A sufficient condition for maintaining data consistency
A sufficient condition for maintaining system-wide consistency
is that conflicting transactions are mutually exclusive with
respect to the version number of the shared atomic data set
accessed by them. That is, data objects belonging to the same
version can be shared by several read transactions, but they
can only be modified by a single update transaction. Under
this condition and our first assumption (i.e., transactions
maintain the consistency of the data objects when executing
alone), a transaction will preserve the date invariants of
each of the accessed atomic data sets. Mutual exclusion with
respect to version number can be obtained by using any

appropriate synchronization method [11,12]. It should be
noted that when semantic knowledge about transactions is
available and dependence relations are multi-valued, mutual
exclusion with respect to version number is not necessary.
For a detailed discussion of this point, see [10]. Although
mutual exclusion with respect to version number does not provide maximum concurrency under some conditions, it has the
properties of freedom from deadlock and rollback as discussed
in Section 2.5.3.

2.5.2. Concurrent updating. The improvement of concurrency
our model provides over the serialization model results from
the fact that the relative ordering requirement of the serialization model is not enforced when the relation among data objects is known to be autonomous. For example, let A, B and C
represent the numbers of jobs on three separate machines.
Transactions, represented at $T_{i,j}$, transfer a job from machine
i to machine j, decrementing the count of jobs at machine i
while incrementing the count at j. Transactions $T_{A,B}$, $T_{B,C}$,
and $T_{C,A}$ each execute and update the values A, B, and C as
follows. $T_{A,B}$ precedes $T_{C,A}$ on A, $T_{B,C}$ precedes $T_{A,B}$ on B and
$T_{C,A}$ precedes $T_{B,C}$ on C. The concurrent execution of these
transactions would violate the relative ordering requirement
of the serialization model. However, our model will permit
this because the relationships among A, B and C are known to
be autonomous. That is, the number of jobs on one machine is
not determined by the number of jobs on another. The serialization model assumes no such knowledge of the relations among
data objects. In order to maintain the dependency relations
in the entire system, the serialization model must enforce
serializability of the execution of transactions even when it
is unnecessary. In other words, the serialization model includes no knowledge of the dependency relations among the data
objects, thus it must be assumed that all data objects are
dependent upon one another.
    In summary: with our model we group the system's data ob-
jects into disjoint subsets (i.e., atomic data sets); data
objects within an atomic data set are related to each other
in the form of either dependent or partially dependent relations. Data objects between different atomic data sets are
autonomous. Transactions can operate on one or more atomic
data sets. Since relations among data objects belonging to
different atomic data sets are autonomous, there is an ordering of operations on each atomic data set, and the relative
ordering of conflicting operations on shared data objects
within an atomic data set must be consistent with the local
total ordering for that set. Thus, we have a partial ordering
instead of the global ordering required by the serialization

model. For example, transaction T_1 precedes transaction T_2 on
all data objects in an atomic data set A, but transactions T_2
can precede T_1 in another atomic data set B. Furthermore,
according to our model, it is possible for the data objects
in an atomic data set to be related in a partially dependent
fashion, requiring that the transactions that execute on the
atomic data set be serialized only part of the time. Since
non-serializable concurrent executions are allowed for data
objects belonging to different atomic data sets, it is often
desirable to decompose system objects into smaller atomic
data sets whenever possible.

Within an atomic data set, a transaction can only update
data objects with the same version number (i.e., a transaction
can only operate on a particular atomic data set version).
However, there can be N concurrent updates on an atomic data
set of N data objects. Mutual exclusion with respect to version
number means that transactions can concurrently update different data objects of the same atomic data set, as long as these
data objects are in different versions. For example, imagine
an atomic data set consisting of data objects A and B; transaction T_1 works on A[1] (producing A[2]), and then begins work
on B[1]. This would permit a transaction T_2 to begin work on
A[2] while T_1 is still working on B[1]. Note that transaction
T_2 is working on a non-existent (by our definition) version
of the atomic data set (i.e., not all the data objects with
this version number are known to exist). Thus, this work will
have to be aborted if T_1 cannot complete the production of
this version of the atomic data set.

To support N concurrent updates to an atomic data set with
N data objects, one can simply use multiple versions of the
data objects (if their size is considered small). In this case
one can simply retain the most recent consistent version of
the data objects, and discard the previous versions. However,
two copies for each of the N data objects is sufficient to
support N concurrent updates. In this case, one set of copies
is used for the atomic data set checkpoint version, while
another set is used to store the most recent versions of the
data objects. As transactions update the data objects in the
atomic data set, the current versions of the data objects
could be different.

Although mutual exclusion with respect to versions prevents
both synchronization induced deadlock and rollback as discussed in the next section, transactions can still abort for
reasons such as the failure of a processing node. Aborting an
earlier transaction will lead to the cascaded abortion of
later transactions operating on data objects with later version
numbers. The trade-off between increased concurrency and the
potential for cascaded aborts is an important design issue.

Assuming that all the transactions following the checkpoint
version are kept in a recovery log, the system can always
recover to the checkpoint version after a system failure. A
new checkpoint version can be made whenever the current
versions of all the constituent data objects in the atomic
data set have the same version number. However, if a fixed
interval between checkpoints is desired, then either some
concurrency in the updating process must be sacrificed, or
additional state saving operations will be required. For example, if the checkpoint version is 5 and the next checkpoint
is 10. When one of the data objects reaches version 10, access
to it must be withheld until all of the data objects reach
version 10 and the transaction producing version 10 is committed. In summary, a small amount of additional storage for
the version numbers makes it possible to have both better
concurrency and ease of recovery, even when cascaded aborts
are involved.

2.5.3. Deadlock and rollback avoidance. In the time-stamp
approach to the maintenance of system-wide serializability,
rollback is used as a means to ensure the relative ordering
of transactions is consistent with a total ordering, and
therefore to ensure the serializability. When the sufficient
condition of conformity is enforced, each conflict transaction
will have a unique version to work on and will produce a new
version for next transaction. There is no possibility that the
synchronization process itself will cause a rollback. However,
rollbacks may still exist in the system, but for reasons such
as a node involved in a transaction crashing.
    Synchronization induced deadlock is also a problem which
our approach avoids. The data invariants of each of the atomic
data sets can be satisfied independently of other atomic data
sets, and each of these transactions can autonomously produce
new versions of the atomic data sets. This cannot cause deadlock, because the generation of new versions makes versions
of the atomic data sets available to other transactions. However, a distinction must be made between synchronization
induced deadlock, and the deadlock problem in general. For
example, let B_1 and B_2 be pools of buffers on machines one
and two, respectively. Let D_1 and D_2 be two distributed variables representing the number of empty buffers in B_1 and B_2.
D_1 and D_2 are autonomous data objects, i.e., they are atomic
data sets consisting of one object each. Therefore, in our
model any transaction requesting resources from B_1 and B_2,
can assess D_1 and D_2 in any arbitrary relative order and no
deadlock or rollback will occur as a result of the synchronization activity. However, in the serialization model, if a
transaction accesses D_1 first and waits to access D_2, while

another accesses D_2 before accessing D_1, deadlock will result
if two-phase lock is used, and a rollback will occur if a
time-stamp scheme is used even if there are sufficient buffers.
Although our approach has eliminated deadlock induced by synchronizing access to D_1 and D_2, the absence of resources in
the pools (B_1) can still cause deadlock, or require the
abortion of a transaction.

2.5.4. Commit management. Commit management is a process which
produces a new version of an atomic data set despite the failure of nodes involved in the transaction. The commit management for an atomic data set that is updated by transactions
not accessing multiple atomic data sets is relatively simple.
In the case of multiple version concurrent updating, when a
transaction completes its computation and produces a new
version, the synchronization mechanism can start the first
phase of the two-phase commit protocol (i.e., copy the new
version into stable storage). When the first phase is completed, the second phase of the commit can be started. When
the two-copy concurrent update protocol is used, only the
"would-be" check-point version can be committed. For example,
let the current committed check-point version of an atomic
data set be 5 and the next check-point version be 10. The
concurrent updating of data objects by transactions can proceed until version 10. Transactions later than the one producing version 10 must wait for the complete commit of version
10 before they can start. When all the data objects reach
version 10, the synchronization mechanism can start the two-
phase commit as before. Note that in this case, we are actuall⁻
committing five transactions at a time, i.e., the transactions
that are producing versions 11 to 15.

     When transactions update multiple atomic data sets, the
complexity of commit management increases. The problem is that
there can be cyclical dependency relations in the commit
management process. For example, let A and B be two atomic
data sets with only one data object. Suppose that transaction
T_1 updates $A[10]$ and $B[21]$ and transaction T_2 updates $A[11]$
and $B[20]$. From the relational model of data consistency, we
know that this is permissible because there are no data invariants across atomic data sets A and B. Therefore the result
of the completed computation is valid although the relative
ordering requirement of serializability is violated. However,
the commit of T_1 and T_2 cannot be performed independently.
This is because if one of them aborts, so must the other.
Although T_1 and T_2 can start the first phase commit when they
finish their computation, they cannot start the second phase
commit on their own. The second phase commit can start only
after both of them complete their first phase commit. In

general, a transaction can start its second phase commit when
all the transactions it is waiting for, finish their first
phase commit. When there is no cyclical dependency, a transaction can simply wait until all the transactions it depends
on finish their entire two-phase commit. However, there can
be cyclical waits, therefore one must time-out waits and start
tracing the dependency cycle. Hence, managing the distributed
commit of conformal transactions across multiple atomic data
sets is similar to the problem of managing deadlocks in serializable transactions. However, the important difference is
that in the case of deadlock, once the cycle is detected at
least one of the transactions must be aborted to break the
waiting cycle. In the case of commit management, once it is
found that all transactions are finished with their first
phase commits and are waiting for others, transactions could
start the second phase commit. To illustrate how the second
phase commit proceeds and breaks the waiting cycle, consider
the example above. Once the second phase starts, A[10] and
B[20] can be committed, making the second phase commit on
A[11] and B[21] possible.

Finally, we want to make two comments. First, when atomic
data sets are involved in transactions crossing multiple
atomic data sets, the two-copy concurrent updating scheme
might further complicate the multiple atomic data set commit
management, and the multiple version method is generally
preferable. Second, if all the transactions are commutative,
then commit management can be simplified. This is because we
can develop a compensating transaction to undo the effect of
aborting a preceding transaction [7].

3. CO-OPERATING PROCESSES

3.1. A New Formulation

The synchronization of co-operating processes is an important
aspect of an operating system. When the processes are physically dispersed, classical centralized techniques are usually
not cost-effective. Our model of data consistency (unlike the
serialization model) is able to handle this because the relationships among distributed co-operating processes are
represented as partially dependent relations among the state
variables of co-operating processes. The synchronization of
co-operating processes is thus defined as the maintenance of
these dependency relations. This paper provides an intuitive
overview of this perspective, leaving formalism to appear in
[10].

According to this model, co-operating processes generally
have two phases - an autonomous phase and a dependent phase.

In the autonomous phase, the state variables of the co-
operating processes take on values that belong to the set of
the cartesian products of the subsets of the domains of these
state variables. For example, let the domains of the state
variables of processes P_1 and P_2 both be $\{0,1,2,3\}$, and let
the relation between them be $\{\{0,1\} \times \{0,1\}, <2,2>, <3,3>\}$.
That is, processes P_1 and P_2 can change their states autonomously, as long as their state variables take on values from
the set of the cartesian products $\{\{0,1\} \times \{0,1\}\}$.
    In the dependent phase, all state variables in a process
must take on values according to the data invariants - e.g.,
the state variables of P_1 and P_2 above must both have values
of either 2 or 3. The problem of ensuring that a set of processes, e.g., P_1 and P_2, will enter their dependent (e.g.,
identical) states is a matter of maintaining the data invariants "$P_1 = P_2$, $2 \leq P_1$, $P_2 \leq 3$". This can be done by requiring that the manipulation of the state variables of processes P_1 and P_2 satisfy the conformity condition.
    In the autonomous phase, it is possible to allow these two
processes to maintain a probabilistic relationship among their
state variables. This can be accomplished by assigning a joint
probability distribution over the set of cartesian products of
the processes' state variables. From this joint distribution,
we can derive conditional distributions to interpret the
probabilistic relationships among the states of processes co-
operating in the autonomous phase. In practice, instead of
trying to obtain the exact distribution a priori, one often
designs a probabilistic algorithm, observes (e.g., through
simulation) the induced probability distribution, and iterates
until the resulting distribution is satisfactory. For example,
we can have the following conditional distributions regarding
processes P_1 and P_2.

$$P[p_2=0 \mid p_1=0] = 0.8, \quad P[p_2=0 \mid p_1=1] = 0.2,$$
$$P[p_2=1 \mid p_1=0] = 0.2, \quad P[p_2=1 \mid p_1=1] = 0.8$$

    This can be interpreted as P_1 requesting P_2 to be in the
same state as P_1, and although P_2 is not obligated to honour
P_1's request, P_2 does give P_1's request favourable consideration. Therefore, when P_1 is in state 0 (or 1), P_2 is likely
to be in state 0 (or 1).
    The need for probabilistic co-operation often arises due
to the communication delays in physically dispersed systems.
It may be less expensive to maintain certain relationships
among data objects indeterministically and recover when
necessary, than to force those relationships to always be
deterministic.
    We now turn to the subject of phase transitions. The tran-
sition from the autonomous phase to the dependent phase

requires the establishment of a dependency relationship among state variables. Since dependency relationships are defined on version numbers, their establishment includes equalizing the version numbers of each state variable (for instance, by resetting them to zero), and assigning appropriate values to the state variables. In general, a state transition is carried out in three stages. First, if there is more than one process requesting that the transition be made, one of the requesting processes is selected. Next, all of the co-operating processes must be instructed to complete (or abort) any current outstanding autonomous manipulation of state variables, and not to initiate further autonomous manipulation. Finally, values must be assigned to each of the state variables according to the selected processes' requirements, and the version numbers of the state variables must be reset.

The transition of processes from the dependent phase to the autonomous phase is a simple matter. Once a process obtains the right to manipulate the current version of the atomic data set, it can bring the co-operating processes to an autonomous phase by assigning appropriate values from the set of cartesian products to the state variables.

Although there are many different algorithms to implement process phase transition and synchronization activities, we have found that (in a variety of applications) the use of a synchronization path is an effective technique. In the example above, processes P_1 and P_2 co-operate probabilistically in states 0 and 1. Suppose now that P_1 wants P_2 to jointly enter state 2, while P_2 wants P_1 to jointly enter state 3. To resolve such a conflict, a synchronization path could be defined as follows. Any request for dependent co-operation must first be submitted to P_1. If more than one request is received at P_1, one will be honored and forwarded to P_2 where it will also be honored. Requests that were not selected by P_1 will be queued to be selected at later times. The following example illustrates the use of synchronization paths.

3.2. Example: Remote Process Interruption and Abortion

The purpose of this example is to illustrate the use of synchronization paths and to compare the remote procedure call paradigm with the co-operating process paradigm. This example arose in the context of the Spice graphic package, Canvas [13], which consists of two co-operating processes running on the Accent network operating system. One process is a remote server while the other is a user interface process. The user interface is local to the user's machine and relays user commands to the remote server via messages. For our discussion, we abstract the user interface into four basic commands:

EXECUTE, INTERRUPT, CONTINUE and ABORT.

The two basic requirements for this task are: first, it is desirable to minimize message traffic between the two processes; and second, the results of remote service can not be made permanent until the user is informed that the job is done - that is, the user is given a chance to abort or interrupt the remote process up until the point where he is notified that the job is done. From an implementation point of view, this requirement implies that the user's request should take precedence when there is a conflict between a remote server that is trying to make a result permanent, and a user who is trying to abort (or interrupt) an outstanding server process.

Initially, a remote procedure call based solution was considered because, intuitively, tasks with a remote server seemed to fit this paradigm well. However, it was soon discovered that the conflict between the server process and the user made the remote procedure call approach difficult to use. This is because in a remote procedure call environment, control is passed from the requesting process when the server process is called, and is returned when the server has completed processing the request (or the system detects that the server has failed). The concept of asynchronously interrupting an executing server process is counter to the remote procedure call paradigm. Thus, the problem defined above cannot be easily solved with a classical remote procedure call approach. In this example, the initial attempt to use remote procedure calls resulted in an overly complex implementation. Furthermore, a remote procedure call approach also generates more message traffic, as all inquiries must be forwarded to the remote server for a response, due to the fact that the state of the remote server changes asynchronously with respect to the state of the user server process.

In general the remote procedure call paradigm is appropriate for tasks with master/slave (i.e., hierarchical) control structures, but it becomes much less so for peer processes having symmetrical control relationships. An approach based on our model does not impose such a restrictive control structure on the co-operating processes, and permits the use of local information to reduce the communication overhead. Let the state variable of the interface process be S_u and the state variable of the remote server be S_g. If we maintain data invariants in the form of "$S_u = S_g$", the user interface process can provide the user rapid response by looking only at its local state variable S_u. To ensure that the user-issued ABORT and INTERRUPT commands win any conflicts, we define a synchronization path such that any command must first update the state variable of the user interface process.

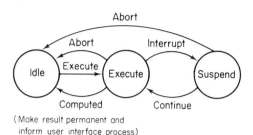

FIG. 1 *State transition diagram of the remote server and the
user interface processes.*

The basic states of the remote server and the user interface processes are called Idle, Suspend and Execute and are
labelled as state zero, one and two respectively. The state
diagram in Fig. 1 indicates the defined state transitions,
and other command occurrences not defined there will have no
effect.

When the system is initialized, $S_u[0] = S_g[0] = 0$. Then,
when a user issues an EXECUTE command, S_u will be updated
first and $S_u[1] = 2$. The EXECUTE command updates $S_u[0]$, and
also updates $S_g[0]$ (via messages), resulting in $S_g[1] = 2$.
That is, both the virtual and remote servers go to the Execute
state. Suppose that suddenly a user discovers that something
is wrong and he issues an ABORT command, while at the same
time the server issues a COMPUTED signal (indicating that the
computation is done and the result is ready to be made permanent). At this point, there is a conflict between the COMPUTED
signal and the ABORT command. Since S_u must be updated first
and is local to the user, the ABORT command is applied to
$S_u[1]$ first, making $S_u[2] = 0$. When the COMPUTED signal reaches
the user interface it will find that S_u is in the Idle state,
and will have no effect. On the other hand, the ABORT command,
after updating $S_u[1]$, will update $S_g[1]$ and cause $S_g[2] = 0$.
Therefore, the ABORT command wins the conflict, resulting in
the system returning to the Idle state. Suppose now that the
user accidentally issues an INTERRUPT command. The interface
process would check its state variable and find that $S_u[2] = 0$.
Thus, the INTERRUPT command would be considered invalid and
the interface process would warn the user based on its local
information alone, and the server would not be affected. Thus,
traffic is minimized; there will be no messages between the
two processes unless they bring about the state transitions.

3.3. Example: Process Creation and Destruction

This example illustrates the two phases in co-operating processes: probabilistic co-operation in the autonomous phase, and deterministic behavior in the dependent phase. This example arose from the Spice remote file server [14] running on the Accent network operating system, with Unix as the local host operating system. The basic structure of the remote file server consists of a parent process and a set of child processes created to handle users' file manipulation messages. A child process maintains a data port for each of the opened files. The maximum number of such ports that can be supported by a child process is twenty, due to the limitation of Unix on the maximum number of open files a process may have. When a user first sends a request to open a file, a child process will be created for him. When the user wants to open more than twenty files, an additional child process will be created for him. A child process should be destroyed when it has closed all its ports.

Since the creation and destruction of a child process is a function of the number of ports, the parent process must keep a record of the number of ports that each child process currently has. Thus, let $C1.n$ be a local variable which counts the number of ports at child $C1$, and let $P1.n$ be the parent's local variable which indicates the number of ports in $C1$. The standard solution is to construct an atomic data set consisting of $\{C1.n, P1.n\}$, with the data invariant "$C1.n = P1.n$". This data invariant can be maintained by requiring all conflicting transactions to be mutually exclusive with respect to the version numbers of the data objects.

However, there is a problem with this standard solution: it keeps a parent's record consistent with the actual number of ports at the child process for all the values. The OPEN FILE and CLOSE FILE command pair associated with each accessed file causes the number of ports at the child process to be incremented and decremented. This results in two sets of conformal operations to update a parent's record. There is one parent process for many children, and the creation and destruction of ports occurs frequently, so the number of conformal operations needed tends to be large. Thus, the parent process becomes a performance bottle-neck.

This raises the question of whether $P1.n$ has to equal $C1.n$ at all times and for all values. In fact, most of the message traffic is generated to maintain a non-critical relation that could be more efficiently maintained probabilistically. Note that there are only two important values of the port-count, zero and twenty. A port-count of zero requires the destruction of the child process, while a count of twenty requires the

creation of a new child when a user wants to open more files.
Furthermore, we only need P1.n equal to C1.n with some probability when the port-count is twenty. If the parent underesti-
mates the number of ports, additional open file requests will
be sent to the child process. However, the child process can
return the requests to the parent saying that he already has
twenty ports. If the parent overestimates the number of ports,
a new child might be unnecessarily created. The time and resources required for that are acceptable in this application.
In particular, the probability of creating unnecessary child
processes is small because most users need less than twenty
ports.

A port-count of zero, however, is critical because serious
abnormalities could occur as a result of the premature destruction of a child process. For example, a child process with
ports could be destroyed. Since a child cannot predict the
arrival time of a new OPEN FILE command from a user, the child
could create a new port after sending a message to the parent
process indicating that it has closed all the ports. If a
child cannot inform its parent of his status change in time,
it could be destroyed by the parent who thinks that the child
has no more ports. Note that this problem cannot be solved by
letting the parent wait a bit longer after he is informed that
the child has no more ports. This is because the arrival time
of a new OPEN FILE command from a user is unpredictable. In
fact, until the user logs out, the system cannot predict when
a user will issue a new OPEN FILE command.

Since a port-count of zero is the only critical value, we
can formulate a partial dependency relation as follows. A
child and its parent process are in an autonomous phase as
the port-count varies from one to twenty, and they are in a
dependent phase when the port-count is zero. In addition, when
a child has twenty ports, we want its parent process to have
a port-count of twenty with relatively high probability. This
is summarized as:

> P1.n = C1.n - with higher probability,
> when the child process enters or
> leaves the state of twenty ports.

> P1.n = C1.n - deterministically,
> when the child process enters or
> leaves the state of zero ports.

This could be implemented by having the child process send
a port-count message to its parent process when it enters or
leaves the state of twenty ports. No effort is made to guarantee that P1.n is equal to C1.n with respect to all concurrent
accesses. When the child process enters or leaves the state

of zero ports, it initiates a conformal transaction that
brings about a phase transition and guarantees P1.n equal to
C1.n with respect to all concurrent accesses. When a child
has ports between two and nineteen, it will not automatically
send any messages to its parent because these values are not
relevant to the creation or destruction of the child process.
However, when a child is interrogated by its parent, it will
report its current number of ports via a simple message. This
is to permit the operating system to sample the number of
opened files for reasons other than process creation and
destruction.

By introducing probabilistic co-operation, the communication
between the parent and the child for the purpose of process
creation and destruction is dramatically reduced. There is
essentially one transaction needed during the life time of a
child process, independent of the number of files accessed by
a user. That transaction is the one that destroys a child
process and alters its parent's record. Only in the rare instances when some users need more than twenty outstanding
open files are there additional message exchanges among
parents and their child processes. Actual implementation and
testing has confirmed that this formulation solves the synchronization problem with a significant improvement in performance (due to the reduced message traffic and message processing time in parent processes).

This example demonstrates that in a message based system
the cost of keeping state variables consistent all the time
could be high, even on a uni-processor. We believe that in a
distributed system the cost of keeping distributed state
variables consistent is much higher. Therefore, it is worth-
while to have mechanisms, such as distributed co-operating
processes, that permit the separation of the critical parts
of relationships that need to be preserved deterministically
from the non-critical parts that can be preserved probabilistically.

3.4. A New Concept

Atomic transactions are vital to distributed database systems
because they allow the consistency constraints of distributed
data objects to be preserved despite the failure of individual
pieces of the system. A decentralized global operating system
requires the same kind of failure atomicity, and so must be
constructed with a transaction facility in its kernel [15].

Unfortunately, the serialization model developed for distributed database systems places a fundamental limitation on the
use of transactions; i.e., they can model only sequential
actions or concurrent actions that are logically equivalent

to sequential actions. Yet, a significant part of operating system software takes the form of co-operating processes. The two-way communications among co-operating processes make it impossible to transform co-operating processes into co-operating transactions without violating the relative ordering requirement of the serialization model. One of the achievements of our relational model of data consistency is that it provides a foundation for formulating co-operating transactions. This new notion is informally introduced here; its characterization and application will be formally elaborated in [10].

From an application point of view, the need for co-operating transactions arises from the desire to make the actions of co-operating processes atomic. For example, consider the hypothetical case of loan activities within a group of independent banks whose computers are connected by a network. Normally, a bank would handle loan applications by itself; however, if an acceptable loan requires more than 10% of the bank's current capital, the bank must (because of government regulations) ask other banks to syndicate the loan. We can model this as a set of co-operating processes, each of which encapsulates its own confidential financial database. Normally, a process operates in the autonomous phase to handle loan applications by itself. The co-operation starts when a process is asked to join the loan syndication. Once asked, a server will examine its own loan portfolio to determine whether it should accept, refuse, or try to negotiate the terms. Although the formulation of co-operating processes models the loan activity well (i.e., a group of independent processes who sometimes co-operate), it has a reliability problem. When a computer involved in a syndicated loan crashes, the financial database containing the banking accounts involved in the loan activities might be in an inconsistent state. This is not acceptable, and these process interactions must be made atomic to help eliminate this problem.

Co-operating transactions are transactions that communicate with each other and satisfy the conformity condition. There are two types of data objects manipulated by co-operating transactions. The first is the state variables of co-operating transactions. As with co-operating processes, the partial dependency relations among state variables define the co-operation. The operands of the co-operating transactions are the second type of data object. The manipulation of operands represents the external effects visible to the users. Since operands are organized in the form of disjoint atomic data sets, co-operating transactions can be structured in the form of nested transactions. Each of the sub-transactions of a co-operating transaction operates on one or more atomic data sets and satisfies the conformity condition.

Now we turn to the subject of managing the commit process of a co-operating transaction. A sub-transaction can be committed if and only if the action invariants of both the sub-transaction and all the levels of the co-operating transactions are satisfied. Therefore, an invoked sub-transaction can perform only the first phase of a two-phase commit protocol and must leave the final decision of whether to complete or abort the commit to the co-operating transaction. For example, suppose that in the loan syndication problem, bank A originates the loan syndication request and bank B agrees to participate. The sub-transactions invoked in A and B for handling that loan, such as the transferring M_1 dollars from B to A, and transferring the total amount of M_2 dollars to the customer, must be all done in order to conclude the loan. When all the sub-transactions invoked by A and B have completed their first phase commit, A (the originator of the syndicate) will follow a distributed two-phase commit protocol [1] to conclude the loan syndication.

We would like to make two comments on this example. First, the reliability problem per se can also be solved by viewing the financial records of each bank as a shared database and using conventional serializable transactions. However, in a typical database approach such as in [1], once an external transaction obtains the write lock, the database is directly manipulated by the transactions. In our approach, external transactions can only indirectly manipulate another bank's financial database via requests to the active local server. It is often important to restrict external users from direct access to another user's (or system) data in order to provide some degree of system sécurity. Secondly, co-operating transactions also provide better concurrency due to the fact that non-serializable concurrent actions are permitted.

3.5. Example: Graceful Degradation

This example is to illustrate the basic idea of co-operating transactions. It arose from the need to provide a reliable authentication service in the Accent network operating system. Since the database managed by the authentication servers is vital to the integrity of the entire system, it is required that the loss of an individual system element results only in the loss of some performance. Our approach to solving this problem is to use co-operating transactions. The three basic issues in defining co-operating transactions are: 1) the operand atomic data sets; 2) the partial dependency relations among co-operating servers; 3) the definition of sub-transactions. In this case, there are two types of operand atomic

data sets. The first is a capability list of users organized
as access group lists. The second is records of users' registered ports, which identify processes as having the access
rights of their users. The user capability list is partitioned
to improve the concurrency of accessing. For reliability
reasons, each part of the capability list and the record of
a user's registered ports are replicated and distributed in
two physically independent machines.

The system authentication servers are organized into a
mutual back-up ring. Suppose that there are three servers,
S_1, S_2 and S_3, residing on machines one, two and three, respectively. Let the partitioned and duplicated capability
lists be $\{L_{1,1}, L_{1,2}\}$, $\{L_{2,2}, L_{2,3}\}$ and $\{L_{3,3}, L_{3,1}\}$, where
the first subscript corresponds to the server who is respon-
sible for the set of the two copies of a partitioned list,
and the second refers to the location of the host machine.
For example, the set $\{L_{2,2}, L_{2,3}\}$ resides on machine two and
three, and is maintained by server S_2. A server also has the
capability to manipulate the portion of the atomic data sets
that resides on his machine so that it can take over the task
of a failed server. For example, server two, in addition to
maintaining the set $\{L_{2,2}, L_{2,3}\}$, also takes care of $L_{1,2}$
should server one crash. In addition to the management of the
capability list, a server also maintains the records of registered ports. These records are managed in the same way as the
capability lists.

The partial dependency relation among servers is as follows.
Normally, servers are working independently. Each of them
maintains the atomic data sets for which it is responsible.
Co-operation among servers is triggered by the events representing the failure or recovery of a server. In Accent, the
interprocess communication sub-system automatically monitors,
and polls if necessary, each process. Once the failure of a
process is detected, the interprocess communication facility
will inform the relevant parties. The neighbors of a failed
server will co-operatively close the mutual back-up ring. For
example, if S_2 crashes, S_1 will recover the atomic data set
(such as $L_{2,3}$) by getting copies from S_3. Furthermore, S_1
will ask S_3 to recreate lost redundant files (such as $L_{1,2}$)
on machine three. The co-operation associated with the closing
of the ring completes when all the relevant atomic data sets
are reconstructed. From that point on, S_1 (or S_3) will then
manage the atomic data sets that were managed by S_2. When a
server process recovers, it will inform its neighbors to
transfer the updated atomic data sets back to it. When all
the file transfers are done, the recovered server resumes its
duty.

The definition of the sub-transactions for this example is

straightforward. A sub-transaction is needed to manage the
capability list, another is needed to manage records of registered ports and a final one is needed to perform file management. The first two sub-transactions are used in normal operations, while the file management sub-transactions are used in
reconstructing the atomic data sets during the failure and
recovery procedures of a server. The action invariants at the
server level (i.e., the co-operating transaction level) is
simply that all invoked sub-transactions for a task must be
all done. For example, when a recovered server is inserted
back into the ring, there are two file transfer sub-transactions transferring files back to the recovered one from its
two neighbors which must all be completed in order to conclude
the insertion.

3.6. Example: Distributed Load Leveling

This example was conceived to illustrate the communications
involved in, and the probabilistic behavior of, co-operating
transactions. In this example we examine the problem of distributed load leveling for a point-to-point computer network.
In any load leveling scheme, there are two major problems
that must be addressed - the first is providing atomic transfer of work items between work queues, and the second is
ensuring the stability of the load leveling operation. The
atomicity requirement arises from the need to guarantee that
work items will not be lost or duplicated should a node crash
during an instance of load leveling. Instability may result
from the lack of co-operation among load leveling activities.
For example, a pair of heavily loaded nodes (nodes A and B)
share a common, lightly loaded neighbor (node C). Nodes A and
B might simultaneously observe that node C is lightly loaded
and attempt to off-load some of their work onto it. This
would result in node C becoming heavily loaded and it may then
choose to redistribute its load with nodes A and B. This could
clearly result in a pathological condition in which work items
are repeatedly distributed.
    Thus, for distributed load leveling, it is necessary to
have both atomicity of work item transfers and a form of
demand-driven co-operation that is able to adapt to a changing
environment. The co-operating transactions paradigm is a
formalism that provides a method of meeting these requirements
while permitting highly concurrent execution of the nodes'
load leveling functions. The demand-driven, adaptive co-
operation between transactions may be represented by probabilistic relations among the state variables of the transactions. The co-operating transaction responsible for load
leveling at each node typically operates in an autonomous

fashion managing the node's work queue and exchanging load
information with other nodes. At some point in time, a node
may decide that it is in the best interest of the system to
engage in an instance of load leveling. A node would then
attempt to enter into a co-operative state with some of its
nearest neighbors. This phase of the load leveling function
is probabilistic in as far as the neighboring nodes are not
constrained to enter into a co-operative state whenever requested to do so. This is because the load information at
each node is partial and inaccurate. In the event that none
of the neighboring nodes agree to enter into co-operation
with the requesting node, the request must be withdrawn and
(possibly) reattempted at a later point in time. On the other
hand, should a node be successful in entering a co-operative
state with one or more of its neighbors, the group of co-
operating nodes collectively enter into a negotiation phase
in which it is determined how the load associated with the
group should be distributed in order to best accomplish load
leveling. It should be noted that the group of nodes involved
in co-operation with the node initiating the load leveling
attempt could extend beyond its nearest neighbors if a non-
neighboring node simultaneously entered into a co-operative
state with a common neighboring node.

   In general, nodes in the co-operating group will carry out
decisions that result from the negotiation within the group.
However, due to the dynamic nature of local work item generation and consumption, a node's load could be substantially
different at the time a load transfer is attempted from when
the group plan was devised. It is therefore desirable for the
system to permit local adjustment to the group plan whenever
the situation warrants. Allowing local adjustment is another
example of the probabilistic co-operation in this example, in
that there is no absolute guarantee that the original load
leveling scheme will be carried out as planned. For example,
the original group plan might require that node A transfer
ten work items to node B. However, before the transfer is
complete, node B receives a block of locally generated work
items. In this situation it may be subsequently determined
that the interests of the system are best served by transferring only five of the ten work items. An advantage of using
co-operating transactions in such a case is that they permit
co-operation (communication) during the execution of the
transactions, and thus are able to adapt to environments that
change quickly with respect to their execution.

   In the co-operating transaction formulation, each node's
work queue represents an operand atomic data set which is
encapsulated by the co-operating transaction that implements
a node's load leveling function. The basic sub-transactions

involved in the manipulation of nodes' work queues are ADD,
DELETE and TRANSFER. The ADD and DELETE sub-transactions are
used to atomically insert and delete items from local work
queues. The TRANSFER sub-transaction carries out specified
transfers of work items by invoking the destination node's
ADD sub-transaction, sending the work items, and invoking the
source node's DELETE sub-transaction. The action invariant of
the TRANSFER sub-transaction is that both the remove and insert operations must be successfully completed. Since job
queues are encapsulated locally, when the sender's transfer
sub-transaction attempts to invoke the receiver's ADD sub-
transaction, the receiver may modify the parameters of the
ADD sub-transaction. In the above example, ten jobs are sent
from node A to node B. However, node B takes five work items
instead of ten, and informs node A accordingly. Although node
A can reject B's modification by aborting the transaction, A
may well re-execute the local ADD sub-transaction and commit
the modified transfer. This is clearly more efficient than
blindly carrying out the original plan and having to remedy
it later.

   Finally, it should be noted that the atomicity of work
item transfers per se can be solved by using a typical database approach based on the serialization model. However, this
would be done at the cost of concurrency, protection and performance. The loss of concurrency is due to the relative
ordering requirement imposed by the serialization model which
is unnecessary for work item transfers. In the co-operating
transaction formulation, the relationships between any two
work queues are autonomous. The integrity of work item transfers are represented by the action invariant "both the destination node's ADD sub-transaction and the source node's DELETE
sub-transaction must be done or neither is done". The work
item transfer sub-transactions can be done in any relative
order and may or may not be serializable. The degree of protection is enhanced because, with co-operating transactions,
each work queue is encapsulated by a local load leveling
transaction which controls access to, and maintains the consistency of, the queues. In a typical database approach, one's
own work queue may be arbitrarily manipulated by any transaction that obtains a write lock. Finally, performance is
sacrificed with serializable transactions due to the fact that
they are not able to adapt to a changing environment, as can
co-operating transactions which may communicate in the course
of their operation.

4. CONCLUSION

This paper has informally outlined some of our initial ideas on synchronization in distributed systems. More formality and elaboration will appear in forthcoming publications.

Our initial experiments with applying these ideas to distributed operating systems have been very encouraging. We believe they are valuable in network operating systems but essential in a decentralized operating system such as ArchOS [16] will be. The kinds of interaction amenable to our approach to co-operating processes and transactions are not yet delineated. Neither is it yet very clear what all the implications of these concepts could be on suitable operating system structures. Our research and experiments are continuing and will be reported in the literature.

ACKNOWLEDGEMENT

We wish to thank our many colleagues who contributed to this work in one way or another. In particular we are grateful to John Lehoczky for his assistance with the relational model of data consistency, Norm Pleszkoch for his diligent criticism and editing, Alex Schaffer for his work with the process creation and destruction example, and James Allchin, Martin McKendry, Mickey Merritt and Alfred Spector for their helpful comments and suggestions.

This work was sponsored in part by: the USAF Rome Air Development Center under contract F30602-81-C-0297; and the US Naval Ocean Systems Center under contract number N66001-81-C-0484; and the US Defense Advanced Research Projects Agency under contract F33615-81-K-1539.

REFERENCES

1. Bernstein, P.A. and Goodman, N. (1980). Fundamental algorithms for concurrent control in distributed database systems. Technical Report CCA-08-05, Computer Corporation of America.
2. Papadimitriou, C.H., Bernstein, P.A. and Rothnie, J.B. Jr (1977). Some computational problems related to database concurrency control. In "Proc. Conf. on Theoretical Computer Science".
3. Kung, H.T. and Papadimitriou, C.H. (1979). An optimal theory of concurrency control for databases. In "Proc. SIGMOD Conf. on Management of Data", pp.116-126, ACM.
4. Lamport, L. (1976). Towards a theory of correctness for multi-user database systems. Technical Report CA-7610-07-12, Massachusetts Computer Associates Inc.
5. Kung, H.T. and Lehman, P.L. (1979). A concurrent database problem: binary search trees. Technical Report, Dept. of Computer Science, Carnegie-Mellon University, Pittsburgh, USA.

6. Schwarz, P.M. and Spector, A.Z. (1982). Synchronizing shared abstract types. Technical Report CMU-CS-82-128, Dept. of Computer Science, Carnegie-Mellon University, Pittsburgh, USA.
7. Garcia-Molina, H. (1982). Using semantic knowledge for transaction processing in a distributed database. Technical Report, Dept. of Electrical Engineering and Computer Science, Princeton University.
8. Allchin, J.E. and McKendry, M.S. (1982). Object based synchronization and recovery. Technical Report GIT-ICS-82/15, School of Information and Computer Science, Georgia Institute of Technology.
9. Sha, L. (1983). Synchronization in distributed operating systems. PhD thesis, Dept. of Electrical Engineering, Carnegie-Mellon University, Pittsburgh, USA. (In preparation.)
10. Sha, L. *et al.* (1983). Non-serializable transactions in distributed operating systems - a relational approach. (In preparation.)
11. Reed, D.P. and Kanodia, R.K. (1979). Synchronization with eventcounts and sequencers. *Comm. ACM* 22, 115-123.
12. Thomas, R.H. (1979). A majority consensus approach to concurrency control for multiple copy database. *ACM Transactions on Data Base Systems* 4, 180-209.
13. Ball, J.E. (1982). Canvas - the Spice graphic package. Technical Report, Dept. of Computer Science, Carnegie-Mellon University, Pittsburgh, USA.
14. Schaffer, A. (1982). LUCIFER: a mechanism for transparent file access in a Unix network. Technical Report, Dept. of Computer Science, Carnegie-Mellon University, Pittsburgh, USA.
15. Jensen, E.D. (1980). Distributed computer systems. *In* "Computer Science Research Review", pp.53-63. Carnegie-Mellon University, Pittsburgh, USA.
16. Jensen, E.D. (1982). Decentralized executive control of computers. *In* "Proc. 3rd Int. Conf. on Distributed Computing Systems", pp.31-35. IEEE.

Towards a Systematic Approach to Implement Distributed Control of Synchronization

1. CONCEPT OF A SYNCHRONIZATION CONTROLLER

1.1. Introduction

In a distributed system, proofs concerning algorithms of synchronization control are often difficult to establish; the
variable delays in communication cause uncertainty about the
real system state [1], and have resulted in increased complexity of protocols for co-operation among controllers [2,3,
4].

To obtain more easily a set of correct algorithms, we
suggest the adoption of the following steps, portrayed in
Fig. 1:

1) At the beginning, one gives an expression which we qual-
ify as being abstract, of the problem posed. This expression, independent of the distributed characteristics
of the target machine, only translates the logic of the
problem. Its principal advantage is that it permits ana-
lytical validation (absence of starvation, etc.) independent of all hypotheses concerning communications among
processes.

2) The abstract expression is then translated with the aid
of a standard procedure which is proved once and for all.
These procedures depend on the target machine, and the
algorithm obtained uses elementary tools of synchronization specially adapted: common memory and mutual exclusion for centralized systems, time stamping [5] and
broadcasting for distributed systems.

Distributed Computing Systems
ISBN 0-12-543970-9

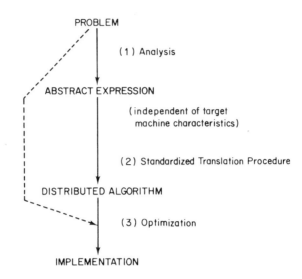

FIG. 1 *Conceptualization of a synchronization controller.*

3) Finally, the particular characteristics of the problem at
hand can open possibilities for improvements and optimizations.

The search for general procedures to translate abstract
synchronization expressions is just beginning [6]. We propose
in this article a method adapted to a particular language of
abstract expressions: the modules of control [7]. In Section
1.2 we present this language, as well as its application to
two classic problems. In Section 2 we state precisely our
hypothesis of distribution as well as the general principles
of the method of translation developed in Section 3.

1.2. Abstract Synchronization Expressions

The language for expression of synchronization we have chosen
permits the definition of a set of controlled procedures [7].
The real synchronizations are carried out when a process calls
or exits the execution of one of these procedures. For each
controlled procedure P two counters register information on
the history of the system:

1) #AUTH(P) represents the number of processes who have been
    authorized to execute procedure P.
2) #TERM(P) represents the number of processes whose ex-
    ecution of P has already terminated.

Remark:

We have chosen for the sake of simplicity to limit our system
to two counters. In reality, to resolve certain problems, it
is useful to add the counter #REQ(P), which represents the
number of processes which have requested execution of procedure P, and it is also convenient to manipulate two auxiliary counters:

$$\#ACTIVE(P) = \#AUTH(P) - \#TERM(P) \quad \text{and}$$
$$\#WAIT(P) = \#REQ(P) - \#AUTH(P)$$

which represent respectively the number of processes actually
executing procedure P and the number waiting to execute P.
The results we establish with the aid of the two principal
counters can be easily adapted to include the #REQ(P) counter
and the two auxiliary counters.

   With each procedure is associated an Authorization Condition, which is a predicate based on the state of the
counters.

   Example 1. The producer-consumer problem with a shared
buffer divided into N slots can be expressed as:

$$CONDITION(CONS) = \#AUTH(CONS) - \#TERM(PROD) < 0 \quad \text{and}$$
$$CONDITION(PROD) = \#AUTH(PROD) - \#TERM(CONS) < N$$

where CONS and PROD are the procedures utilized respectively
as the consumer and producer processes.

   Example 2. The management of a class of resources which
exist in R separate instantiations can be expressed as:

$$CONDITION(U) = \#AUTH(U) - \#TERM(U) < R$$

where U is the procedure which manipulates one instance of
resource R.

   In the following discussion, we consider conditions of the
form

$$CONDITION(P) = \sum \alpha_j Cj < K \qquad (1)$$

where $\alpha_j = \pm 1$ and Cj is one of the counters associated with
the controlled procedure.

   This type of expression represents a large enough number
for the cases encountered in practice. To streamline the
notation, we will prefer to work with the two examples previously cited. We will then systematically take the counter
#AUTH(P) as having a positive coefficient in the condition
statements, and the counter #TERM(P) as having a negative
coefficient. Thus we need only consider conditions of the
form:

$$CONDITION(P) = \sum_i \#AUTH(P_i) - \sum_j \#TERM(P_j) < K \qquad (1')$$

This artifice only aims to clarify the exposition; in
general it is the coefficient which determines the mode of
the distribution of the counter Cj.

2. SYNCHRONIZATION AND DISTRIBUTED SYSTEMS

2.1. Definition

We define a distributed system as a set of co-operating processes installed on a multiprocessor architecture without a
common memory. Each processor with its local memory forms a
site, and the sites are connected by physical communication
channels such that any pair of processors can exchange information. In choosing such an organization, we aim to satisfy
two principal objectives:

1) to augment system performance as much by exploiting local
   properties (a process and the data it handles may be installed on the same site) as by the possibility of parallel execution by diverse processors;
2) to augment the availability of the system by ensuring
   that after the failure of any site, the system can continue, possibly degraded, on the sites which remain intact

Nonetheless, since the processes co-operate with a common
goal, the processes in a system are induced to synchronize
with each other. The synchronization tools implemented in a
centralized system, of which semaphores [8] and monitors [9]
constitute the two typical forms, are unfit because they
depend, in general, on the existence of a common memory among
all the processes.

On an architecture without a common memory, a solution for
a problem of synchronization as given consists of maintaining
a single process, the controller, which, by the skewing of
message exchanges, co-ordinates the activities of the processes
in the system. This solution, which we term "centralized control" fails to satisfy objectives 1) and 2) above because:

1) The processes are slowed up by the exchange of messages
   with the controller, since in the general case it is on
   a remote site.
2) If the site containing the controller process malfunctions
   the entire system ceases to function.

Another way, that of "distributed control", consists of
installing on each site a process controller which manages
local processes and which periodically co-ordinates its operation with the controller processes of the other sites.

To distribute control, one adopts the following principles

1) A controller is installed on each site to verify the conditions which apply to the processes it controls.
2) As the conditions can occur using counters whose exact
   value is known only to a remote site, we replace each
   abstract expression with a stricter local condition. To
   do this, it is sufficient for each site to provide, for
   each counter affected, a positive coefficient (respectively negative) with a value which is always greater
   (respectively smaller).

2.2. System Organization

The system we consider is composed of N sites. On each site
i are installed the processes PRij, which must be synchronized in order to use the set of procedures Pk whose local-
ization is unspecified. We are not concerned with either the
manner in which the processes designate these procedures nor
with the underlying scheme of execution (such as remote call
implemented by an exchange of messages). A detailed exposition
of the diverse techniques which can be used is to be found in
[10].

The abstract expression of the problem of synchronization
is given by some number of conditions which respect the general form given in (1') above. An implementation of the
abstract expression with the aid of a centralized controller
is simple: the process controller manages the necessary counters in accordance with the messages sent to it by the controlled processes. The set of these counters thus gives an
exact representation of the state of the system and in ju-
diciously evaluating all the conditions, the controller can
block and unblock the processes.

To distribute the control, one installs on each site a
local controller, CTLi, which manages a set of variables
which we term the approximate representation of the state of
the system. This representation should be sufficient to enable
CTLi to synchronize all processes PRij, which are installed
in its site. The maintenance of the approximate representation
presupposes some co-operation among the local controllers. To
this end, they are tied logically by a virtual communication
ring [1] such that CTLi can send messages to its successor
site, and receive messages from its predecessor site in the
ring. The system is portrayed in Fig. 2.

We have yet to specify what it is that constitutes the
approximate representation of the system state as well as
what authorization conditions are evaluated by the local controllers.

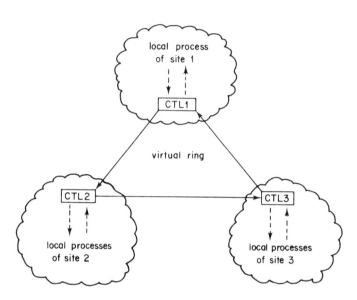

FIG. 2 *Distribution of control*

2.3. Local Control

2.3.1. Introductory example. As an informal example of distributed control, we can use the management of a bank account held in common by two persons, A and B, each possessing his own cheque book. The constraint imposed by the bank is that after any expenditure, one must verify the condition:

(Sum of expenditures) - (Sum of past deposits) <= 0.

A and B see each other periodically to exchange messages, but each desires for most of the time to conserve a certain autonomy in control of their expenditures.

Person A, for example, knows exactly the total of his expenditures as well as his deposits. As for those of B, A can only estimate. If these estimations meet verifiably at all times the conditions:

(Estimation of deposits by B) <=
                         (Actual sum of past deposits by B)

and

(Estimation of expenditures by B) >=
                      (Actual sum of past expenditures by B)

then A is certain never to write any bad cheques so long as he verifies before each new expenditure that:

((Sum of past expenditures of A) +
          (Estimation of past expenditures by B)) -
((Sum of past deposits of A) +
          (Estimation of past deposits by B)) < 0.

2.3.2. General principles. In the same manner as the preceding example, the total number of expenditures is broken
up into a subtotal of expenditures by A and another subtotal
of expenditures by B, each of which is known locally and
estimated elsewhere. To distribute control, one will split
each counter (both authorization and termination) into as
many instances (local counters) as there are sites. For
example, the local counter #AUTH(P) represents the number of
authorizations of execution of procedure P already permitted
by CTLi. Thus we have:

$$\sum_i \#\mathrm{authi}(P) = \#\mathrm{AUTH}(P)$$

and   (2)

$$\sum_i \#\mathrm{termi}(P) = \#\mathrm{TERM}(P)$$

If for each counter #AUTH(P) we know how to manage at each
site i a counter #M.authi(P) (called the lower bounded approximation) which equals or exceeds the sum of all the local
counters #authk(P) at the other sites, and inversely if for
each counter #TERM(P) we can manage at each site i a counter
#m.termi(P) (called the upper bounded approximation) which is
less than or equal to the sum of all local counters #termk(P),
then one can deduce for all abstract conditions of the form
(1') a stronger local condition (see Proposition 1).
This condition is expressed as a function of the local counters of the site as well as the lower bounded (#M.---) and
upper bounded (#m.---) approximations (counters) which are
also managed locally.
     Thus in example 2, the abstract condition:

CONDITION(U) = #AUTH(U) - #TERM(U) < R

can be replaced by the local condition:

conditioni(U) = (#authi(U) + #M.authi(U)) -
                         (#termi(U) + #m.termi(U)) < R.

     Evidently, one need only install at each site i those
counters which are strictly necessary for the control of local
processes and furthermore one is not obliged to manage all of
these conditions, all of the counters, nor all the upper and
lower bounded approximation counters.
     Proposition 1 is quite evident in light of the form im-
posed on all the CONDITIONs.

PROPOSITION 1

If the management of the lower bounded and upper bounded
approximation counters is correctly implemented, that is
to say if it can verify at any given moment at every site
the truth of the following inequalities:

$$\#m.termi(P) <= \sum_{k\neq i} \#termk(P) \qquad (3)$$

and

$$\#M.authi(P) >= \sum_{k\neq i} \#authk(P) \qquad (4)$$

then we assert that for each site i,

$$conditioni(P) \implies CONDITION(P)$$

The local controllers only authorize execution of a controlled procedure if the local condition associated with the
procedure is satisfied. Furthermore, Proposition 1 assures
that this distributed behaviour effectively implements the
abstract synchronization expression.

3. MANAGEMENT OF APPROXIMATE REPRESENTATIONS

We treat in this section the management of the upper bounded
and lower bounded approximation counters ($\#m.termi(P)$ and
$\#M.authi(P)$ respectively) in the absence of site failures.

3.1. Management of Upper Bounded Approximations

Referring back to the introductory example, let us suppose
that B sends to A the sum of his deposits to the account.
Then A can use this information received from B as an estimation of the past deposits of B. The delays in the message-
sending mechanism lead us to suspect that this estimation is
not necessarily exact by the time A receives it, but since it
is based on known reality it will amply suffice. It is always
less than or equal to the real figure, and, therefore, upper
bounded.

It is clear that one can manage the variables $\#m.termi(P)$
in the same manner. This behaviour is taken from [11]. It is
combined with the results in [12] under regular conditions.
Its principle is simple:

1) At each incrementation of a counter $\#termi(P)$, CTLi transmits along the ring a message of augmentation of all
   $\#m.termk$ upper bounded approximations, i.e. a message of
   the form: << +m.term(P), i >>.
2) Site i, upon receiving a message of the form << +m.term
   (P), k >>, and upon verifying i ≠ k, performs the incrementation on its local copy, m.termi(P), and retransmits

TABLE 1 *Management of upper bounded approximations.*

SITE	APPROXIMATE REPRESENTATIONS	LOCAL CONDITIONS
1	#auth1(PROD), #term1(PROD) #m.term1(CONS)	condition1(PROD) = #auth1(PROD) - #m.term1(CONS) < N
2	#auth2(CONS)m #term2(CONS) #m.term2(PROD)	condition2(CONS) = #auth2(CONS) - #m.term2(PROD) < 0

the message to its successor on the ring.

Thus we have at any given instant:

$$\#m.termi(P) = \sum_{k \neq i} (\#termk(P) - nbr\ of\ <<+m.term(P),k>>\ messages\ in\ transit\ between\ k\ and\ i) \qquad (5)$$

which suffices to establish invariant (3) (provided that at system initialization all of the #termi(P) variables and the #m.termi(P) upper bounded approximations are initialized to zero).

In the case where the producer process is installed at Site 1 and the consumer process is at Site 2, the variables and the applicable local conditions can be depicted as in Table 1.

3.2. Management of Lower Bounded Approximations

For the management of the #M.xxx lower bounded counters, the requirements are slightly more complex. In the case of the introductory example, A can no longer be content with a delayed knowledge of B's expenditures! However if B has signalled to A that he does not plan in the near future to spend more than some fixed sum, then this figure can serve as A's estimation of B's expenditures for that period. As long as B stays within the limits of his projected expenditures, he can function autonomously. But if he desires to surpass that value, he must do so in co-ordination with A, that is he must await A's response to his request to increase the value (which response may be a simple acknowledgement of receipt of the message). The waiting delay for the response assures that if two demands are made simultaneously by A and B which together

are inconsistent with the current account balance, the account
will not be debited. On the other hand, it could be that
neither expenditure can be made individually: thus one of the
two must cancel his request (and signal the cancellation to
the other) and reformulate it at a later time when financial
conditions become more favourable.

We can use these principles as the basis for managing the
#M.xxx lower bounded approximation counters. To each local
counter #authi(P), we will associate a variable #max.authi(P),
called the local allotment, which represents the degree of
freedom to be tolerated in the autonomous evolution of the
local counter #authi(P). In other words, if #max.authi(P) -
#authi(P) = c, then the controller at site i refrains from
authorizing in the near future more than c executions of
procedure P. (These obviously occur in the framework of the
local conditions.) We will say that CTLi has at its disposal
an allotment of credit of c authorizations of procedure P.

The system of service messages assures that the value of
#M.authi(P) very closely tracks the value $\sum_{k \neq i}$ #max.authk(P).

3.2.1. **Augmenting the local allotment of credits.** The first
sort of service message permits the local controllers to increase their allotment (or award) of credits in the following
steps:

1) site i transmits along the ring the message << +M.auth(P),
   i >>
2) upon receiving this message, each site k will increment
   its local counter #M.authk(P) and pass the message along
   the ring
3) when site i recovers its message, after one complete
   circuit on the ring, all the local lower bounded approximation counters will have been incremented by 1. Thus i
   can augment its local allotment of credits for P,
   #max.authi(P), by 1 also.

The uncertainty factor present in this method of managing
the lower bounded variables causes the risk of system deadlock. In example 2 it is discovered that as a result of an
excessive number of augmentations of local allotments, all
the #M. authi(P) local counters become superior to R, and,
therefore, no further authorizations can be awarded. This
possibility necessitates a mechanism for diminution of allotments of credits.

3.2.2. **Diminution of local allotments of credit.** The diminution by CTLi of a local allotment (i.e. the cancellation of
a credit) proceeds according to the following scenario:

1) If the diminution is possible (i.e. if #authi(P) <
    #max.authi(P)) then site i decrements its local allotment
    and subsequently transmits this message along the ring:
    << -M.auth(P), i >>.
2) During the circulation of the message on the ring, each
    site k will decrement #M.authk(P) and pass the message on
    to its successor on the ring.
3) When the message finishes its circuit, site i removes the
    message from circulation.

Thanks to this possibility, we can avoid system deadlock.
An exhaustive treatment of the subject would be long and
tedious, and we deem it preferable for our purposes here to
delineate the problem with respect to the particular synchronization problems already posed. For this reason we are content
to outline the principles of a general method (to show that
the problem is at least solvable) in which the elements can
be drawn out for resolution in the particular cases sited.
Bearing in mind that some of the requests for augmentation
may enter into conflict, in order to avoid system deadlock it
is necessary to cancel all the conflicting requests except
for one (otherwise one risks entering an infinite cycle of
augmentation/diminution requests).
We now know techniques which ensure that such cancellations
are consistent among themselves (see "wait/die system" in [3]).
To do this one attributes to each message a unique number of
logical date (for example the time-stamp in [5]). Each controller retains an image of the augmentation messages that it
receives (the list of these images is the "trace" maintained
by the controller). The controller also retains the logical
date of each such request in the trace. Each controller removes the image of a message from its trace when it receives
a termination message bearing the same logical date.
  · Whenever all the local conditions have remained false for
a given fixed period of time (a time-out countdown which
signals the possibility of a deadlocked system), each CTLi
will examine its trace for an augmentation message which
antecedes his own, and if one is found, will commence the
systematic diminution of his local allotment of credit. The
awards of credit thus cancelled are retransmitted (with the
original logical date) when they arrive at the head of the
trace (i.e. when each becomes the oldest outstanding augmentation message).
  Example 3. Let us consider the classic "reader/writer"
problem [13]. The two controlling procedures are R (read) and
W (write). The rules (constraining conditions) of synchronization are:

$$\text{CONDITION}(R) = \#\text{AUTH}(W) - \#\text{TERM}(W) < 1 \text{ and}$$
$$\text{CONDITION}(W) = (\#\text{AUTH}(W) - \#\text{TERM}(W) +$$
$$(\#\text{AUTH}(R) - \#\text{TERM}(R)) < 1 \qquad (6)$$

All awards of credit for reading impede awards of credit for writing, and vice versa. During periods without outstanding requests for writing, the credits for reading can be awarded without restrictions, implying an almost autonomous operation for the local controller. The first award of credit for writing (transmission of the message $<< +\text{M.auth}(W), i >>$) will be cancelled if there remain unused older credits for reading. Meanwhile, the presence of this message in the traces of the various controllers prohibits any acquisition of new awards of credit for reading. When a sufficient number of terminations of reading have been requested, the message $<< +\text{M.auth}(W), i >>$ will become the oldest entry in the traces of the CTLi and then the writing operation will be allowed to proceed

3.3. Global Operation

The method of management of the upper bounded approximation counters implies that at any given instant:

$$\#\text{M.authi}(P) = \sum_{k \neq i} (\#\text{max.authk}(P) + \qquad (7)$$
$$\text{(the nbr of } << +\text{M.auth}(P),k >> \text{ messages}$$
$$\text{in transit between i and k)}$$
$$+ \text{ (the nbr of } << -\text{M.auth}(P),k >> \text{ messages}$$
$$\text{in transit between k and i))}$$

and thus that

$$\#\text{M.authi}(P) >= \sum_{k \neq i} \#\text{max.authk}(P) \qquad (8)$$

Thus by the definition of the local allotments, $\#\text{max.authk}(P) >= \#\text{authk}(P)$, the invariant (4) is established, if at the starting point of the system the variables $\#\text{authi}(P)$, $\#\text{M.authi}(P)$, and $\#\text{max.authi}(P)$ are initialized to zero.

Since we have shown above in Section 3 that the invariant (3) is also satisfied, Proposition 1 as established in Section 2 is sufficient to prove the correct behaviour of this method of distributed control.

Example: To manage a resource composed of R identical instances of a resource, we install at each site i the variables $\#\text{authi}(U)$, $\#\text{max.authi}(U)$, $\#\text{M.authi}(U)$, $\#\text{term}(U)$ and $\#\text{m.term}(U)$. Then the local conditions become:

$$\text{CONDITION}(U) = (\#\text{authi}(U) + \#\text{M.authi}(U)) -$$
$$(\#\text{termi}(U) - \#\text{m.termi}(U)) < R \qquad (9)$$
$$\text{AND} \quad \#\text{authi}(U) < \#\text{max.authi}(U)$$

TABLE 2 *Management of lower bounded approximation variables.*

Message received	Cause	Effect
$<+m.term(p),k{\neq}i>$	augmentation of #m.termk(P)	#m.termi(P):= #m.termi(P)+1; pass message on the ring
$<+M.auth(P),k{\neq}i>$	augmentation of #max.authk(P)	#M.authi(P):= #M.authi(P)+1; pass message on the ring
$<-M.auth(P),k{\neq}i>$	diminution of #max.authk(P)	#M.authi(P):= #M.authi(P)-1; pass message on the ring
	augmentation of #termi(P)	send $<<+m.auth(P),i>>$ along the ring
	desire to augment #max.authi(P)	send $<<+M.auth(P),i>>$ along the ring
	desire to diminish #max.authi(P)	#max.authi(P):= #max.authi(P)-1; send $<<-M.auth(P),i>>$ along the ring
$<+m.term(P),i>$	circulation complete	
$<+M.auth(P),i>$	circulation complete	#max.authi(P):= #max.authi(P)+1;
$<-M.auth(P),i>$	circulation complete	

The service messages exchanged among the sites on the virtual ring, as well as their semantics in causing action, are summarized in Table 2.

4. CONCLUSIONS

The method we have just described for the distribution of

a controller is a general one. Its applicability, however, encounters two sorts of difficulties. The first one is eased by the power of the chosen language of abstract expressions. One can find in [14,15] some examples of problems which are unsolvable using the system of counters described in Section 2.1, as one can also find there some proposals for adequate extensions to the system.

The second type of difficulties consists of quantitative problems: certain rules of synchronization aim at reducing the parallelism of the system to such an extent that the solution of a distributed controller can hardly be justified. The problem of mutual exclusion certainly pertains to this class; the relative independence of local controllers is illusory since, in any case, only one process requesting a given resource can be active at any given time. The choice of a centralized controller appears to be the most legitimate alternative, even though in order to satisfy the objective of reliability, it becomes necessary to build a recovery protocol to replace the controller (using a deputy controller for example).

In return, the management of R instantiations of a resource (example 2) lends itself well to distribution if R is much greater than N (R >> N). Each controller has at its disposal an allotment of credit for k instances of the resource, allowing for the possibility of autonomous operation. The size of the credit, k, varies (thanks to the mechanism of augmentation/diminution) and one can expect that it will change dynamically to adapt to instantaneous fluctuations in workloads.

In conclusion, we return to example 3 (reader/writer problem). If the characteristics of the system are such that requests for writing are frequent, the solution of a centralized controller would seem preferable. (See preceding remarks on mutual exclusion.) If, on the other hand, writing is rare or infrequent, the choice of a distributed controller is seductive: during periods free of requests for writing, allotments of credit for reading can be taken in large numbers, and the functioning of each local controller will be practically autonomous. The first demand for writing will inhibit pending requests for credits for reading, and exclusive access for the writer is assured within a finite and estimable delay.

5. ACKNOWLEDGEMENTS

The author wishes to thank C. Pinkard for the translation of this paper from the original French version.

REFERENCES

1. Le Lann, G. (1977). Distributed systems: towards a formal approach. *In* "Information Processing 77", pp.155-160. North-Holland, Netherlands.
2. Le Lann, G. (1978). Algorithms for distributed data-sharing systems which use tickets. *In* "Proc. 3rd Workshop on Distributed Data Management and Computer Networks". Berkeley, California.
3. Rosenkranz, D., Stearns, R. and Lewis, P. (1978). System level concurrency control for distributed database systems. *ACM Transactions on Database Systems*.
4. Seguin, J., Sergeant, G. and Wilms, P. (1979). A majority consensus algorithm for the consistency of duplicated and distributed information. *In* "Proc. First Int. Conf. on Distributed Computing Systems". Huntsville.
5. Lamport, L. (1978). Time, clocks and the ordering of events in a distrubuted system. *Comm. ACM* **21**, 7.
6. Carvalho, O.S.F. and Roucairol, G. (1982). On the distribution of an assertion. *In* "Proc. ACM-SIGACT-SIGOPS Symp. on Principles of Distributed Computing". Ottawa, Canada.
7. Robert, P. and Verjus, J.-P. (1977). Towards autonomous description of synchronization modules. *In* "Information Processing 77". North-Holland, Netherlands.
8. Dijkstra, E.W. (1968). Cooperating sequential processes. *In* "Programming Languages", (Ed. F. Genuys). Academic Press, New York.
9. Hoare, C.A.R. (1974). Monitors: an operating system structuring concept. *Comm. ACM* **17**, 11.
10. Cornafion (1981). Systèmes Informatiques Répartis - Concepts et Techniques. DUNOD.
11. André, F., Herman, D. and Verjus, J.-P. (1980). Contrôle du parallélisme et de la répartition, AFCET Summer School, July 1980. Aix-en-Provence, France.
12. Bochman, G.V. (1979). Towards an understanding of distributed and parallel systems. P.I. No.317. University of Montreal, Montreal, Canada.
13. Courtois, P.J., Heymans, I. and Parnas, D.I. (1971). Concurrent control with readers and writers. *Comm. ACM* **14**, 10.
14. Latteux, M. (1980). Synchronisation de processus. *RAIRO Informatique* **14**, 2.
15. Verjus, J.-P. (1978). Expression du contrôle à l'aide d'invariants. Bulletin AFCET Groplan, Vol.4.

Assertion, Decomposition and Partial Correctness of Distributed Control Algorithms

Osvaldo S.F. Carvalho and Gerard Roucairol

1. INTRODUCTION

1.1. Distributed Systems

The accelerated development in recent years of computer networks and multiprocessor technology provokes an increasing
interest in the programming of distributed systems. Many advantages come from decentralization; however, the opinion
that the art of distributed systems programming is still not
mastered, is widely accepted. Evidently the characteristics
of distributed systems, which distinguish them from centralized ones, are at the origin of the difficulties found by the
designer of distributed programs. But even these characteristics are not easy to specify precisely: there are countless
definitions of what is, or what should be a distributed system. That being so, let us state here what we think their
main features are.

A network (by this term we mean any distributed system) is
formed by a set of nodes that are physically independent;
there are no physical means for a node to force or to hinder
any action by any other node. A local controller drives each
node, following a local program. Global coherence and co-
operation can only be obtained through "diplomatic" ways,
using agreements - protocols - normally fixed when programming
the controllers. Each node has a local memory with exclusive
access, where it may store information about the rest of the
network. This information can only come through the network
communication lines by means of message exchanges between the
nodes. In particular no common clock is accessible.

Distributed Computing Systems
ISBN 0-12-543970-9

Difficulties with communication by messages are well known:
non-negligible, variable travelling times, non-existence of
direct communication lines between certain pairs of nodes,
possibility of transmission errors and of losses of messages,
and even line and node crashes. Effectively, this context
contributes to direct a large part of distributed systems
literature to the solution of problems created by their own
implementation.

In this paper we avoid most of these troubles and study
the design of algorithms in networks with the following
properties:

1) the nodes never fail
2) each node can always exchange messages with any other
    node
3) message contents are never truncated by its transmission.

We will not examine here all the kinds of algorithms that
can be executed by a network. Our interest concentrates on
the design of distributed algorithms that intend to maintain
the validity of an assertion over all possible combinations
of the states of the nodes of a network. Examples of such
assertions are: the reservations made by all the agencies of
an airline company must be such that one seat in a flight
cannot be booked to more than one passenger, or, the sum of
the deposits minus the sum of the withdrawals made by a client
in all agencies of a bank should always be positive. Many
resource managing problems of a distributed operating system
can also be put in this form.

A solution for this kind of problem is partially correct
if its execution never leads to situations where the correctness assertion is violated. To be totally correct, an algorithm must be deadlock-free and starvation-free. Finally, a
solution will be satisfactory if it fulfils some performance
criteria, such as the minimization of the number of message
exchanges, or the maximization of the load factor of some
resource.

This paper is mainly concerned with a method for the design of partially correct distributed algorithms. This goal
is complicated by the nature of the communication by messages,
which forces the information that a node has about the others
to be always approximate. Some care is needed to keep this
information reliable, even being approximate.

We propose herein a systematic procedure for the design of
data structures that represent the relevant information that
a node should have about the others, as well as a set of rules
for controller programming that assures their partial correctness. This preoccupation being reduced, the programmer may
then dedicate more attention to the total correctness and

and performance goals.

1.2. Paper Contents

This paper is organized as follows. In Section 2 we first examine the case of a very basic correctness assertion called a "lower-upper bounds couple". As we shall see in the following sections, any other correctness assertion can be decomposed in such a way that all resulting non-local assertions will be of this elementary form.

A "lower-upper bounds couple" is formed by two variables x_1 and x_2, localized at two nodes 1 and 2, ranging over the same partially ordered domain D, and linked by the assertion $x_1 \leq x_2$. In this context we characterize events (updates of the variables and message exchanges) with respect to their safety, this characterization being based on the shape of the common domain D. Then we propose a set of rules, using the notion of acceptance thresholds for messages, that assures the partial correctness of any protocol with respect to the assertion $x_1 \leq x_2$.

In a lower-upper bounds couple we may consider that x_1 represents, at node 1, a knowledge about the situation of node 2, and vice versa: x_1 is an underestimation, kept at node 1, of the current state of node 2, while x_2 is an overestimation, kept at node 2 of the current state of node 1. Thus in this case, the value of x_1 or x_2 represents both the current state of a node and the knowledge that it has about the other one.

In subsection 2.6 we separate these concepts and we confine the information that each node has about the other inside an "interface module". The correctness assertion is decomposed into two "local assertions" and one "communication assertion". A local assertion relates the current state of a node with the data in its interface; the communication assertion relates data in both interfaces. The resulting communication assertion will also be in the form of a lower-upper bounds couple. Consequently the acceptance thresholds method can also be used to keep it.

In Section 3 we deal with networks with 2 nodes linked by any correctness assertion. It is shown that any problem of this kind can be reduced to a lower-upper bounds couple. The correctness assertion is initially decomposed into two local assertions and two communication assertions, through algebraic manipulations based on the notion of Galois connections from lattice theory. The resulting communication assertions are also of the form of lower-upper bounds couples, where the variables x_1 and x_2 are representations of subsets of the sets of states of the nodes. The partial ordering is given by the subset inclusion relation.

Using other results from Galois connections theory, we show that we may consider only "relevant" subsets of states, and also coalesce the two communication assertions into a single lower-upper bounds couple. As an application example we develop a distributed algorithm for mutual exclusion in 2-node networks.

Networks with n-nodes are seen in Section 4. We propose a decomposition of the correctness assertion such that the resulting communication assertions will also be lower-upper bounds couples. We use this decomposition to get a solution for the 2-out-of-3 problem.

2. LOWER-UPPER BOUNDS COUPLES

Consider a network with two nodes 1 and 2, that store in their local memories two variables x_1 and x_2 respectively. If these variables have the same range of values given by a partially ordered domain D, and if the correctness of the network is given by the assertion $x_1 \leqq x_2$, then we call x_1 and x_2 a lower-upper bounds couple.

Besides their simplicity, lower-upper bounds couples are interesting because any other assertion keeping problem can be decomposed in order to have assertions of the form $x_1 \leqq x_2$ as subproblems. In this section we propose a set of rules for the design of partially correct protocols that keep lower-upper bounds couples. To do that we begin by characterizing events in these networks and by classifying them with respect to their safety.

2.1. Events, Controllers, Protocols

An event consists of a change in the value of one or more variables and can also include the sending and/or the reception of a message. Its characterization can be made based on the following hypothesis:

1) Events occur one at a time at precise instants $t_0 < t_1 < \ldots$
2) Each event is localized at a single node: every updated variable and every emission and reception of messages associated with an event are localized at the same node.
3) Every event is submitted to some satisfiability condition and then can be thought as the execution of a guarded command [1].

It can be verified that these hypotheses do not hide any critical phenomenon.

The controller of a node is made up of all guarded commands of this node. Together the two controllers form the network protocol.

For a lower-upper bounds couple, an event arriving at an instant t_k where $x_1(t_{k-1}) \leqq x_2(t_{k-1})$ will be safe if and only if $x_1(t_k) \leqq x_2(t_k)$, i.e., if the situation of the network remains correct after its occurrence. If a protocol permits only the occurrence of safe events, every situation derived from an initially correct one will be correct too, insuring its partial correctness.

Due to the locality hypothesis we have $x_2(t_k) = x_2(t_{k-1})$ for an event localized at node 1. This allows us to write the safety condition for events at node 1.

Safety condition 1: an event localized at node 1 at instant t_k will be safe if and only if

$$x_2(t_k) \geqq \text{lub}(x_1(t_{k-1}), x_1(t_k)), \quad \text{(lub: least upper bound)}$$

given that $x_2(t_{k-1}) = x_2(t_k) \geqq x_1(t_{k-1})$.

This condition allows for a classification of events localized at node 1 with respect to their safety. Events that make $x_1(t_k) \leqq x_1(t_{k-1})$ are trivially safe, since they satisfy automatically the safety condition. Trivially non-safe events are those for which $\text{lub}(x_1(t_k), x_1(t_{k-1}))$ does not exist in the domain D. For such events, the validity of $x_1 \leqq x_2$ would only be achieved by a perfect synchronization of the two nodes, but this contradicts our hypothesis about the non-accessibility of a common clock. When an event is such that $\text{lub}(x_1(t_k), x_1(t_{k-1}))$ exists and differs from $x_1(t_{k-1})$ it is classified as dangerous.

Events localized at node 2 are classified in the same way by means of the symmetrical safety condition below.

Safety condition 2: an event localized at node 2 at instant t_k will be safe if and only if

$$x_1(t_k) \leqq \text{glb}(x_2(t_{k-1}), x_2(t_k)), \quad \text{(glb: greatest lower bound)}$$

given that $x_1(t_k) = x_1(t_{k-1}) \leqq x_2(t_{k-1})$.

A partially correct protocol should then:

1) prevent completely the arrival of trivially non-safe events, and
2) have the guards of the commands that may provoke dangerous events strong enough to guarantee their safety conditions.

Commands that can only provoke trivially safe events must be examined only for total correctness and performance optimization purposes.

2.2. The Acceptance Thresholds Method

The safety conditions above are not suitable for direct use

as guards for the commands of the controllers, since they involve variables localized at distinct nodes. To solve this problem we propose the acceptance thresholds method, which conciliates the information needs for the safety conditions with the constraints imposed by the communication by messages.

This method exploits the idea of a "treaty" between the nodes, using fixed rules that, on one side, delimit the conditions for the sending of a message and, on the other side, associate the occurrence of dangerous events to the reception of "satisfactory" messages. At least in principle a node can maintain a list with all messages it sent up to the current instant (this list is an upper bound for the list of received messages of the other node), and a list with all received messages (that is a lower bound for the list of sent messages of the other node). Based on these lists and also on the fixed rules, each node can keep a reliable estimation of the other node's current state, that will perhaps satisfy the safety condition required for the occurrence of dangerous events.

Normally only the most recently exchanged messages present interest and it is not necessary for a node to keep the complete lists. In this sense we shall use two auxiliary variables TH_1 and TH_2 that will range over the same totally ordered domain. They will be localized at nodes 1 and 2 respectively, and will be used to stamp all sent messages as well as to identify outdated arriving messages. TH stands for acceptance threshold. The partial correctness of protocols that use this method is guaranteed in case of varying travelling times for messages, order inversions in their delivery and even in case of message losses. However, they can lead to situations where no event is allowed. It is up to the programmer to complete them in order to avoid such situations. The rules to be employed are:

R1:   consecutive values of the acceptance threshold of each node should always form ascending chains. For any event arriving at instant t_k we have $TH_i(t_k) \geq TH_i(t_{k-1})$ for $i = 1,2$.

R2:   every message sent by node i (i=1,2) at instant t_s has the form $<TH, X_i,...>$, where $TH = TH_i(t_s)$ and $X_i = x_i(t_s)$ Data in possible extra fields do not concern partial correctness (this rule characterizes a message as a sample of the situation at the sending node at the sending instant).

R3:   the guard of a command at node 1 that can provoke an event for which $x_1(t_r) \neq x_1(t_{r-1})$, where t_r is the instant of occurrence of the event must require the reception of a message $<TH, X_2,...>$ such that

   1. $TH > TH_1(t_{r-1})$

CONTROL ALGORITHMS 73

2. $X_2 \geq \text{lub}(x_1(t_{r-1}), x_1(t_r))$

R4: symmetric to R3

R5: the current acceptance threshold of node i must be
greater than the greatest TH field present at any message
sent to or received from node j up to the current instant
(for i,j = 1,2 ; i ≠ j).

Using these rules, a protocol will allow uniquely the
occurrence of safe events. This is so because every dangerous
event must obey rule R3 or R4. Requirements 1 and 2 of R3
will guarantee that $x_2(t_r) \geq X_2 \geq \text{lub}(x_1(t_{r-1}), x_1(t_r))$, the
safety condition for an event allowed by it. The arrival at
node 1 at instant t_r of a message $\langle TH, X_2 \rangle$ satisfying requirements 1 and 2 of R3 means that at a past instant $t_s < t_r$ - at
the sending instant t_s - we had $TH_2(t_s) = TH$ and $x_2(t_s) = X_2$.
Until t_r, all messages sent by node 1 carried a threshold
field that was (by R1 and R2) less than $TH_1(t_{r-1})$. Since by
requirement 1 of R3 we have $TH_1(t_{r-1}) < TH = TH_2(t_s)$, by requirement 1 of R4 none of the messages sent by node 1 until
t_r could provoke a non-trivially safe event at node 2 after
t_s. The occurrence of events at node 2 in the interval
$[t_s, t_r]$ is limited in this way to trivially safe ones. Consecutive values of x_2 in this interval must then form an
ascending chain, assuring that $x_2(t_r) \geq X_2$. By symmetrical
arguments we can show that all events allowed by R4 are also
safe. Rule R5 is not necessary from the strict point of view
of partial correctness. However, its adoption prevents a node
sending messages that would be blocked by the other node's
acceptance threshold, and also dispenses with the nodes
having to examine arriving messages carrying old news. But
perhaps its greatest advantage is the approximation that is
caused between the properties of the acceptance thresholds
and of the logical clocks and timestamps described in [2].
The former are indeed inspired by the latter and the two
concepts present identical properties in 2-node networks. In
more complex networks each node must keep one acceptance
threshold relative to each other node with which it partici-
pates in a lower-upper bounds couple. In this case it is the
greatest current value among all acceptance thresholds of a
node that will present the properties of the logical clocks.
Those properties can be used to impose an ordering of priorities for the resolution of conflicts that may prevent
deadlock and starvation phenomena [2,3].

2.3. Local and Communication Assertions

Suppose that the domain D of a lower-upper bounds couple is
given by the integers between 1 and 5. If node 1 remains

through a long time interval in the state $x_1 = 2$, and if node
2 executes a cycle $x_2 = 3,4,3,4,\ldots$ during this interval, by
our rules each transition $4 \to 3$ (a dangerous event) will require a message exchange. To avoid this, we add a variable L
to node 1, a variable U to node 2 and we decompose the correctness assertion into three others: $x_1 \leq L$, $L \leq U$ and $U \leq x_2$.
Assertion $L \leq U$ is a lower-upper bounds couple too, and can
be maintained by a protocol using the acceptance threshold
method. If a situation arrives where $L = U = 3$, in a time
interval like the one described above, no communication between the nodes would be necessary.

   Without the variables L and U, all the knowledge that a
node has about the other is contained in its own state: x_1
works as a lower bound for x_2 and vice versa. The separation
in a node of its state from the information that it has about
the rest of the network is always possible, and can furnish
many advantages.

   An algorithm that uses this separation works roughly in
this way: the information that a node has about the rest of
the network is represented in a data structure that we call
interface (L and U are the interfaces of node 1 and 2 in the
above example). The correctness assertion is decomposed into
"local assertions" (ex. : $x_1 \leq L$ and $x_2 \geq U$) and "communication assertions" (ex. : $L \leq U$). The conjunction of the resulting assertions must imply the network correctness. The
current state of a node is related to data in its interface
by its local assertion. Communication assertions relate the
interfaces between themselves.

   The controllers are responsible for the maintenance of both
local and communication assertions, being consequently submitted to internal and external pressures. Every state transition of a node needs an authorization from the controller,
that verifies whether the validity of the local assertion
will be kept with the new state. If it is, the transition is
approved, otherwise some modification in the interface data
is needed. Since these data are linked with the other interfaces by the communication assertions, the controller must
start negotiations with the other nodes through a protocol,
in order to try to obtain the desired modifications. Evidently
the communication assertions must be invariants of these
protocols.

   External pressures come through messages that arrive at the
node with requests for modifications on interface data. Then
the procedure is inverse: the controller consults the current
state of the node to verify if it is compatible with the requested modification. If it is, the modification is done, and
communicated to the requesting node through a message. If not
the reply is deferred until the node reaches a state compatibl

with the requested modification.
There are many possibilities of conflicts in this schema:
conflicts between a "desired" and a "requested" modification,
between the current state and several requests, etc. The designer of a distributed algorithm must provide means to solve
all of them with a view to the total correctness and performance goals.
With this section we hope we have shown that lower-upper
bounds couple problems allow an easy identification of dangerous events with a simple method that assures the partial
correctness of the protocols that employ it. The proposed
acceptance thresholds method is not unique: many other possibilities may be considered. Advantages of the presented version are in its resistance to some failures, in the easiness
of its application and in the possibility of collateral gains
with its use to obtain total correctness. The idea of the
separation into local and communication assertions is applied
in the next sections to networks with assertions of any type.
It is shown that this separation can always be made in such a
way that the resulting communication assertion will always be
in the form of lower-upper bounds couples.

3. THE 2-NODE NETWORK

3.1. Problem Statement and Subset Transformations

Consider a network with two nodes 1 and 2; suppose that E_i,
for i=1,2, is the set of all possible states of node i, and
that the network correctness is given by an assertion G :
$E_1 \times E_2 \rightarrow \{true,false\}$. Sometimes we also consider the
associated binary relation $\Gamma \subseteq E_1 \times E_2$ that contains all correct couples.
Example 1: suppose that nodes 1 and 2 share two resources
A and B in the following way:

1) node 1 uses at most one resource at a time
2) node 2 may use resources A and B simultaneously; furthermore it must be using at least one resource every time.

The sets of possible states may be written

$$E_1 = \{0, A_1, B_1\} \qquad E_2 = \{A_2, B_2, AB\}$$

with obvious meanings.
The correctness assertion is then given by

$$G = (e_1 = A_1 \Rightarrow e_2 = B_2) \wedge (e_1 = B_1 \Rightarrow e_2 = A_2)$$

where e_i is the current state of node i. The relation Γ is
given by

$$\Gamma = \{(0,A_2),(0,B_2),(0,AB),(A_1,B_2),(B_1,A_2)\}$$

In this section we show that every 2-node network problem is reducible to a lower-upper bounds couple. We do this through some algebraic manipulations based on the notation of subset transformations defined below, which comes from Galois connections theory [4,5,6].

Given a subset S_1 of E_1 and a subset S_2 of E_2, we define the transform by G of S_1 (denoted $\overline{G}_1^2(S_1)$) and of S_2 (denoted $\overline{G}_2^1(S_2)$) by

$$\overline{G}_1^2(S_1) = \{e_2 \in E_2 \mid \forall\, e_1 \in S_1 \ (e_1,e_2) \in \Gamma\} \quad \text{if } S_1 \ne \phi_1$$

$$\overline{G}_1^2(\phi_1) = E_2$$

$$\overline{G}_2^1(S_2) = \{e_1 \in E_1 \mid \forall\, e_2 \in S_2 \ (e_1,e_2) \in \Gamma\} \quad \text{if } S_2 \ne \phi_2$$

$$\overline{G}_2^1(\phi_2) = E_1$$

where ϕ_i represent the empty subset of E_i.

Properties P1 and P2 below, valid for any non-empty subsets S_1 and S_2, are direct consequences of these definitions.

$$S_1 \times S_2 \subseteq \Gamma \iff S_1 \subseteq \overline{G}_2^1(S_2) \iff S_2 \subseteq \overline{G}_1^2(S_1) \tag{P1}$$

$$S_i \subseteq S_i' \implies \overline{G}_i^j(S_i) \supseteq \overline{G}_i^j(S_i') \tag{P2}$$

We may interpret the transform of a subset S_i of E_i as the greatest subset of E_j which is completely compatible with S_i.

Some transforms in Example 1 are:

$$\overline{G}_1^2(\{0\}) = \{A_2,B_2,AB\} = E_2 = \overline{G}_1^2(\phi_1)$$

$$\overline{G}_1^2(\{0,A_1,B_1\}) = \phi_2$$

$$\overline{G}_2^1(\{AB\}) = \{0\} = \overline{G}_2^1(\{A_2,B_2,AB\})$$

Transformation $\overline{G}_1^2$ is an application from the subset lattice of E_1 to the subset lattice of E_2; $\overline{G}_2^1$ is an application between the same lattices but in the inverse sense. Together they define a Galois connection between the two subset lattices. We shall see many consequences of this fact.

3.2. Distribution of the Assertion

We now propose a way to distribute an assertion over a 2-node network. The knowledge that node i has about node j is given by two special variables M_i^j and W_i^j that form its interface. At each instant, M_i^j can be interpreted as an upper-bound for the subset of E_j composed by all states where currently node j can be. W_i^j is interpreted as a lower-bound for the subset of E_i composed by all states where node j expects that node i can be.

Local assertions for node i can then be expressed by this formula:

$$e_i \in \overline{G}_j^i(M_i^j) \cap W_i^j \qquad i,j = 1,2 \; ; \; i \neq j \qquad (1)$$

The transform of the M term means that each node must be in a state compatible with all current states of the other nodes. The W term means that each node can not risk breaking the expectations that the other node has over it.

These local assertions and interpretations will work if the validity of the following communications assertions is kept:

$$M_1^2 \supseteq W_2^1 \quad (a) \qquad\qquad W_1^2 \subseteq M_2^1 \quad (b) \qquad (2)$$

It is not difficult to verify (using P1 and P2) that the conjunction of the local and the communication assertions always implies G.

The two variables in (2a) range over the subset lattice of E_2, and the variables in (2b) range over the subset lattice of E_1. Both are partially ordered domains with respect to the subset inclusion relation; consequently assertions (2) are lower-upper bounds couples.

3.3. Range Reductions and Simplifications

Not all subsets of E_1 and E_2 are suitable as "values" for the M and W variables. In this subsection we show that their range can be significantly reduced to contain only "relevant" subsets. This reduction points out a strong symmetry between them which allows the two communication assertions to coalesce into a single one.

The "current territory" of a node is the set of states that satisfy its local assertion for the current value of data in its interface. We shall use this notion while introducing the concept of "relevance".

Looking at Example 1, suppose that in a given situation we have $M_1^2 = \{AB\}$. If we choose the values of the other inter-face variables (these values being compatible with local and communication assertions) in order to give the nodes the widest possible freedom, the resulting territories will be $\{0\}$ for node 1 and $\{AB\}$ for node 2. If we start from $M_1^2 = \{A_2, B_2, AB\}$ and repeat this procedure, node 1 will remain in the same situation, but node 2 will have its territory ex-panded to $\{A_2, B_2, AB\}$. We remark that the passage of the value of M_1^2 from $\{AB\}$ to $\{A_2, B_2, AB\}$ is a trivially safe event with respect to the lower-upper bounds couple (2a) and also that node 1 does not lose anything with the occurrence of this event. The best thing to do is simply not to consider subsets as $\{AB\}$ as possible values for M_1^2 and W_2^1.

The advantage that $\{A_2, B_2, AB\}$ presents over $\{AB\}$ comes from the fact that it contains $\{AB\}$ though its transform is the same subset $\{0\}$ of E_1. It is not difficult to show that, given any subset S_i of E_i, $\overline{G}_j^i \, \overline{G}_i^j (S_i)$ has the same transform as S_i, and that any other subset of E_i whose transform is $\overline{G}_i^j (S_i)$ will be contained in $\overline{G}_j^i \overline{G}_i^j (S_i)$. There is a theorem from Galois connections theory about these special subsets [4,5] which states that:

1) The subsets of the form $\overline{G}_j^i \overline{G}_i^j (S_i)$, for $S_i \subseteq E_i$, compose a lattice that is a sub-lattice of the subset lattice of E_i with respect to the intersection operation.
2) There is a dual isomorphism between the lattice of ele-ments $\overline{G}_2^1 \overline{G}_1^2 (S_1)$ and the lattice of elements $\overline{G}_1^2 \overline{G}_2^1 (S_2)$. The one-to-one correspondence between these special subsets is given by the transformation $\overline{G}_1^2$ in one sense, and $\overline{G}_2^1$ in the other.

Therefore if we reduce the range of the the M_i^j and W_j^i variables to the subsets of the form $\overline{G}_i^j \overline{G}_j^i (S_j)$ we will have the following advantages:

1) useless losses on freedom degrees, like the one described above, will be eliminated;
2) the communication assertions will remain as upper-lower bounds couples;

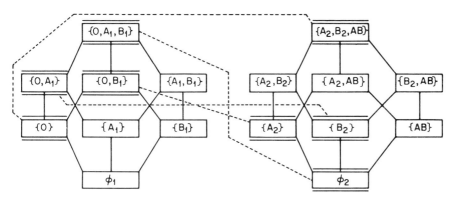

FIG. 1 *Subset lattices for Example 1*

3) the representation needs – the cardinality of the type of the variables chosen in an implementation to represent M_i^j and W_j^i – may be considerably reduced;

4) the range of possible territories for node j will also be limited to subsets of the form $\overline{G}_i^j \overline{G}_j^i(S_j)$;

5) within the reduced ranges, we can say that any representation for say, M_1^2 (a subset of E_2) is also a representation for its unique correspondent $\overline{G}_2^1(M_1^2)$, which is a subset of E_1.

Figure 1 shows the complete state subset lattice for Example 1. The subsets of the form $G_i^j G_j^i(S_j)$ are pointed out, and the one-to-one correspondence between them is indicated by dashed lines.

As in Example 1, in some cases the empty subset of one or both state sets may be of the form $\overline{G}_i^j \overline{G}_j^i(S_j)$, as well as a subset with empty transform (if it is the case, it will always be E_1 or E_2. Why?). In real algorithms none of these values can be assigned to the M or W variables, for at least one node would have an empty territory.

So, we will consider as the "final" range of variables M_i^j and W_j^i the lattice composed by all subsets of the form $\overline{G}_i^j \overline{G}_j^i(S_j)$, with exception – if it is the case – of the empty subsets and of the subsets with empty transform. The remaining subsets are called "relevant" subsets. Figure 2 shows the relevant subsets for Example 1.

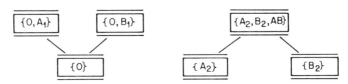

FIG. 2 *Relevant subsets for Example 1*

After all these reductions on their range, assertion (2a) looks so much like assertion (2b) that one wonders if they could not be coalesced into a single communication assertion. Effectively we can do it. Through a reasoning similar to the one used for the range reductions, we can cause any variation of M_i^j to become a corresponding variation of W_i^j in the inverse sense, and vice versa. Without any loss in flexibility we can force each interface to work always with its variables coupled by $W_i^j = \bar{G}_i^j(M_i^j)$ or, equivalently, by $M_i^j = \bar{G}_i^j(W_i^j)$ (we remark tha when working only with relevant subsets, we have $\bar{G}_i^j = (\bar{G}_j^i)^{-1}$).

There are several ways to use this linkage to simplify assertions (1) and (2) through suitable substitutions. We give here three possible variants. In the first one we eliminate the M variables:

$$e_i \in W_i^j \quad i,j = 1,2 \; ; \; i \neq j \quad \text{(local assertions)}$$
$$W_1^2 \subseteq \bar{G}_2^1(W_2^1) \quad \text{(communication assertion)} \tag{3}$$

In the second variant we eliminate the W variables:

$$e_i \in \bar{G}_j^i(M_i^j) \quad i,j = 1,2 \; ; \; i \neq j \quad \text{(local assertion)}$$
$$M_1^2 \supseteq \bar{G}_1^2(M_2^1) \quad \text{(communication assertion)} \tag{4}$$

Finally we eliminate W_1^2 at node 1, and M_2^1 at node 2:

$$e_1 \in \bar{G}_2^1(M_1^2) \; ; \; e_2 \in W_2^1 \quad \text{(local assertion)}$$
$$M_1^2 \supseteq W_2^1 \quad \text{(communication assertion)} \tag{5}$$

The reader should convince himself that all these variants can be seen as lower-upper bounds couples, through a suitable choice of the partial ordering relation.

3.4. The Mutual Exclusion Problem

In this section we give a complete algorithm to solve the distributed mutual exclusion problem for 2-node networks. With this we intend to: (1) give a practical example of the application of our method on the design of distributed solution and (2) show how it can - and must - be completed to arrive at a final algorithm.

An informal description of this problem is: a resource that can only serve one node at a time is shared by a 2-node network. How should we program these nodes in order to:

1) prevent simultaneous use of the resource by the two nodes and

2) assure that each node requesting the resource will eventually obtain it.

Distributed algorithms for this problem may be found in [2,3, 7,8]. All these papers present solutions for networks with n nodes. The algorithm we show here is an improved specialization of [8] for 2-node networks. The solution in [7] uses global agreements over a circularly connected network; it is not in the scope of this work to examine this kind of algorithm.

The three other solutions may be compared by the number of messages exchanged per critical section invocation. [2] uses approximately $3.(n-1)$ messages, [3] uses systematically $2.(n-1)$ messages, and [8] exchanges a number of messages varying between 0 and $2.(n-1)$ per critical section invocation. This last result has been obtained with the use of local and communication assertions. This does not mean that this technique leads automatically to better solutions but it indicates that with the partial correctness aspects under control, the algorithm designer can dedicate more attention to political choices.

Analysis: each node i, for i = 1,2, can be in one of two states: either it is using the resource ($e_i=1$) or not ($e_i=0$). So we have:

$$E_i = \{0,1\} \qquad i = 1,2$$

The correctness assertion is given by:

$$G = (e_1 = 0) \lor (e_2 = 0)$$

The reader can verify that:

$$\overline{G}_i^j(\phi_i) = \overline{G}_i^j(\{0\}) = \{0,1\}$$

$$\overline{G}_i^j(\{1\}) = \overline{G}_i^j(\{0,1\}) = \{0\}$$

$$i,j = 1,2 \; ; \; i \neq j$$

So the relevant subsets for each node are $\{0\}$ and $\{0,1\}$. To distribute the correctness assertion we shall use formula (3). The resulting local assertions are:

$$e_i \in W_i^j \rightarrow USING_i \Rightarrow w_i^j$$

where the boolean variable $USING_i$ represents the state of node i, and the boolean variable w_i^j represents W_i^j with values false and true for $\{0\}$ and $\{0,1\}$ respectively.

Since $\{0\} \subset \{0,1\}$, dangerous events are those where w_i^j changes its value from false to true.

The statements that can provoke such events must be examined in order to verify if they fulfil the conditions exposed in Section 2.

Algorithm: the algorithm we propose is intended to work in a network without message losses. It is resistant to varying travelling times and to order inversions in message delivering. Each request operation needs between 0 and 2 message exchanges. Integer sequence numbers are used to implement the acceptance thresholds, with the same properties of the logical clocks [2]. These properties are used to solve conflicts between requesting operations as in [2] and [3]. The reader should consult these references to see an explanation of this technique.

In order to make the algorithm more readable, messages are grouped into "types" that absorb some fields with fixed values at every sending instant. We use two types of messages: <REQUEST(TH)> and <RELEASE(TH)>. All messages are sent by node i only when w_i^j = false. A message of type REQUEST also indicates the existence of a non-satisfied demand at its sending instant.

The two controllers are almost identical. They assume the existence of two processes at each node:

1) One of them actually uses the resource. It calls cyclically the REQUEST.RESOURCE and RELEASE.RESOURCE procedures to do that.

2) The other one treats the received messages. According to their type, it calls the TREAT-REQUEST-MESSAGE or the TREAT-RELEASE-MESSAGE procedures.

The algorithm is presented here in the form of an abstract data structure, with a common data base shared by the four procedures above. Except for the "waitfor" statement, the procedures are indivisible. The "verify" statement re-evaluates the expression contained in the waitfor statement. In the case of a positive result, and if there is some process waiting for it, the control is transferred to that process.

If there is no waiting process the statement is innocuous. Full details can be seen directly in the algorithm.

controller MUTEX:

begin

    {shared data}

    constant i,   {this node unique number}

          j;   {other node number; i ≠ j}

    integer OSN initial (0),   {Our Sequence Number}

           TH initial (0);   {acceptance THreshold}

    logical USING initial (false),

           WAITING initial (false),

           W initial (false),

           REP_DEF initial (false);   {REPly DEFerred}

    {shared procedures}

procedure REQUEST_RESOURCE:

begin

    WAITING := true;

    if W = false

    then TH := OSN := TH+1;

          send to j <REQUEST(TH)>

    fi;

    waitfor (W);

    WAITING := false; USING := true

end REQUEST_RESOURCE.

procedure RELEASE_RESOURCE:

begin

    USING := false;

    if REP_DEF

    then W := false; TH := TH+1;

          send to j <RELEASE(TH)>

    fi

end RELEASE_RESOURCE.

procedure TREAT_REQUEST_MESSAGE (TSN):
begin
  if TSN ≧ TH
  then TH := TSN;
    if WAITING
    then if (TSN > OSN) v (TSN = OSN ∧ i < j)
      then REP_DEF := true; W := true; verify
      fi
    else if USING
      then REP_DEF := true
      else W := false; TH := TH+1;
        send to j <RELEASE(TH)>
      fi
    fi
  fi
end TREAT_REQUEST_MESSAGE.

procedure TREAT_RELEASE_MESSAGE (TSN):
begin
  if TSN > TH
  then TH := TSN; W := true;
    verify
  fi
end TREAT_RELEASE_MESSAGE.

4. THE n-NODE NETWORK

4.1. Decomposition of the Correctness Assertion

Consider a completely connected network whose n nodes are uniquely numbered from 1 to n. Suppose that the set of possible states of each node is E_i, and that the global correctness is given by an assertion

$$G: \underset{i=1}{\overset{n}{\times}} E_i \rightarrow \{\underline{true}, \underline{false}\}$$

In this section we propose a decomposition of G such that all resulting communication assertions will be lower-upper bounds couples. Firstly we extend our notation and transform definitions in order to deal with n-node networks. Then we give formulae for local and communication assertions and we discuss some consequences of this decomposition. Throughout this section we refer to the example below:

Example 2 (the 2-out-of-3 problem): A resource that can serve at most two nodes simultaneously is shared by three nodes of a network. Then we may consider that each node i, for i = 1,2,3, can be in one of two states: either it is using the resource (e_i = 1) or not (e_i = 0), and we may write

$$E_i = \{0,1\} \qquad \text{for i = 1,2,3.}$$

$$G = (e_1 = 0) \vee (e_2 = 0) \vee (e_3 = 0)$$

We now introduce the following extensions to our notation. We write [n] for the complete set of node indexes, i.e., [n] = {1,...,n}. If I is some subset of [n] we write:

.S_I for a subset of $\underset{i \in I}{\times} E_i$;

.e_I for an element of $\underset{i \in I}{\times} E_i$. We call e_I an I-tuple.

.$e_I \; // \; e_J$ for J ⊂ [n], J ∩ I = φ, for the (I ∪ J)-tuple resulting from a coherent merge, preserving the index order, of the I-tuple e_I with the J-tuple e_J;

.$\overline{I}$ for the complement subset of I ($\overline{I}$ = [n] - I);

.Γ for the n-ary correctness relation;

.$Γ_I$ for the projection of Γ over I. We have:

$$Γ_I = \underline{proj}_{|I}(Γ) = \{e_I | \; \exists \; e_{\overline{I}} \text{ such that } (e_I \; // \; e_{\overline{I}}) \in Γ\}$$

Using this notation we can now express a general transformation by G between any two disjoint parts I and J of the network.

$$\overline{G}_I^J(S_I) = \{e_J \; | \; \forall \; e_I \in S_I \quad (e_I \; // \; e_J) \in Γ_{I \cup J}\} \quad \text{if } S_I \neq φ_I;$$

$$\overline{G}_I^J(φ_I) = \underset{j \in J}{\times} E_j.$$

This application takes a subset of states of the nodes in I (any collection of I-tuples) and transforms it into a completely compatible subset of states of J (a collection of J-tuples). The compatibility between an I-tuple and a J-tuple is given by the projection of Γ over $I \cup J$. Some transforms in Example 2 are:

$$\overline{G}_1^{23}(\{0\}) = \{(0,0),(0,1),(1,0),(1,1)\} = E_2 \times E_3 = \overline{G}_1^{23}(\phi_1)$$

$$\overline{G}_1^{23}(\{1\}) = \{(0,0),(0,1),(1,0)\} = \overline{G}_1^{23}(\{0,1\})$$

$$\overline{G}_1^{2}(\{0,1\}) = \{0,1\}$$

It is not difficult to show that $\overline{G}_I^J$ and $\overline{G}_J^I$ together define a Galois connection between the subset lattice of $\underset{i \in I}{\times} E_i$ and the subset lattice of $\underset{j \in J}{\times} E_j$. In particular there will be a Galois connection between the lattice of subsets of states of any node and the lattice of subsets of states of the rest of the network. Based on this fact we can say that the relevant subsets of states of a node i are the subsets of the form

$$\overline{G}_{\{\overline{i}\}}^{\{i\}}(\overline{G}_{\{i\}}^{\{\overline{i}\}}(S_i))$$

where S_i is any subset of E_i. The reader may verify that the relevant subsets for any node i in Example 2 are $\{0\}$ and $\{0,1\}$.

In order to get lower-upper bounds couples as communication assertions, the knowledge that each node will have about the rest of the network will be given by n-1 separate data, concerning each one of the other n-1 nodes. The part of the interface of a node i relative to a node j will be formed by two variables M_i^j and W_i^j. Like in a 2-node network, M_i^j will be interpreted as an upper bound for the subset of E_j composed by all states where currently node j can be, and W_i^j will be interpreted as a lower bound for the subset of E_i composed by all states where node j expects that node i can be. At each node i the product $\underset{j \in \{\overline{i}\}}{\times} M_i^j$ is an upper bound for the subset of $\underset{j \in \{\overline{i}\}}{\times} E_j$ where the rest of the network can currently be.

Without proof we now give formulae for the decomposition

of G. As expected, the communication assertions will be:

$$M^j_i \supseteq W^i_J \qquad \text{for all } i,j \in [n], \; i \neq j \qquad (6)$$

The two variables in each communication assertion will range over the relevant subsets of E_j. The local assertions will be:

$$e_i \in \bigcap_{j \in \{\bar{i}\}} W^j_i \cap \overline{G}^{\{i\}}_{\{\bar{i}\}} (\underset{j \in \{\bar{i}\}}{\times} M^j_i \cap \Gamma_{\{\bar{i}\}}) \qquad \text{for all } i \in [n] \qquad (7)$$

We may interpret the local assertions in the following

way: the term $\bigcap_{j \in \{\bar{i}\}} W^j_i$ means that node i cannot risk breaking
the expectations of any other node; the transform term means that node i must be in a state compatible with all states where the rest of the network can be, but – owing to the intersection with $\Gamma_{\{\bar{i}\}}$ – it does not need to take care of the $\{\bar{i}\}$-tuples that are intrinsically wrong, even when they are

contained in $\underset{j \in \{\bar{i}\}}{\times} M^j_i$.

The decomposition proposed above is not necessarily the best solution for n-node problems. In some cases circular or tree arrangements would be preferable for performance reasons, even when we have a completely connected network. It is not in the scope of this work to examine other ways to decompose an assertion, nor the criteria for optimal decomposition. We just remark that the distribution proposed here permits a concurrent treatment of requests which may be a decisive advantage in cases like the n-node mutual exclusion problem.

4.2. An Algorithm for the 2-out-of-3 Problem

In this subsection we propose a complete algorithm to solve the 2-out-of-3 problem. Since we have only three nodes in our network, formula (7) reduces to

$$e_i \quad \overline{G}^i_{jk}((M^j_i \times M^k_i) \cap \Gamma_{jk}) \cap W^j_i \cap W^k_i$$

where $i,j,k, \in \{1,2,3\}$ and $i \neq j$, $i \neq k$, $j \neq k$. We have

$$\Gamma_{jk} = \{(0,0),(0,1),(1,0),(1,1)\}$$

Therefore Γ_{jk} will always contain $M^j_i \times M^k_i$. As we have seen,

the relevant subsets for each node are $\{0\}$ and $\{0,1\}$. Using boolean variables m_i^j and w_i^j to represent these subsets by the values false and true respectively, the local assertion for node i reduces to

$$e_i = 1 \Rightarrow \neg(m_i^j \wedge m_i^k) \wedge w_i^j \wedge w_i^k$$

The algorithm uses three types of messages:

1) <RELEASE(SENDER,TH)>, sent by node i to node j only when m_i^j = true and w_i^j = false;

2) <REQUEST(SENDER,TH)>, sent only when m_i^j = true and w_i^j = false; it also indicates the existence of a non-satisfied demand at its sending instant; and

3) <PERMIT(SENDER,TH)>, sent only when m_i^j = true and w_i^j = true.

The explicit fields SENDER and TH have obvious meanings in all types of messages.

Each node keeps a variable HSN whose value always equals the currently greatest valued acceptance threshold. It is used to solve conflicts between request operations, as in [2,3], but the first-come-first-served discipline is not necessarily respected. Each request operation requires between 0 and 7 message exchanges. The same linguistic remarks made for the mutual exclusion controller are valid for this algorithm.

In [5] we propose another solution to this problem. Differences between the two algorithms are the introduction of the message type PERMIT - a difference of syntactical order only - and in the modificated reactions to the arrival of REQUEST and RELEASE messages. These last modifications have been introduced in order to avoid the following case that has been kindly pointed out by J.-P. Verjus and A. Schipper. Using the first version, when a node i uses a part of the resource for a relatively long time period, after some initial exchanges the system will be blocked until the release of the resource by node i. The modifications introduced here allow the sharing of the remaining part of the resource by nodes j and k during such an interval, at the cost of some extra exchanges of messages.

```
controller TWO-OUT-OF-THREE
begin
    {shared data}
    constant i,          {this node unique number}
             j,k;        {numbers of the other nodes; j<k}

    integer OSN initial (0),        {Our Sequence Number}
            HSN initial (0),        {Highest Sequence Number}
            TH[j:k] initial (0);    {acceptance THresholds}

    boolean m[j:k] initial (true),
            w[j:k] initial (false),
            REP_DEF[j:k] initial (false),    {REPly DEFerred}
            USING initial (false),
            WAITING initial (false);

    {shared procedures}

    procedure REQUEST:
    begin integer r;
        OSN := HSN := HSN + 1;  WAITING := true;
        for r := j,k do
            if ¬w[r]
            then TH[r] := HSN;
                 send to r <REQUEST(i,TH[r])>
            fi
        od;

        waitfor (w[j] ∧ w[k] ∧ ¬(m[j] ∧ m[k]));

        WAITING := false;   USING := true;
        if m[j] = m[k] = false
        then if REP_DEF[j]
             then m[j] := true;  TH[j] := HSN := HSN + 1;
                  send to j <PERMIT(i, TH[j])>
             else if REP_DEF[k]
                  then m[k] := true; TH[k] := HSN := HSN + 1;
                       send to k <PERMIT(i, TH[k])>
                  fi
             fi
        fi
    end REQUEST.
```

```
procedure RELEASE:
begin integer r;
   USING := false;
   for r := j,k do
      if REP_DEF[r]
      then TH[r] := HSN := HSN+1; m[r]:= true; w[r]:= false;
           send to r <RELEASE(i, TH[r])>;
           REP_DEF[r] := false
      fi
   od
end RELEASE.

procedure TREAT_RELEASE_MESSAGE(SENDER, TSN):
begin integer r;
   if TSN > TH[SENDER]
   then TH[SENDER] := TSN;  HSN := max(HSN, SN);
        m[SENDER] := false;  w[SENDER] := true;
        for r := j,k do
           if REP_DEF[r]
           then if r ≠ SENDER
                then m[r] := true;  TH[r] := HSN := HSN+1;
                     send to r <PERMIT(i, TH[r])>
                else REP_DEF[r] := false
                fi
           fi
        od;
        verify
   fi
end TREAT_RELEASE_MESSAGE.

procedure TREAT_PERMIT_MESSAGE (SENDER, TSN):
begin
   if TSN > TH[SENDER]
   then TH[SENDER] := TSN; HSN := max(HSN,TSN);
        w[SENDER]:= true;  verify
   fi
end TREAT_PERMIT_MESSAGE.
```

```
procedure TREAT_REQUEST_MESSAGE:
begin integer r
   if SN > TH[SENDER]
   then TH[SENDER] := SN; HSN := max(HSN,TSN);
        if WAITING
        then if OSN < TSN ∨ (OSN = TSN ∧ i < SENDER)
             then REP_DEF[SENDER] := true;
                  m[SENDER]:= false;  w[SENDER] := true;
                  verify
             else m[SENDER] := true;
                  if w[SENDER]
                  then w[SENDER] := false;  TH[SENDER] := HSN := HSN+1;
                       send to SENDER <REQUEST(i,TH[SENDER])>
                  fi
             fi
        else if USING
             then REP_DEF[SENDER] := true;
                  if m[j] = m[k] = false
                  then m[SENDER] := true;
                       TH[SENDER] := HSN := HSN+1;
                       send to SENDER <PERMIT(i,TH[SENDER])>
                  fi
             else for r := j,k do
                      if r = SENDER v (r = SENDER ∧ ¬m[r] ∧ w[r])
                      then m[r] := true; w[r] := false; TH[r] := HSN := HSN+1;
                           send to r <RELEASE(i,TH[r])>
                      fi
                  od
             fi
        fi
   fi
end TREAT_REQUEST_MESSAGE.
end TWO-OUT-OF-THREE.
```

5. CONCLUSIONS

We have presented an attempt to improve the degree of systematization of the programming of distributed control algorithms satisfying some global assertion over the states of a network. We proposed formulae for the decomposition of the global assertion into a collection of local and communication assertions; all assertions in this last group are in the elementary form of lower-upper bounds couples, that allow for an easy identification of dangerous events. Using this fact, the partial correctness of protocols for lower-upper bounds couples - and consequently of any protocol that works with the suggested decomposition - may be guaranteed by a simple set of rules for message exchanges. The design of data structures representing only relevant information for node interfaces is also a direct product of the process of decomposition of the correctness assertion.

As an example we proposed a distributed algorithm to get mutual exclusion in 2-node networks. Even if we were not concerned with performance aspects, the solution given needs fewer messages per critical section invocation than the algorithm presented in [3].

REFERENCES

1. Dijkstra, E.W. (1975). Guarded commands, nondeterminacy and formal derivation of programs. *Comm. ACM* 18, 8.
2. Lamport, L. (1978). Time, clocks and the ordering of events in distributed systems. *Comm. ACM* 21, 7.
3. Ricart, G. and Agrawala, A. (1981). An optimal algorithm for mutual exclusion in computer networks. *Comm. ACM* 24, 1.
4. Ore, O. (1944). Galois connections. *Trans. Amer. Math. Soc.* 55, 493-513.
5. Szasz, G. (1963). "Introduction to Lattice Theory". Academic Press, New York, London.
6. Birkhoff, G. (1948). "Lattice Theory". Amer. Math. Soc. Colloquium Publ. 25. (Revised edition.)
7. Le Lann, G. (1977). Distributed systems - towards a formal approach. *In* "Information Processing 77", pp.155-160. North-Holland Publishing Co., Amsterdam, The Netherlands.
8. Carvalho, O.S.F. and Roucairol, G. (1981). Une amélioration de l'algorithme d'exclusion mutuelle de Ricart et Agrawala. Laboratoire Informatique Théorique et Programmation. Internal Report no.81-58.
9. Carvalho, O.S.F. and Roucairol, G. (1982). On the distribution of an assertion. *In* "Proc. ACM-SIGACT-SIGOPS Symposium on Principles of Distributed Computing". Ottawa, Canada.

Specification of a Communication System

Carroll Morgan

1. INTRODUCTION

The formal specification of a communication system is presented. The design of the communication system is regarded as
experimental and might, for example, be applicable to distributed computing systems. The specification makes use of non-
constructive techniques, which make it considerably simpler
than constructive techniques alone would have allowed.

The specification language consists mainly of mathematical
set theory; special notations are kept to a minimum. An
appendix provides a glossary of the mathematical symbols used.

The description of a communication system is given as an
example of non-constructive formal specification. Non-constructive specifications are distinguished by their ability
to present properties rather than necessarily constructs. For
example, of the following specifications of a real number x:

$$(1) \quad 3x^2 + 5x + 2 = 0$$

$$(2) \quad x = \frac{-5 \pm \sqrt{5^2 - 4(3x2)}}{2x3}$$

the former is non-constructive, the latter constructive.

Part of the value of the non-constructive style is that it
furthers the separation of specification and implementation –
and this separation can be vital. Not only can a constructive
style prejudice a specification towards a particular implementation technique, but the difficulty in some cases of producing a constructive specification can be mistaken to be a
barrier to producing any specification at all:

Distributed Computing Systems
ISBN 0-12-543970-9

(1) $ax^5 + bx^4 + cx^3 + dx^2 + ex + f = 0$

(2) ???

The communication system presented is a futuristic telephone system, whose design is motivated by utility rather than available technology. As distributed computer systems, for example, have many unexplored technical capabilities, such a design technique is one way of avoiding needless perpetuation of limitations appropriate only to non-distributed systems. Thus this telephone system can be regarded as an experimental design of a distributed systems communication facility.

While the system will be described in more detail below, an outline of its unconventional aspects is given here:

1) It is possible for a subscriber to make himself available at any telephones he may physically access; any attempt to call that subscriber will be routed to one of those telephones.
2) A subscriber may request a number of calls which are to be connected automatically as the called subscribers become available. In this way, he need not continually redial a subscriber who is "engaged" or "absent" - the telephone system will ring both phones when the connection is made.

The informal specification below gives an introduction to the telephone system's design. The need for formalism is then discussed, and a formal specification is given. Finally, the informal and formal approaches are related.

2. THE TELEPHONE SYSTEM - INFORMALLY

Every subscriber to the telephone system is given a "card" (perhaps by the "telephone authority") which is to be used in his interactions with the system. Among other data, his card contains his own identification - that is, it contains the datum which another subscriber would use to request a conversation with him.

Telephones themselves each consist of at least:

1) a handset - for speaking and listening.
2) a display - giving the identifications of all subscribers in any conversation which this telephone is supporting. When the telephone is not supporting a conversation, its display is blank.
3) a keyboard - with which the identifications of subscribers may be entered when making calls. The keyboard also includes keys which are used to perform some of the operations described below.

4) a slot - into which a subscriber's card may be inserted. This is how the subscriber identifies himself to the telephone system.

The telephone system provides the following facilities for permitting conversations among its subscribers; these facilities may be accessed through any telephone:

1) plug-in: by inserting his card into the slot and pressing plug-in the subscriber informs the telephone system that requests for conversations with him can be directed to this telephone. This is not cancelled by his removing the card; it is cancelled by unplugging (see below).

2) call: to request a conversation, the subscriber's card must be inserted; he may then serially enter the identification(s) of the other subscribers with whom he wishes to speak. Pressing the call key terminates the entry.

   Often, a requested conversation will involve only two subscribers, but this need not be so - conference calls can be requested.

   A subscriber may request as many conversations as he likes, and the telephone system will set up those conversations as their subscribers become available. A subscriber is available when he is plugged in to a telephone which isn't at the time supporting another conversation.

3) cancel: a subscriber may cancel his request for a conversation as long as that conversation hasn't started.

4) ding-dong: once a conversation has started, all supporting telephones will display the identifications of the subscribers in the conversation.

5) hang-up: a conversation is concluded when any of the supporting telephones' handsets is replaced in its cradle.

6) unplug: while his card is inserted, by pressing the unplug key a subscriber may inform the telephone system that he is no longer available at this telephone. (On a "public" telephone, perhaps the unplug operation would be automatic on removal of the card.)

3. THE ROLE OF FORMALISM

The informal specification given above is intended to present an easily comprehended description of the facilities which the telephone system provides. However, realistic documentation - as supplied, for example, to the general public - would have to include also step-by-step instructions on how to make a call, how to be available for calling, and so on. Thus the description above is insufficient in that it is not basic enough.

On the other hand, there are many questions which the informal specification doesn't answer - and due to its use of natural language, it might even not be fully understood. Thus it is not sufficiently precise.

The formal specification is to supply the required precision. In being precise, however, a formal specification is absolutely precise - and this can reveal quite complex issues which the informal specification might have left to the reader's intuition. This characteristic of formal specification makes it very attractive.

Where complex issues are revealed, their treatment often can be considerably simplified by the use of non-constructive techniques.

The making and breaking of connections is a potentially complex issue in the telephone system. Below is given a summary of the operations which could lead to this sort of activity (which activity, therefore, must be described as part of each operation's specification):

	make	break
plug-in	x	
call	x	
cancel		
ding-dong		
hang-up	x	x
unplug		?

The hang-up operation, for example, can make a connection because it might free a telephone for which a connection request exists. And there is already a question unanswered by the informal specification: what happens if a subscriber unplugs without hanging-up?

A formal specification will reveal questions such as the one above and allow them to be answered conclusively.

4. THE TELEPHONE SYSTEM - FORMALLY

The specification given here is in a style currently in use at the Programming Research Group; it is based on the Z specification language of J.-R. Abrial [1,2]. In Z, the techniques and notation of standard typed set theory are exploited as far as possible - the "language" as such is quite small.

4.1. Primitives

The first step is to decide which concepts will be primitive in the specification - that is, of what objects is it necessary to know only their existence, but not their structure or properties? In this specification, there are three primitive sets:

SUBSCRIBER - the set of subscribers
PHONE   - the set of telephones
DOCKET   - a set used to make unique reference to
             conversation requests

The details of these sets are not required at this level of abstraction; they simply are named. (The use of upper case has no significance except that it conventionally indicates that the named object has a global relevance in the specification.)

Having identified the primitive sets it's now possible to build other sets from them. The first of these is the set of conversations; a conversation is a set of subscribers - that is, those who are having it:

$$\boxed{\begin{array}{l}\text{CONVERSATION} \\ \hline \mathbb{P}\ \text{SUBSCRIBER} \end{array}}$$

The box is called a schema: it indicates a textual equivalence between its contents ($\mathbb{P}$ SUBSCRIBER) and its name (CONVERSATION). Conference calls are conversations with more than two elements.

Requests for conversations have two components:

$$\boxed{\begin{array}{l}\text{REQUEST} \\ \hline \text{subscriber:}\quad \text{SUBSCRIBER} \\ \text{conversation: CONVERSATION} \end{array}}$$

Subscriber is who made the request, and conversation is what he requested. Although it usually will be the case, subscriber ε conversation is not required in general.

Finally, a connection provided by the telephone system is represented by a triple:

$$\boxed{\begin{array}{l}\text{CONNECTION} \\ \hline \text{phones:}\qquad\quad \mathbb{P}\ \text{PHONE} \\ \text{subscribers: } \mathbb{P}\ \text{SUBSCRIBER} \\ \text{using:}\qquad\quad\ \text{SUBSCRIBER} \longrightarrow \text{PHONE} \\ \hline \text{dom using = subscribers} \\ \text{ran using = phones} \end{array}}$$

Phones is the set of phones which are connected; subscribers is the conversation which the connected phones collectively support; using records for each subscriber in the conversation which phone he is using. The horizontal line

separating the signature and predicates of the schema is read
"such that".

The components phones and subscribers in the schema
CONNECTION are redundant in that their values always can be
determined from the value of using. Such components are
called derived; here, their introduction is to allow simpler
expression below.

The use of a schema name is in every way equivalent to the
use of its contents. The following are conventional uses of
this equivalence:

1) ∀conversation:CONVERSATION. ...
    for all conversations ...

2) {REQUEST│ card conversation > 2}
    the set of requests for conference calls.

3) ∃CONNECTION. thisphone ε phones
    there is a connection of which thisphone is a part.

4) λCONNECTION. phones
    The projection function of type

$$CONNECTION \longrightarrow \mathbb{P}\ PHONE$$

which maps a connection onto its phones component.

Set brackets ({}) around a schema name may be omitted if
context makes their need clear.

At this stage, very little has been said. But what has
been said will have a profound influence on the specification
to follow: it provides a framework on which to hang the detail

4.2. System State

The schema notation may be used also to describe states –
here, the possible states of the telephone system:

```
TS
    sites:        SUBSCRIBER ⟷ PHONE
    requests:     DOCKET ⇸ REQUEST
    connections: DOCKET ⇸ CONNECTION

    disjoint ran(phones˙connections)

    subscribers˙connections ⊆ conversation˙requests

    ∪using ⦇ran connectionsD⦈ ⊆ sites
```

Sites records for each subscriber the phones he's plugged
in to. Phones may be shared between subscribers, and each
subscriber may be plugged into several phones.

For each request a unique docket is used to distinguish it
from all others; it will be shown below how this (electronic)
docket is issued by the telephone system when the request is

made. requests gives for each issued docket its corresponding
request.

Each connection is in response to a request identified by
such a docket; connections gives this association. At any
time, ran connections is the set of connections the telephone
system has made.

The predicates express the relationships which hold between the three state components:

1) no phone may be a part of more than one connection at a
   time. (The use of a component name (e.g. phones) as a
   function refers to the appropriate projection function);
2) each connection must support exactly the conversation in
   its corresponding request;
3) each subscriber in a conversation must be plugged in to
   a phone in its supporting connection.

4.3. General Operations on States

The operations which may be performed on the telephone system
will be presented as schemas also. The domain of an operation
will include a system state (TS) together with any input
parameters required:

> TS
> input_parameter: in_type

The range of an operation will include a system state
again (the new state after the operation), and possibly
results of the operation:

> TS'
> results': out_type

The undashed names conventionally indicate inputs to the
operation, and dashed names indicate outputs from it. The
effect of decorating a schema name is to so decorate every
component within it - thus the components of TS' are sites',
requests', and connections', and are themselves properly
decorated to be in the range part of an operation.

When one schema is included in the description of another
(as are TS and TS' below), its components and predicates
join any others of the enclosing schema, with equal status.
There is no hierarchical structure implied.

ΔTS ——————————————————————————————————
┌─────────────────────────────────────
│ TS
│ TS'
│
│ me: SUBSCRIBER
│ thisphone: PHONE
│ ─────────────
│ ∄ TS".
│   sites'   = sites"
│   requests' = requests"
│
│   connections' ∩ connections ⊂
│   connections" ∩ connections
└─────────────────────────────────────

ΔTS is intended to give the common properties of all telephone system operations, and so it states that me and thisphone are domain components of each one – that is, who is
performing the operation, and on what telephone it is being
performed.

The predicate part expresses formally that in any operation
the set of connections must change "as little as possible" –
that is, that

                connections ∩ connections'

is maximal.

That the set of connections should change as little as
possible is important due to the great liberty the telephone
system enjoys in choosing which conversation to enable. For
example,

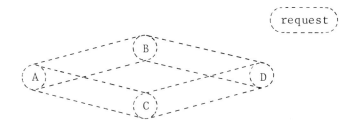

could lead to

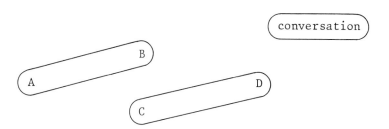

but could also lead to

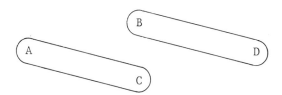

Without the predicate in ΔTS, the telephone system could capriciously leap among these possibilities. That is, the predicate is to assure that, for example,

In state

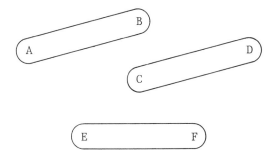

E's hanging up can not lead directly to

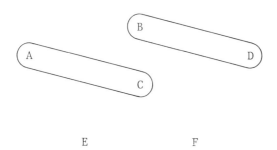

E   F

Operations which do not make deliberate change to the
telephone system state are called observations; the following
schema describes them.

```
ΦTS _____
    |  ΔTS
    |  _____
    |
    |  sites'    = sites
    |  requests' = requests
    |_____
```

The ΔTS predicate ensures that no connection can be broken
by an observation.

4.4. Specific Operations and Observations

The schema inclusion device is used heavily in this section.
ΔTS supplies not only the "automatic" input parameters me
and thisphone, but imposes the non-caprice condition as well.

```
plug_in _____
    |  ΔTS
    |  _____
    |
    |  sites'    = sites ∪ [me⊢→thisphone]
    |  requests' = requests
    |_____
```

Plug_in associates the subscriber and the phone he's
plugging in to. The set of requested conversations isn't
altered.

call_____

    ΔTS
    request: REQUEST
    docket': DOCKET
    ───────────

    subscriber request = me
    docket' ∉ dom requests

    sites'   = sites
    requests' = requests ⊕ [docket'↦request]
_____

Call accepts a request and returns a docket with which it
is uniquely associated. It is possible for a subscriber to
request conversations of which he isn't a part; the restriction of this facility to authorised subscribers could be
expressed by adding the following predicate

        me ∉ conversation request ⟹ me ε TELECOM

where TELECOM is some subset of SUBSCRIBER.

cancel_____

    ΔTS
    docket: DOCKET
    ───────────

    docket ∉ dom connections
    subscriber·requests (docket) = me

    sites'   = sites
    requests' = requests \ {docket}
_____

Cancel allows a subscriber to withdraw his conversation
request if the conversation isn't already in progress. He
can cancel only requests he himself has made.

ding_dong!_____

    ΦTS
    docket': DOCKET
    ───────────

    thisphone ε phones·connections (docket')
_____

Ding_dong! returns the docket associated with the conversation this phone is supporting. While there is no such conversation, ding_dong cannot occur.

```
request?_____
    ΦTS
    docket:   DOCKET
    request': REQUEST
   _____
    request' = requests docket
_____
```

Request? allows a subscriber to determine the request, if any, associated with a docket. This could be, for example, the docket he received from ding_dong.

```
hang_up_____
   _____
    ΔTS
   _____
    sites'    = sites
    requests' = requests \ {docket}

    where docket: DOCKET| thisphone ε
                          phones·connections (docket)
_____
```

Hanging up removes the request associated with the conversation the phone is supporting. The TS invariant causes the connection to be broken.

```
unplug._____
   _____
    ΔTS
   _____
    sites'    = sites - [me⊢→thisphone]
    requests' = requests
_____
```

Unplug removes the association of the subscriber and the telephone he unplugged from. The requests are unchanged.

4.5. Efficiency of Service

The specification so far gives a non-deterministic description of which connections actually are made - and in fact, making no connections at all is one of the possibilities. That is, the function connections may be empty. Rather than call such a system invalid, it is more realistic to call it inefficient. An efficiency measure is now incorporated into the specification.

The most efficient telephone system would be one which made every connection it could; it would constantly be in a state where connections was maximal. This schema describes such states.

$$
\begin{array}{|l}
\hline
\text{maxTS} \\
\quad \text{TS} \\
\hline
\quad \exists\,\text{TS}. \\
\qquad \text{sites} \quad = \underline{\text{sites}} \\
\qquad \text{requests} = \underline{\text{requests}} \\
\\
\qquad \text{connections} \subset \underline{\text{connections}} \\
\hline
\end{array}
$$

A system's efficiency will be a measure of how closely it approaches such a state.

In the following redefinition of TS, a new component – efficiency – is added. The use of TS within the definition indicates substitution of its previous value; there is no recursion implied.

$$
\begin{array}{|l}
\hline
\text{TS} \\
\quad \text{TS} \\
\quad \text{efficiency: } \mathbb{R} \\
\hline
\quad \exists\,\text{maxTS}''. \\
\qquad \text{sites} \quad = \text{sites}'' \\
\qquad \text{requests} \quad = \text{requests}'' \\
\qquad \text{connections} \subset \text{connections}'' \\
\\
\qquad \text{efficiency} \leq \dfrac{\text{card connections}}{\text{card connections}''} \\
\hline
\end{array}
$$

Efficiency constraints may now be succinctly expressed – for example,

$$
\begin{array}{|l}
\hline
\text{TS} \\
\quad \text{TS} \\
\hline
\quad \text{efficiency} \geq 75\% \\
\hline
\end{array}
$$

5. WHAT HAS BEEN GAINED BY FORMALISM

One of the immediate effects of a formal specification often is that it forces a decision to be made on every issue, however small (even if that decision is "not to decide"). Mathematical notation, by its very nature, can't be vague (though it can be surprising – like all concise notation).

Below are discussed several points of detail which the informal specification failed to cover - and, significantly, which its writing gave no urge to cover. The formal specification supplies an answer in each case.

1) What happens if a subscriber who is in a conversation unplugs without hanging up?

The call is disconnected. However, the request for that conversation isn't cancelled, and it may be reconnected subsequently.

2) Can two subscribers call each other?

Yes - but the connections made are distinct.

3) Can a subscriber call himself?

Yes - the connection made might include only one telephone. This could be a useful diagnostic facility.

4) Can a subscriber be involved in more than one call at a time?

Yes - but each requires a separate telephone.

5) What happens if the calling and called subscriber are plugged into the same phone?

That phone alone could support a conversation between them.

Further advantages of a formal specification, especially in a mathematical framework, are that it allows mathematical experiments (in the form of postulates and proofs) to be performed on the object specified. The results of these experiments can be used in the design process much earlier (and much more cheaply) than otherwise would have been possible.

Finally, a formal specification has a much greater possibility of effectively being shown to be satisfied by proposed implementations - indeed, techniques exist for the mathematical proof of this as well.

ACKNOWLEDGEMENT

Tony Hoare suggested specifying a telephone system, and provided a great deal of necessary guidance. Tim Clement, Paul Fertig, Roger Gimson, Steve Schumann, Ib Sørensen and Bernard Sufrin all made valuable suggestions as the specification developed.

REFERENCES

1. Abrial, J.-R. (1980). The specification language Z: basic
   library. Specification Group Working Paper, Programming
   Research Group, Oxford.
2. Sufrin, B.A. (In press). Formal system specifications -
   notation and examples. *In* "Tools and Notations for Program
   Construction" (Ed. D. Néel). Cambridge University Press,
   Cambridge.

APPENDIX

Glossary of mathematical symbols

$\wedge$	Logical conjunction
$\vee$	Logical disjunction
$\Longrightarrow$	Logical implication
$\forall$	Universal quantifier. For all ...
$\exists$	Existential quantifier. There exists ...
$\mathbb{R}$	The set of real numbers
$\subseteq$	Set inclusion
$\subset$	Strict set inclusion
$\cup$	Set union
$\cap$	Set intersection
$-$	Set difference
ε	Set membership
$\{\}$	The empty set
$\{term1 | term2\}$	The set of term1 such that term2
card	The cardinality of a set
$\mathbb{P}$	Powerset

$$\mathbb{P}\,S \equiv \{s \mid s \subseteq S\}$$

disjoint   Pairwise disjoint

for $\underline{A}$: $\mathbb{P}\,\mathbb{P}\,A$

disjoint $\underline{A} \equiv$

$\forall a,a':\underline{A}.\ a\cap a' \neq \{\} \Longrightarrow a=a'$

$A \longrightarrow B$	The set of total functions from A to B
$A \longrightarrow\!\!\!\!\rightarrow B$	The set of partial functions from A to B
$A \longleftrightarrow B$	The set of relations from A to B
$[a \mapsto b]$	The function $\{(a,b)\}$
λ	Lambda abstraction

$$\lambda a:A.term \equiv \{(a,term) \mid a: A\}$$

dom   The domain of a relation (or function)
               for R: A $\longleftrightarrow$ B
               dom R $\equiv$ {a:A| $\exists$b:B. a R b}

ran   The range of a relation (or function)
               for R: A $\longleftrightarrow$ B
               ran R $\equiv$ {b:B| $\exists$a:A. a R b}

·   Relational (or functional) composition

⟮ ⟯   Relational application
               for R: A $\longleftrightarrow$ B; A: $\mathbb{P}$ A
               R⟮$\underline{A}$⟯ $\equiv$ {b:B|$\exists\underline{a}$:$\underline{A}$. $\underline{a}$ R b}

\   Domain restriction
               for f: A $\twoheadrightarrow$ B; A: $\mathbb{P}$ A.
               f\$\underline{A}$ $\equiv$ {(a,b):f|$^-$a $\notin$ $\underline{A}$}

⊕   Functional overriding.
               for f,g: A $\twoheadrightarrow$ B.
               f ⊕ g $\equiv$ (f \ dom g) $\cup$ g

Computer System Dossiers

Peter E. Lauer

1. INTRODUCTION

Concurrent systems are more difficult to specify and analyse
than sequential ones, because they require the conceptualisation not only of their sequential subsystems, but also of the
complex interactions between them. It follows that the programmer's intuition is not enough, being unreliable in cases
of high complexity. Here solution of the problem of verification of correct behaviour of the design becomes crucial,
and a satisfactory conceptual apparatus for rigorous verification becomes essential.

In such an apparatus, reduction of complexity, by abstract-
ing away from all irrelevant detail specific to some implementation of a concurrent and distributed system strategy, is
desirable. But it must be easy to obtain implementations from
the abstract specification of a strategy, given enough information about the synchronisation mechanisms of the concrete
system on which it is to be implemented. We therefore need a
notion of "system" sufficiently abstract to allow analysis
only of those aspects of systems arising from their concurrency and yet capable of being readily translated into
practical terms.

We have developed such a conceptual apparatus called COSY
(from COncurrent SYstems) to a great level of sophistication.
The results we have obtained are outlined below and are
treated in detail in the references. Analysis based on the
COSY formalism often involves extensive mechanical transformations of programs and their corresponding semantical objects,
a laborious process which inhibits thorough exploration of

more than one or two alternative designs. Judicious use of
the computer for performing these mechanical tasks would thus
greatly extend the practical utility of the method.
Some of the uses one can made of the COSY formalism are:

1) Specification: To specify the synchronisation aspects of
    systems of congreable (co-operating) concurrent behaviours

2) Abstraction: To abstract to the synchronisation aspects
    of programs (implementations). That is, rather than ex-
    pressing "how" a set of concurrent behaviours is enforced
    by means of the synchronisational elements of a program,
    one expresses "what" the set of synchronised concurrent
    behaviours is.

3) Implementation: To translate a specification of synchron-
    ised concurrent behaviours into a program involving syn-
    chronisation primitives in such a way as to enforce the
    behaviour specified when the program is executed. That is
    we have the inverse of abstraction, rather than expressin;
    "what" the set of synchronised concurrent behaviours is,
    we are to express "how" a set of synchronised concurrent
    behaviours is enforced by the synchronisational elements
    of a program of some implemented programming language.

4) Verification:
    a. Implementation (program) satisfies specification.
    b. Specification is implemented by program.

5) Transformation: To translate one specification into
    another which is more or less concurrent and/or distri-
    buted but defines the same interleaved or pseudo-con-
    current behaviours.

6) Comparison: To compare two different programs implementin
    some synchronisation strategy by comparing their corres-
    ponding abstract specifications in COSY. Comparisons may
    be made with regard to their degree of concurrency and
    distribution. However, the abstractions must preserve
    concurrency and distribution.

7) Evaluation: To evaluate programming languages with respec
    to their ability to support concurrency and distribution.
    Hence, specification1 may be transformed to a more con-
    current and/or distributed specification2, but it may
    not be possible to implement it by means of a correspond-
    ing program2 which has the same degree of concurrency anc
    distribution.

8) Realisation: To obtain a means of executing specificatior
    by either:
    a. direct implementation of specification in VLSI; or
    b. implementation in the sense of point 3 above; or
    c. combining the specification grammar with the grammar
       for a more conventional algorithmic programming langua

Full system COSY notation including the distinction between
specification and implementation was developed to support the
processes of abstraction and implementation (programming,
coding, translating). Verification requires that there exist
formal methods for determining the "meaning" of both the
specification part and the implementation part. If there is
a formal semantics associated with the implementation part
then its meaning can be determined and must be shown to determine the same behaviours in some sense as the specification.
We have developed a suite of computer programs which constitute a system design and analysis environment for basic COSY
called BCS. This environment is intended to reduce the mechanical labour of manipulating COSY specifications of example
systems during the various uses mentioned above.

Given the BCS environment it is possible to produce a lot
of information about a system formulated in COSY and it becomes necessary to devise a means for organising this information in a way which facilitates the analysis of the system
formulated and allows ready comparison between different
system designs. For this purpose, we introduced the notion of
a system dossier as a framework for organising one's information about a system. This notion is particularly helpful if
one has several complementary but differing viewpoints supported by formalisms and automated procedures with the help
of which one is gathering and analysing this information.

In the process of developing the dossier notion it became
apparent that it would be presumptuous if we fixed the possible
viewpoints constituting a dossier *a priori*. Hence, the dossier
notation was introduced as an extendable notation. In this
notation it is possible to introduce new viewpoints provided
each viewpoint is adequately defined particularly with respect
to its interface with other viewpoints which have already been
defined.

Furthermore, since the dossier is a rather general notion
it should not only be applicable to systems developed in COSY
but should also serve as a means for describing the COSY formalism itself, the BCS environment and even the dossier concept itself.

Finally, we envisage the dossier notation as eventually
being implemented and if it were then "compiled" this would
mean, for example:

1) certain communication paths are established between, for
example, the user and maintainer or designer of the
system;
2) interconnections between suite components are made which
allow, for instance:
a. output of one component to become input to another

component;

b. systems descriptions written in a combination of
   notations from different components, e.g. ALGOL 68
   programs and COSY specifications, to be interpreted
   using the semantics of the components involved. It
   might even be possible to run a program written, e.g.
   in a combination of ALGOL 68 and CONCURRENT PASCAL,
   by linking the respective compilers in appropriate
   ways.

Hence, the dossier concept is intended to combine aspects
of a programming language construct, an operating system construct, a communication system construct and even a text processing construct.

Our present formulation of the concept is only tentative
and works tolerably well for our purposes in this paper, but
we hope that a more definitive concept will emerge eventually
from an interaction of interested colleagues in the field.
Hence, we invite the reader to communicate to us any criti-
cisms and suggestions.

Our purpose in the present paper will be to introduce the
dossier concept and give it an informal meaning by applying
it to the dossier concept in Section 2, to the COSY formalism
and BCS environment in Section 3, and finally to a familiar
synchronisation problem and its solution in Section 4.

2. THE DOSSIER ABOUT THE DOSSIER CONCEPT

dossier   dossier_concept

   description Websters_Unabridged_Dictionary

A dossier is an accumulation of records, reports, miscel-
aneous pertinent data, and documents bearing on a single subject of study or investigation.
   A suite is a series or group of things forming a unit or
constituting a complement or collection.

   enddescription

   description   Computer_system_ dossier

With regard to computing systems (hardware, software and
human components) the dossier concept is intended as a means
for:

a) Organising
   1) information about the system;
   2) communication paths between the designers,

developers, maintainers and users of the system;
b) Integrating the computational facilities, their documen-
    tation, the communication system and the general text
    processing facilities.

It is hoped that such a reorganisation and integration will
significantly increase:

a) the overall effectiveness of the system and the individu-
    als involved with it both as users and service personnel;
b) the effectiveness of communication between users and
    maintainers of a system;
c) the responsiveness of the system to queries, complaints
    and needs of the users;
d) the control system personnel have over how they want
    users to inform them about the behaviour of the system
    as a result of its use;
e) the control managers and project leaders have over the
    form and emphasis of research into and development of
    systems.

By a suite in the narrower sense we shall mean a complementary
set of viewpoints supported by software, hardware and personnel who are responsible for the system and its documentation.

enddescription

syntax
DN1: <dossier>=dossier   dossier_name

                   <viewpoint>+

             enddossier

DN2: <viewpoint>=<dossier> |
                 <description> |
                 <specification> | <syntax> | <program> |
                 <definition> | <semantics> |
                 <verification> |
                 <relation> | <intermediary> |
                 <model>

DN3: <description>=
     description descriptionname
     enddescription

DN4: <specification>=
     specification specificationname
     endspecification

DN5: <syntax>=
     syntax syntaxname
     endsyntax

```
DN6:  <program>=
      program programname
      endprogram

DN7:  <definition>=
      definition definitionname
      enddefinition

DN8:  <semantics>=
      semantics semanticsname
      endsemantics

DN9:  <verification>=
      verification verificationname
      endverification

DN9:  <relation>=
      relation relationname
      endrelation

DN10:<intermediary>=
      intermediary intermediaryname
      endintermediary

DN11:<model>=
      model modelname
      endmodel

      endsyntax
```

semantics

Note: For each of the viewpoints we indicate:

1. rules of composition of dossier text;
    a. manual
    b. automatic
2. suite component.

General form of a COSY dossier

dossier   pure_COSY_dossier

    description descriptionname
Here one writes intuitive descriptions of the system that is
to be specified, implemented, verified, etc.
    enddescription

    specification specificationname
Here one can write an abstract behavioural system specification in the Pure COSY notation
    endspecification

definition definitionname
Here one can write a definition of the concurrent behaviour
corresponding to the specification or to the implementation
using the Vector Firing Semantics notation. This part may also
contain certain kinds of verification as for example a proof
that the behaviours displayed are indeed complete in the sense
that no possible behaviour has been omitted.
enddefinition

verification verificationname
Here we can write rigorous proofs or exhaustive simulations
using the Vector Firing Sequence Model verifying that the
system specified is deadlock or starvation free, or that two
implementations implement the same specification, or that two
specifications are inequivalent with respect to degree of
concurrency and distribution though they can both be considered to "compute" the same relation from input to output,
etc.
endverification

enddossier

We will not give any formal semantics for our COSY dossier
but only indicate the above pattern in the present section.
The two subsequent sections contain fragments of applied COSY
dossiers and they will serve as implicit definitions of the
semantics intended.
endsemantics
enddossier

3. BASIC COSY SYSTEMS

3.1. The Dossier about Basic COSY Systems
dossier   basic_COSY_system

description
A basic COSY system is a collection of cyclic, sequential
and non-deterministic subsystems consisting of elementary
events (also called actions, operations, procedures, etc.).
Each event is capable of giving rise to a number (possibly
zero) of occurrences of that event during any period of
(discrete) behaviour of the system.
    The basis (also called set of operations, or alphabet) of
a system is the set of all events considered to constitute
the system.
    A trace (also called firing sequence) of a sequential sub-
system is any, possibly empty, sequence of event occurrences

which constitutes the history of an actual or potential sequential behaviour of the subsystem from some initial event
occurrence, and to some final event occurrence in the finite
case.

A sequential subsystem is completely determined by the set
of all its traces. From the definition of trace it follows
that for any sequential system:

1) the empty trace is a trace of the system, and
2) every prefix of a trace is a trace.

The behaviour of a sequential subsystem is usually defined
in terms of a set of successful initial traces (also called
cycles previously) by stating that all traces of the system
are all possible prefixes of multiples of successful initial
traces. In the case of a cyclic sequential system we identify
the notion of successful initial trace with the notion of a
trace whose corresponding sequence of event occurrences returns the system to the point which preceded the first occurrence of any of that system's constituent events, or briefly,
in the sequential and centralised case, what would be called
its initial state.

A vector (also called vector firing sequences) of congreable traces of a concurrent system consisting of n sequential subsystems is an n-place vector whose i-th component
is a trace of the i-th subsystem for all i in the range 1 to
n, and in which the traces of all subsystems agree about the
number and order of occurrences of events they share. In
other words, a vector of traces of a concurrent system is any
vector of (finite, possibly empty) sequences of event occurrences which constitutes the history of some actual or potential concurrent behaviour of the system from some (possibly
concurrent) event occurrences, and in the finite case, up to
some (possibly concurrent) event occurrences. The i-th sub-
history of the vector of histories is a history of an actual
or potential sequential behaviour of the i-th sequential subsystem from some event occurrence, and to some event occurrence in the finite case. But in addition, if several subsystems involve the same event then their respective traces
have to agree about the number and order of occurrences of
the event in which they coincide. Hence we talk about vectors
of congreable traces.

A concurrent system is completely determined by the set of
its vectors of congreable traces. Again it follows from the
definition of vector of traces that:

1) the vector of empty traces is a concurrent history of
    the system
2) every prefix (generalised to vectors of traces) of a

vector of traces of the system is a vector of traces of
the system.

More generally, our semantic model divides a view of a
concurrent system into three aspects:

1) the individual view of the sequential subsystems independent of their combination into a single concurrent system,
i.e. the traces of the subsystems considered independently
of whether they share events;
2) the common view of the combined concurrent system which
all sequential subsystems must share if they are to constitute a single system, independent of their view of
their own sequential history, i.e. the vectors of "traces"
which agree on the number and order of occurrences of
events subsystems share disregarding the order prescribed
by the traces of the individual subsystems;
3) the combined view of the whole system in which both views
(1) and (2) coincide.

In the application of the COSY formalism, (notation and
semantic model), one will want to be able to start from any
one of these views and obtain any of the other views from
them while developing one's conceptualisation of the system.
Furthermore, one will want to derive specifications to correspond to systems which have been designed by means of the
semantic model alone.

enddescription

syntax

A basic COSY specification is a string derived from the production rules given below. The following meta-language conventions have been used in the syntax rules: the symbols "=",
"{", "}", "/", "*", "+", "@" are used as meta-symbols. The
symbol "=" denotes replacement of its left-hand side by the
string on its right-hand side. The braces "{ }" are used to
group items together, "/" indicates alternate productions,
"{item}*" indicates production of "item" zero or more times,
"{item}+" production of "item" one or more times. The notation

   {item1 @ item2}+

is used as a shorthand for

   item1 {item2 item1}*

In the syntax rules for basic COSY specifications "item2" may
be one of the terminal symbols ";" and ",". Non-underlined

lower case words, except single lower case letters and digits,
are non-terminal symbols, and all other symbols like ";", ",",
"(", ")", "*", underlined lower case words and single lower
case letters and digits are terminal symbols. We shall ad-
ditionally use the following convention: in right parts of
production rules the concatenation of terminals and non-
terminals has precedence over alternation. Thus A B/C means
either A B or C. When necessary we use "{ }" to override the
normal precedence. Thus A {B/C} means either A B or A C.
   The syntax of a basic COSY specification is given by the
following rules:

BN1. basicspecification = specification body endspecification
BN2. body = {path/process}+
BN3. path = path sequence end
BN4. process = process sequence end
BN5. sequence = {orelement @;}+
BN6. orelement = {starelement @,}+
BN7. starelement = element/element*
BN8. element = operation/(sequence)
BN9. operation = simple-op/subscr-op
BN10. simple-op = letter{letter/digit/ }*
BN11. subscr-op = simple-op({integer @,}+)
BN12. letter = a/b/.../z/A/B/.../Z
BN13. digit = 0/1/.../9

endsyntax

semantics

In the regular expressions produced by the non-terminal
"sequence" the symbols ";", and "," denote sequentialisation
and arbitrary choice respectively; the symbol "*" is the
Kleene star, which denotes zero or more repetitions.
   All the regular expressions in paths and processes are
considered to be cyclic in the sense that constituent operations may be executed repeatedly subject to the constraints
of sequentialisation and arbitrary choice. For this reason
the outermost star and parentheses are omitted, their presence
being implicit. The semantics of a basic path P are given in
terms of its set of firing sequences denoted by FS(P). The
infinite set FS(P) is constructed from a set consisting of
the cycles of P by the function "Cyc". The function "Cyc"
applies to syntactic components of basic paths, that is to
say substrings produced by non-terminals. Syntactic component
of paths are denoted by syntactic variables. A path P is
represented by

path SEQ end

where SEQ denotes a sequence, which is represented by

OREL1;...;ORELn

where ORELi for i=1,...,n denote orelements. An orelement is represented by

STAREL1,...,STARELn

where STARELi for i=1,...,n denote starelements. A starelement is represented by

ELEM* or ELEM

where ELEM denotes an element which is represented by

(SEQ)

when it is produced by the second option of the syntax rule for element BN8, or by

OP

when produced by the first option. The function "Cyc" is defined as follows:

Cyc(e)=cases e:

1. path SEQ end $\rightarrow$ Cyc(SEQ)
2. OREL1;...;ORELn $\rightarrow$ Cyc(OREL1) • ... • Cyc(ORELn)
3. STAREL1,...,STARELn $\rightarrow$ Cyc(STAREL1) U...U Cyc(STARELn)
4. ELEM* $\rightarrow$ Cyc(ELEM)*
5. (SEQ) $\rightarrow$ Cyc(SEQ)
6. OP $\rightarrow$ {OP}

In the above definition of "Cyc" the symbol "U" denotes the set-union operator and the symbol"•" the concatenation of sets of strings operator. The operation

X•Y

where X,Y of sets of strings is defined as:

X•Y={x•y|x $\in$ X,y $\in$ Y}

where "•" denotes string concatenation and "$\in$" element of a set.

    In the definition of "Cyc" a starred set X* indicates the set obtained by concatenation of zero or more times of elements of the set X. Formally X* is defined by

$$X* = X^0 \cup X^1 \cup X^2 \cup \ldots$$

where X is a set of strings and X^i is defined recursively by

$$X^i = X^{i-1} \bullet X$$
$$X^0 = \{e\}$$

where "e" denotes the empty string.

From the set Cyc(P) we construct the set of firing sequences of P denoted by FS(P) as follows:

$$FS(P) = Pref(Cyc(P)*)$$

where Pref(X) is defined as

$$Pref(X) = \{x \mid x \bullet y \in X, \text{ for some } y\}$$

where X is a set of strings.

The set FS(P) is the set of sequences of operation executions permitted by the path P. As already mentioned, to model the non-sequential behaviour of a basic specification R consisting of paths P1,...,Pn partial orders of occurrences of operations will be constructed which are represented by vectors of strings. An n-vector $\underline{x}$

$$\underline{x} = (x1, \ldots, xn)$$

is a possible behaviour of R if each xi for $1 \leq i \leq n$ is a possible firing sequence of Pi for i=1,...,n and furthermore, if the xi's agree on the number and the order of occurrences of operations they share.

To formally define the set of possible behaviours or histories of R, vectors of strings are introduced together with a composition operation on them. Let S1,...,Sn be a family of sets of strings and let

$$\overset{n}{\underset{i=1}{X}} Si* = S1* \ x \ldots x \ Sn* = \{ (s1, \ldots, sn) \mid \text{for all } i, \ si \in Si* \}$$

where "X" denotes the cross product operator. If the vectors $\underline{x}$ and $\underline{y}$ belong to the above set then their composition $\underline{x}\tilde{}\underline{y}$ is defined as

$$\underline{x}\tilde{}\underline{y} = (x1, \ldots, xn)\tilde{}(y1, \ldots, yn) = (x1 \bullet y1, \ldots, xn \bullet yn)$$

where "$\tilde{}$" denotes the vector concatenation operation.

To each specification R consisting exclusively of paths

$$R = P1 \ldots Pn$$

we associate its set of operations Ops(R) defined by

$$Ops(R) = Ops(P1) U \ldots U \ Ops(Pn)$$

and its set of vector operations Vops(R) defined as follows: for each operation "a" in R we construct an n-vector $\underline{a}$. The

i'th component of this vector for $1 \leq i \leq n$ denoted by $[\underline{a}]i$ is
given by

$[\underline{a}]i= |$ a if a $\in$ Ops(Pi)

$\qquad |$

$\qquad |$ e otherwise

where "e" denotes the null string. The set of vector operations of R, Vops(R) is then defined as

Vops(R)=$\{\underline{a}|$a $\in$ Ops(R)$\}$

Let us define Vops(R)* to be the submonoid of

$$\begin{array}{l} n \\ X \text{ Ops(Pi)}* \\ i=1 \end{array}$$

by Vops(R) and $\underline{e}$=(e,...,e) under the vector composition
operation. The set of all possible behaviours or histories of
R, the vector firing sequences of R, denoted by VFS(R) is
defined by:

$$\begin{array}{l} n \\ \text{VFS(R)}=(\ X \text{ FS(Pi)}) \cap \text{Vops(R)}* \\ \quad\quad i=1 \end{array}$$

The set

$$\begin{array}{l} n \\ X \text{ FS(Pi)} \\ i=1 \end{array}$$

in the definition of VFS(R) guarantees that each string component of a history $\underline{x} \in$ VFS(R) is a firing sequence of the
corresponding path, $\overline{i}$.e. it represents the individual view,
and the set Vops(R)* guarantees that all these firing sequences agree on the number and order of executions of the
operations they share, i.e. it represents the collective
view. VFS(R) of course represents the combined view.

By the construction of VFS(R) each of its elements $\underline{x}$
represents everything that has happened in some possible
period of activity of R. We may write $\underline{x}$ as a composition of
vector operations $\underline{a1}$,...,$\underline{am}$ of Vops(R)$\overline{\ }$as in (V1)

(V1) $\underline{x}=\underline{a1}^{\sim}...^{\sim}\underline{am}$

Consequently, for every $\underline{x}$=(x1,...,xn) $\in$ Vops(R)*, the symbol
$[\underline{x}]i$ denotes the string $\overline{x}i$, i.e. $[\underline{x}]i$=xi, for i=1,...,n. If
for some operations "ak" and "aℓ" for $1 \leq k, \ell \leq m$ and $k \neq \ell$,
$[\underline{ak}]i \neq e$ implies $[\underline{a\ell}]i$=e for i=1,...,n then the composition
$\underline{ak}^{\sim}\underline{a\ell}$ is the same as $\underline{a\ell}^{\sim}\underline{ak}$. Such operations are said to be
independent and we write $\underline{ind}$(ak,aℓ). If furthermore ℓ=k+1

that is a̲k̲ and a̲ℓ̲ are neighbouring vectors in (V1), as in (V2)

(V2) x̲=a1~...a̲k̲~a̲ℓ̲~...a̲m̲

then x̲ may also be written as (V3)

(V3) x̲=a1~...~a̲ℓ̲~a̲k̲~...~a̲m̲

The commutativity of vector operations in a vector firing sequence is interpreted to mean that the operations corresponding to these vector operations may execute concurrently. We say that two operations "a" and "b" are concurrent at a history x̲ and we write

    a c̲o̲ b a̲t̲ x̲

if i̲n̲d̲(a,b) and x̲~a, x̲~b ∈ VFS(R). This definition implies that only independent operations may execute concurrently. However, independent operations may not always execute concurrently or may never execute concurrently at all.

For the construction of the vector firing sequences of a basic specification R, the following sets need to be constructed directly from R:

1) the cycle sets of all paths in R, and
2) the set of the vector operations in R, Vops(R).

In general, a basic specification R is a string of the form

    R=P1...Pn Q1...Qm

where Pj for j=1,...,n and Qi for i=1,...,m denote paths and processes respectively. Although paths and processes may be intermixed in a basic specification, in the above expressions for convenience, we assumed that all paths are collected before processes.

The semantics of a basic specification involving processes is given by means of the vector firing sequences of an equivalent basic specification R' involving just paths. The conversion of R into R' is denoted by Path(R) and is obtained by the following rule (Path Conversion Rule):

1) For every a ∈ Ops(R) construct a set

    Ia={i│a ∈ Ops(Qi) for 1≤i≤m}

and, if the cardinality of the set Ia denoted by │Ia│ is greater than zero, say ℓ=│Ia│>0 then
 - replace the operation "a" in each path it occurs by the element

    (a&i1,...,a&iℓ)

where ik $\in$ Ia for k=1,...,ℓ
- replace the operation "a" in processes Qik by a&ik for all ik $\in$ Ia.

2) Replace all occurrences of "process" by "path".

Then the semantics of R are given by means of VFS(Path(R)) and are obtained as defined in the previous section. As we have mentioned, a basic COSY specification describes a system by specifying partial orders on the execution of its operations and therefore, the only properties of interest are behavioural in nature.

The formal model of behaviour, the vector firing sequences of path-specifications permit us to speak formally of dynamic properties of a system specified by a path-specification R. All properties of R may be expressed in terms of its corresponding vector firing sequences VFS(R). Such properties fall into two classes, the general and the specific properties.

The general properties are those which apply to any specification, properties such as absence of deadlock or starvation, which may be defined in terms of uninterpreted operations. We say that a path-specification R is deadlock-free if and only if

$$\forall \underline{x} \in \text{VFS}(R) \ \exists a \in \text{Ops}(R):\underline{x}\tilde{\ }\underline{a} \in \text{VFS}(R)$$

that is if and only if every history $\underline{x}$ may be continued. We say that a specification R is adequate if and only if

$$\forall \underline{x} \in \text{VFS}(R) \ \forall a \in \text{Ops}(R) \ \exists \underline{y} \in \text{Vops}(R)*: \ \underline{x}\tilde{\ }\underline{y}\tilde{\ }\underline{a} \in \text{VFS}(R)$$

that is, if and only if every history of R may be continued enabling eventually every operation in R. Adequacy is a property akin to absence of partial system deadlock (see also [1,2]).

The relation $-->\subseteq \text{Vops}(R)* \times \text{Vops}(R)*$, defined as:

$\underline{x}-->\underline{y}:<==> \underline{x}\in\text{VFS}(R)$ &
  $(\exists a1,...,ak\in\text{Ops}(R)) \ \underline{x}\cdot a1.....ak=\underline{y}$
  & $((\forall i=1,...,n) \ \overline{[\underline{y}]i\in\text{FS}(\text{Pi})})$
  & $((\forall j=1,...,k) \ i\neq j --> \underline{\text{ind}}(ai,aj))$

is called the concurrent reachability in one step [3].

It can be proved that VFS(R)={$\underline{x}$: $\underline{e}-->*\underline{x}$}. For every $\underline{x} \in$ VFS(R), let enabled($\underline{x}$) be the following family of action names:

enabled($\underline{x}$)={{a1,...,ak}:{a1,...,ak} $\subseteq$ Ops(R)   &
  $\underline{x}-->\underline{x}\cdot\overline{a1.....ak}$}

and let maxenabled($\underline{x}$) be the family of all maximal elements contained in enabled($\underline{x}$), i.e.

maxenabled($\underline{x}$)={A$\in$ enabled($\underline{x}$):(B$\in$ enabled($\underline{x}$)&A$\subseteq$ B) --> A=B}.

And finally, let $\xrightarrow{M} \subseteq \text{Vops}(R)^* \times \text{Vops}(R)^*$ be the relation
given by:

$$\underline{x}\xrightarrow{M}\underline{y}: \; \Longleftrightarrow \; (\dashv\{a1,\ldots,ak\} \in \text{maxenabled}(\underline{x})) \; \underline{y}=\underline{x}\cdot a1\ldots..ak$$

The relation $\xrightarrow{M}$ is called the maximally concurrent reachability in one step. For more details on the last notions the
reader is referred to [3].

The specific properties involve the interpretation of a
COSY specification as a description of an actual system. The
operations of a COSY specification are interpreted as actions
of a system and the behaviour of the specification as the
behaviour of the system.

Considerable work has been done concerning the verification
of general properties of specifications and in particular re-
lating to adequacy [4,5] and a number of general theorems
have been obtained [5]. For simple comma-free path specifications there is a complete characterisation for adequacy.
Other theorems have been obtained which permit certain
specification transformations which preserve adequacy.

As far as specific properties of specifications are concerned, various specifications have been shown to satisfy
some design requirements. The most involved of these is the
parallel resource releasing mechanism [6,7,14].

endsemantics

3.2. Basic COSY System Program

dossier   BCS

description

The basic COSY system BCS is a program which emphasises the
analysis and simulated execution of concurrent systems. It is
coded in SIMULA, and is of modular design to localise as much
as possible those parts which are unavoidably specific to the
host operating system. From the abstract viewpoint, BCS is
nothing but the implementation of the relation -->. It is
just a device which produces the relation --> for a given path
program R (see [3]). The program has the following principal
functional procedures, or processors:

a)   Compile, which inputs a source specification written in
     the basic COSY syntax, producing an object file which is
     used as input by other processors. The object file in-
     cludes the original text, and also contains the parsing
     tree in a compact form, and tables of operation names

with cross-references to paths and processes.
b) Recompile also produces an object file, but instead of a
    source input, it uses an object file as input, usually
    after editing, and so provides a recycling capability
    which makes the process of refining a COSY specification
    much more efficient than the conventional approach of
    editing source code.
c) Fire generates the firing sequences (cyclic histories) of
    individual paths and processes under interactive user
    control.
d) Simulate is the most powerful of the processors, being a
    mechanism for stepping a simulation of the concurrent
    system, described in COSY notation, through all its per-
    mitted histories.

enddescription

syntax syntaxname
Here we put the syntax of the BCS command language.
endsyntax

semantics
BCS has been written in SIMULA 67, and runs on the Newcastle
IBM 370 computer under the Michigan Terminal System (MTS). By
December 1981, as we then reported in more detail [9], BCS
had been developed to the stage where three principal functions
were in useful working order:
    Compilation: BCS will accept a source specification, written
in the basic COSY notation, which describes a distributed system comprising an arbitrary number of sequential, cyclic and
nondeterministic processes, and from that source construct a
parse-tree representation of the distributed system.
    The tree structure is then written out in a compact object
language to a file, from which the tree may be readily reconstructed by the other functions of BCS.
    Generation of Firing Cycles: the Firing Sequence Generator
(FSG) function of BCS operates on the individual paths or processes of a compiled COSY specification, without regard to
the synchronisation restraints imposed by the coincidence of
operations in different paths. The FSG is mainly useful for
checking the semantics of more complicated paths which are
otherwise difficult to read.
    Simulation: the Simulation function of BCS provides what
is effectively a COSY machine, a mechanism for the simulated
execution of a system of distributed sequential processes.
    The mechanism realises the Vector Firing Sequence semantics
of a COSY specification thus:

1) For each sequential subsystem (path and processes) there

is a pointer to the last operation fired (a null pointer
if no operation has yet fired).
2) There is a variable set of operations which are enabled,
that is, permitted to fire by the constraints implied by
all the path expressions comprising the COSY specification
(A path or process which contains no operation in the
enabled set is blocked, and when the enabled set is empty,
the simulated system is totally deadlocked. Starvation
arises when certain enabled operations fail to be executed
3) From the enabled set of operations (while that set is not
empty) some may be selected to "fire". A firing operation
leaves the enabled set (taking with it all those operation
which are subject to mutual exclusion with it), and becomes the "last operation fired" in each of the sequential
subsystems in which it occurs. All the paths and processes
containing that fired operation now define new (local)
sets of potentially enabled operations, and those
operations now permitted to fire by all the paths citing
them join the enabled set.
4) Each operation fired is stored (effectively as a vector
operation), in a sequential history list.

Driving the simulation of a COSY specification may be done,
at present, in two ways.

a) The current set of enabled operations is displayed as a
list of operation names at the terminal, from which the
user may select one or more (depending on the mutual
exclusion relations among the operations). After the
selected operations have been "fired" and recorded, the
new enabled set is displayed, and the manual selection
made again.
b) The user may choose a number of simulation steps to be
run automatically. At each step, one operation is
selected at random from the current enabled set. Re-
cording of vector firing sequences is done as when in
the manual selection mode.

Playback of the simulated history, which may be accumulated
after arbitrary alternation between the two modes of driving,
can be in two (so far) styles.

a) The "packed" style shows the history of each sequential
path as a simple string of operation names, and does not
emphasise the synchronisation of operations occurring in
several paths at once.
b) The "padded" or "vector" style of replay appears as a
concatenation of column vectors. Such a display is
generally more bulky than the packed display but provides
a very nice illustration of the meaning of concurrency

of operations.

Modelling, Analysing and Developing Specifications. Examples below and in the more detailed paper on BCS [9] illustrate how the semantic routines of BCS may be used to:

a) clarify one's understanding of a specification leading to a possible reformulation which is more readable;
b) reliably obtain particular histories of system behaviour, either by terminal dialogue or automatically, and display them in various forms;
c) semantically correct a specification for which one has obtained a history by (b), for example by transforming the specification to exclude a deadlock (cf. [10] p.324);
d) verify correctness of a specification by

   1) using a theorem (cf. [8] p.11) which says that if there exists a generalised cyclic history in the combined view of the system then it involves no partial system deadlock
   2) using a theorem (cf. [4] p.22) which says when a specification may be reduced to a simpler one with the same deadlock properties by removing parts of the specification which could not contribute to deadlock. If a given specification reduces to the empty specification, the original specification allows no partial system deadlock.

e) analyse and develop the system from any of the three viewpoints, individual, collective, and combined.
f) analyse the concurrency of the system which can be made explicit by using the vector operation representation of a history (see above).

Obviously these approaches may all be combined in the analysis and development of a system. For example, one can use the above method (2) to reduce a specification not to the empty specification, which may not be possible, but to a collection of disjoint sub-specifications each of which can be verified by method (1).

endsemantics

verification

Problem of maximally concurrent simulation.

By maximally concurrent simulation, we mean a simulation where we always perform concurrently as many actions as possible. It turns out that if this kind of simulation is

enough to describe the complete system behaviour, then the
whole verification procedure is easier and less labour-
consuming. Let us start with the following lemma:
Lemma: n,m independent actions and concurrent at some
point:

$$n,m = m,n$$

Proof: depends on argument based on:
i) their independence, i.e. firing of one cannot
disable the other,
ii) neither can make use of any choices which might
arise at the invisible intermediate point.

This lemma tells us that it suffices to request independent
and simultaneously enabled actions be done in one step, by
writing them in one order, to obtain all traces obtainable by
writing them in some other order.
Unfortunately, the following fact is also true:
Fact: Doing two independent and simultaneously enabled
actions in one step, that is, without making use of
choices that might arise after one or the other of
the actions has been completed, is not the same as
doing them in either order but sequentially, that
is, in two steps.

Proof: the specification below and the accompanying trace
generated by taking all possible choices at least
once demonstrate the non-equivalence.

specification
    P1:path a,c;d end
    P2:path b;c,d end
endspecification

Enabled : 1=a 4=b
=1,4
Enabled : 3=d
=3

Enabled : 1=a 4=b
=1
Enabled : 4=b
=4
Enabled : 3=d
=3

```
Enabled : 1=a 4=b
=4
Enabled : *1=a *2=c
=1
Enabled : 3=d
=3

Enabled : 1=a 4=b
=4
Enabled : *1=a *2=c
=2
Enabled : 4=b
=4
Enabled : 3=d
=3

    P1 : a. .d.a. .d. .a.d. .c. .d
    P2 :  .b.d. .b.d.b. .d.b.c.b.d
```

The problem sketched above is precisely studied in [3]. Let us recall some basic results. For every specification R=P1...Pn (if R contains processes we consider Path(R)), let:

$$\text{VMFS}(R) = \{ \underline{x} : \underline{e} \xrightarrow{M} > *\underline{x} \}.$$

VMFS(R) is simply the set of all vectors of firing sequences produced by maximally concurrent performances. R is said to be completely characterised by maximally concurrent simulation if and only if

$$\text{VFS}(R) = \text{Pref}(\text{VMFS}(R)),$$

where here Pref(X) is defined as:

$$\text{Pref}(X) = \{ \underline{x} : \underline{x} \cdot \underline{y} \in X \text{ for some } \underline{y} \}$$

The fact stated above shows that there is an R such that VFS(R) $\neq$ Pref(VMFS(R)).

Let pre, exc, con $\subseteq$ Ops(R) x Ops(R) be the following relations:

$(a,b) \in$ pre $: <==> (\exists i)(\exists x \in \text{FS(Pi)})\ x \cdot a \cdot b \in \text{FS(Pi)}$,

$(a,b) \in$ exc $: <==> (\exists i)(\exists x \in \text{FS(Pi)})\ x \cdot a \in \text{FS(Pi)}\ \&\ x \cdot b \in \text{FS(Pi)}$,

$(a,b) \in$ con $: <==> \underline{\text{ind}}(a,b)\ \&\ (\exists \underline{x} \in \text{VFS(R)})\ \underline{x \cdot a \cdot b} \in \text{VFS(R)}$.

Let PDT(R) $\subseteq$ Ops(R) x Ops(R) x Ops(r) be the relation defined as follows:

$(a,b,c) \in$ PDT(R) $: <==> (a,b) \in (\text{pre} \cup \text{con})\ \&$
$\qquad\qquad\qquad\qquad (b,c) \in \text{exc}\ \&\ (a,c) \in \text{con}.$

The relation PDT(R) is called potentially dangerous triples. In the case of the example considered in the proof of the Fact above we have: (b,c,a) ∈ PDT(R). In [3] the following theorem is proved:

If PDT(R)={ } then VFS(R)=Pref(VMFS(R)),

where { } denotes the empty set.
In other words, if there are no potentially dangerous triples then maximally concurrent simulation alone is enough to describe the complete system behaviour.
endverification

program

Here goes a copy of the SIMULA program BCS#24

endprogram

enddossier
enddossier

4. A COSY SMOKERS DOSSIER

dossier   Smokers

dossier   Smokers_problem

description smoking_analogy

Three smokers are sitting at a table. One of them has tobacco, another has cigarette papers, and the third one has matches; each one has a different ingredient required to roll, light and smoke a cigarette but he may not give any ingredient to another. On the table in front of them, two of the three ingredients will be placed. No new set of ingredients will be placed on the table until some smoker has successfully smoked. Smokers can only pick up ingredients that are on the table sequentially, one after the other. Smokers cannot return ingredients to the table if they discover that the third required ingredient for them to smoke has not been placed on the table. Hence, once the wrong smoker picks up an ingredient which another smoker could successfully use, no smoker can successfully smoke and the smokers are deadlocked.

enddescription

specification semaphore_smokinganalogy

    P1:<u>path</u> tobaccoV;tobaccoP <u>end</u>
    P2:<u>path</u> paperV;paperP <u>end</u>
    P3:<u>path</u> matchV;matchP <u>end</u>
    P4:<u>path</u> smokertV;smokertP <u>end</u>
    P5:<u>path</u> smokerpV;smokerpP <u>end</u>
    P6:<u>path</u> smokermV;smokermP <u>end</u>
    P7:<u>path</u> sP;sV <u>end</u>
    Q1:<u>process</u> sP;paperV;matchV <u>end</u>
    Q2:<u>process</u> sP;tobaccoV;paperV <u>end</u>
    Q3:<u>process</u> sP;matchV;tobaccoV <u>end</u>
    Q4:<u>process</u> smokertP;sV <u>end</u>
    Q5:<u>process</u> smokerpP;sV <u>end</u>
    Q6:<u>process</u> smokermP;sV <u>end</u>
    Q7:<u>process</u> paperP;matchP;smokertV <u>end</u>
    Q8:<u>process</u> tobaccoP;paperP;smokermV <u>end</u>
    Q9:<u>process</u> matchP;tobaccoP;smokerpV <u>end</u>

<u>endspecification</u>

definition semaphore_smokinganalogy

    <u>The Periodic Vector Firing Sequences of the</u>
    <u>Problematic Smokers</u>
    <u>problem dialogue pd1</u>:

    Enabled : *19=sP&1 *20=sP&2 *21=sP&3
    =19
    Enabled : 5=paperV&1
    =5
    Enabled : 7=paperP&7 9=matchV&1
    =7,9
    Enabled : *11=matchP&7 *12=matchP&9
    =11
    Enabled : 13=smokertV&7
    =13
    Enabled : 14=smokertP&4
    =14
    Enabled : 22=sV&4
    =22
    Enabled : *19=sP&1 *20=sP&2 *21=sP&3

problem vector firing sequence pvfs1 "padded":

```
P1 :   .      .      .      .      .        .        .
P2 :   .paperV.paperP.      .      .        .        .
P3 :   .      .      .matchV.matchP.        .        .
P4 :   .      .      .      .      .smokertV.smokertP.
P5 :   .      .      .      .      .        .        .
P6 :   .      .      .      .      .        .        .
P7 : sP.      .      .      .      .        .        .sV
Q1 : sP.paperV.      .matchV.      .        .        .
Q2 :   .      .      .      .      .        .        .
Q3 :   .      .      .      .      .        .        .
Q4 :   .      .      .      .      .        .smokertP.sV
Q5 :   .      .      .      .      .        .        .
Q6 :   .      .      .      .      .        .        .
Q7 :   .      .paperP.      .matchP.smokertV.        .
Q8 :   .      .      .      .      .        .        .
Q9 :   .      .      .      .      .        .        .
```

problem dialogue pd2:

```
Enabled : *19=sP&1 *20=sP&2 *21=sP&3
=20
Enabled : 1=tobaccoV&2
=1
Enabled : 3=tobaccoP&8 6=paperV&2
=3,6
Enabled : *7=paperP&7 *8=paperP&8
=8
Enabled : 17=smokermV&8
=17
Enabled : 18=smokermP&6
=18
Enabled : 24=sV&6
=24
Enabled : *19=sP&1 *20=sP&2 *21=sP&3
```

problem vector firing sequence pvfs2 "padded":

```
P1 :  .tobaccoV.tobaccoP.     .        .          .        .
P2 :    .        .      .paperV.paperP.          .        .
P3 :    .        .      .        .        .        .        .
P4 :    .        .      .        .        .        .        .
P5 :    .        .      .        .        .        .        .
P6 :    .        .      .        .      .smokermV.smokermP.
P7 : sP.        .      .        .        .        .      .sV
Q1 :    .        .      .        .        .        .        .
Q2 : sP.tobaccoV.      .paperV.        .        .        .
Q3 :    .        .      .        .        .        .        .
Q4 :    .        .      .        .        .        .        .
Q5 :    .        .      .        .        .        .        .
Q6 :    .        .      .        .        .      .smokermP.sV
Q7 :    .        .      .        .        .        .        .
Q8 :    .      .tobaccoP.      .paperP.smokermV.        .
Q9 :    .        .      .        .        .        .        .
```

problem dialogue pd3:

```
Enabled : *19=sP&1 *20=sP&2 *21=sP&3
=21
Enabled : 10=matchV&3
=10
Enabled : 2=tobaccoV&3 12=matchP&9
=2,12
Enabled : *3=tobaccoP&8 *4=tobaccoP&9
=4
Enabled : 15=smokerpV&9
=15
Enabled : 16=smokerpP&5
=16
Enabled : 23=sV&5
=23
Enabled : *19=sP&1 *20=sP&2 *21=sP&3
```

problem vector firing sequence pvfs3:

```
P1 :    .      .tobaccoV.      .tobaccoP.        .        .
P2 :    .        .      .        .        .        .        .
P3 : .matchV.        .matchP.        .        .        .
P4 :    .        .      .        .        .        .        .
P5 :    .        .      .        .      .smokerpV.smokerpP.
P6 :    .        .      .        .        .        .        .
P7 : sP.        .      .        .        .        .      .sV
Q1 :    .        .      .        .        .        .        .
Q2 :    .        .      .        .        .        .        .
Q3 : sP.matchV.tobaccoV.      .        .        .        .
Q4 :    .        .      .        .        .        .        .
Q5 :    .        .      .        .      .smokerpP.sV
Q6 :    .        .      .        .        .        .        .
Q7 :    .        .      .        .        .        .        .
Q8 :    .        .      .        .        .        .        .
Q9 :    .        .      .matchP.tobaccoP.smokerpV.        .
```

The non-periodic vector firing sequences of the problematic smokers

problem dialogue pd4:

Enabled : *19=sP&1 *20=sP&2 *21=sP&3
=19
Enabled : 5=paperV&1
=5
Enabled : 7=paperP&7 9=matchV&1
=7,9
Enabled : *11=matchP&7 *12=matchP&9
=12
System deadlocked!

problem vector firing sequence pvfs4 "padded":

```
P1 :   .       .       .       .       .<R>
P2 :   .paperV.paperP.          .       .<R>
P3 :   .       .       .matchV.matchP.<R>
P4 :   .       .       .       .       .<R>
P5 :   .       .       .       .       .<R>
P6 :   .       .       .       .       .<R>
P7 : sP.       .       .       .       .<R>
Q1 : sP.paperV.          .matchV.       .<R>
Q2 :   .       .       .       .       .<R>
Q3 :   .       .       .       .       .<R>
Q4 :   .       .       .       .       .<R>
Q5 :   .       .       .       .       .<R>
Q6 :   .       .       .       .       .<R>
Q7 :   .       .paperP.          .       .<R>
Q8 :   .       .       .       .       .<R>
Q9 :   .       .       .       .matchP.<R>
```

problem dialogue pd5:

Enabled : *19=sP&1 *20=sP&2 *21=sP&3
=20
Enabled : 1=tobaccoV&2
=1
Enabled : 3=tobaccoP&8 6=paperV&2
=3,6
Enabled : *7=paperP&7 *8=paperP&8
=7
System deadlocked!

problem vector firing sequence pvfs5:

```
P1 :  .tobaccoV.tobaccoP.          .        .<R>
P2 :  .        .        .paperV.paperP.<R>
P3 :  .        .        .        .    .<R>
P4 :  .        .        .        .    .<R>
P5 :  .        .        .        .    .<R>
P6 :  .        .        .        .    .<R>
P7 : sP.       .        .        .    .<R>
Q1 :  .        .        .        .    .<R>
Q2 : sP.tobaccoV.       .paperV.      .<R>
Q3 :  .        .        .        .    .<R>
Q4 :  .        .        .        .    .<R>
Q5 :  .        .        .        .    .<R>
Q6 :  .        .        .        .    .<R>
Q7 :  .        .        .        .paperP.<R>
Q8 :  .        .tobaccoP.         .    .<R>
Q9 :  .        .        .        .    .<R>
```

problem dialogue pd6

```
Enabled : *19=sP&1  *20=sP&2  *21=sP&3
=21
Enabled : 10=matchV&3
=10
Enabled : 2=tobaccoV&3  12=matchP&9
=2,12
Enabled : *3=tobaccoP&8  *4=tobaccoP&9
=3
System deadlocked!
```

problem vector firing sequence pvfs6:

```
P1 :  .        .tobaccoV.       .tobaccoP.<R>
P2 :  .        .        .        .    .<R>
P3 :  .matchV.          .matchP.      .<R>
P4 :  .        .        .        .    .<R>
P5 :  .        .        .        .    .<R>
P6 :  .        .        .        .    .<R>
P7 : sP.       .        .        .    .<R>
Q1 :  .        .        .        .    .<R>
Q2 :  .        .        .        .    .<R>
Q3 : sP.matchV.tobaccoV.          .   .<R>
Q4 :  .        .        .        .    .<R>
Q5 :  .        .        .        .    .<R>
Q6 :  .        .        .        .    .<R>
Q7 :  .        .        .        .    .<R>
Q8 :  .        .        .        .tobaccoP.<R>
Q9 :  .        .        .matchP.       .<R>
```

In the two definitions of the smokers problem given above we
have exhibited six vector firing sequences and we have implicitly claimed that these six vector firing sequences completely define all possible behaviours of the system of problematic smokers. We now prove that our implicit assumption is
justified. One can easily prove by inspection that the
interesting part of the relations con and exc are the
following:

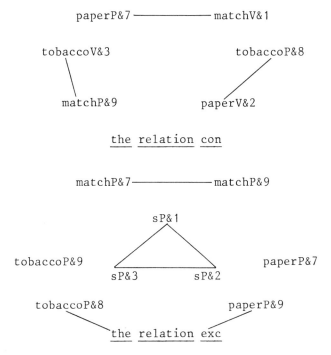

the relation con

the relation exc

The relation pre is much more complicated but it is not
necessary to consider the whole relation pre. Let us consider

$\{a:(a,paperP\&7) \in pre$ or $(paperP\&7,a) \in pre\}$

and denote it by pre(paperP&7). It is very easy to show by
inspection (see the form of the process Q7), that:

pre(paperP&7)=smokerV&7 paperP&7 matchP&7

Now we have:

(paperP&7,matchP&7) $\in$ pre & (matchP&7,matchP&9) $\in$ exc but
(paperP&7,matchP&9) $\notin$ con;

and

(smokerV&7,paperP&7) $\in$ pre & (paperP&7,paperP&9) $\in$ exc but
(smokerV&7,paperP&9) $\notin$ con;

thus there is no potentially dangerous triple containing the action paperP&7.

In a similar way we may prove that the remaining actions from the domain of con, i.e. matchV&1, tobaccoP&8, paperV&2, matchP&9, tobaccoV&3, do not belong to any potentially dangerous triples. But this means that there is no potentially dangerous triple so by the theorem we obtain that the maximally concurrent simulation given above completely characterises the whole behaviour of the problematic smokers.

enddefinition

dossier   Patil's problem

    description Patil's problem statement

To inform the smokers about the ingredients which are placed on the table, three binary semaphores representing tobacco, paper and matches are provided. On placing the ingredients on the table the corresponding semaphore is incremented by performing a V() operation. On the smoker's side semaphores smokert, smokerp and smokerm are used to signal that a cigarette has been smoked. The smoker who completes smoking a cigarette performs the operation V() on the corresponding semaphore [11].

    enddescription

    specification Patil's problematic smokers

Rtobacco	Rpaper	Rmatch	the agent
rt:P(s)	rp:P(s)	rm:P(s)	
V(paper)	V(tobacco)	V(match)	
V(match)	V(match)	V(paper)	
goto rt	goto rp	goto rm	
bt:P(smokert)	bp:P(smokerp)	bm:P(smokerm)	
V(s)	V(s)	V(s)	
goto bt	goto bp	goto bm	
smokert	smokerp	smokerm	
at:P(paper)	ap:P(tobacco)	am:P(tobacco)	the smokers
P(match)	P(match)	P(paper)	
**	**	**	
V(smokert)	V(smokerp)	V(smokerm)	
goto at	goto ap	goto am	

  -- initially: s=1, tobacco=paper=match=smokert=smokerp=smokerm=0
** stands for some operation performed by the process
    endspecification

definition definitionname

A binary semaphore is a variable whose value can only be 0 or
1. Instruction P(s) decrements the value of the semaphore s
by 1 and if the value of the semaphore is 0, the execution of
the instruction is held up until it becomes 1. This provides
a way to allow a process to wait until other processes catch
up. Furthermore, if the value of the semaphore is 1 and
several processes try to execute P(s) then only one of the
processes is permitted to complete execution of P(s) and
others are held waiting for the value of the semaphore to
become 1. The instruction V(s) just increments the value of
the semaphore by 1.

Go to statements to simple labels are used to indicate cycli-
city of the processes. All the processes are cyclic.

enddefinition

enddossier

verification abstraction_correctness1

Here we need to verify that the specification semaphore_
smokinganalogy in some more abstract sense is equivalent to
the specification Patil's_problematic_smokers. In the paper
[15] we have shown how to do this formally, but here we will
only state that:

1) A binary semaphore s=1 initially, an exclusion semaphore,
    can be represented by path sP:sV end.
2) A binary semaphore s=0 initially, a sequencing semaphore,
    can be represented by path sV;sP end.
3) Cyclic processes consisting of sequences of semaphore
    instructions can be directly modelled by COSY processes.

Note: There is a slight permutation of the sequential actions
of the smoker with paper "smokerp". It seemed to us that two
of the smokers, namely, smokerp and smokerm should not both
start with the same initial action, since this makes the
possible interactions between the three processes unnecessaril
unsymetric. So though the original deadlock discussed above is
no longer possible, it is represented by three distinct deadlocks in the transformed specification.

endverification

enddossier

<u>dossier</u>   smokers_solution

<u>description</u> descriptionname

Three processes, the pushers, are added to the problematic
smokers which pick up the ingredients from the table and they
pass the ingredients to the appropriate smoker and then signal
him to smoke.

<u>enddescription</u>

<u>specification</u> Janicki_Parnas_solution
  P1:<u>path</u> tobaccoV;tobaccoP <u>end</u>
  P2:<u>path</u> paperV;paperP <u>end</u>
  P3:<u>path</u> matchV;matchP <u>end</u>
  P4:<u>path</u> smokertV;smokertP <u>end</u>
  P5:<u>path</u> smokerpV;smokerpP <u>end</u>
  P6:<u>path</u> smokermV;smokermP <u>end</u>
  P7:<u>path</u> sP;sV <u>end</u>
  P8:<u>path</u> mutexP;mutexV <u>end</u>
  P9:<u>path</u> VS(1);PS(1) <u>end</u>
  P10:<u>path</u> VS(2);PS(2) <u>end</u>
  P11:<u>path</u> VS(3);PS(3) <u>end</u>
  P12:<u>path</u> VS(4);PS(4) <u>end</u>
  P13:<u>path</u> VS(5);PS(5) <u>end</u>
  P14:<u>path</u> VS(6);PS(6) <u>end</u>
  P15:<u>path</u> (VS(1);VS(3),VS(5)),(VS(2);VS(3),VS(6)),
        (VS(4);VS(5),VS(6)) <u>end</u>
  Q1:<u>process</u> sP;paperV;matchV <u>end</u>
  Q2:<u>process</u> sP;tobaccoV;paperV <u>end</u>
  Q3:<u>process</u> sP;matchV;tobaccoV <u>end</u>
  Q4:<u>process</u> smokertP;sV <u>end</u>
  Q5:<u>process</u> smokerpP;sV <u>end</u>
  Q6:<u>process</u> smokermP;sV <u>end</u>
  Q7:<u>process</u> tobaccoP;mutexP;VS(1),VS(3),VS(5);mutexV <u>end</u>
  Q8:<u>process</u> paperP;mutexP;VS(2),VS(3),VS(6);mutexV <u>end</u>
  Q9:<u>process</u> matchP;mutexP;VS(4),VS(5),VS(6);mutexV <u>end</u>
  Q10:<u>process</u> PS(6);smokertV <u>end</u>
  Q11:<u>process</u> PS(3);smokermV <u>end</u>
  Q12:<u>process</u> PS(5);smokerpV <u>end</u>
  Q13:<u>process</u> PS(1) <u>end</u>
  Q14:<u>process</u> PS(2) <u>end</u>
  Q15:<u>process</u> PS(4) <u>end</u>
<u>endspecification</u>

```
specification    Campbell_Lauer_solution
  P1:path tobaccoV;tobaccoP end
  P2:path paperV;paperP end
  P3:path matchV;matchP end
  P4:path smokertV;smokertP end
  P5:path smokerpV;smokerpP end
  P6:path smokermV;smokermP end
  P7:path sP;sV end
  P8:path (tobaccoP;((paperP;smokermV),(matchP;smokerpV))),
          (paperP;((tobaccoP;smokermV),(matchP;smokertV))),
          (matchP;((tobaccoP;smokerpV),(paperP;smokertV))) end
  Q1:process sP;paperV;matchV end
  Q2:process sP;tobaccoV;paperV end
  Q3:process sP;matchV;tobaccoV end
  Q4:process smokertP;sV end
  Q5:process smokerpP;sV end
  Q6:process smokermP;sV end
  Q7:process smokertV end
  Q8:process smokermV end
  Q9:process smokerpV end
  Q10:process tobaccoP end
  Q11:process paperP end
  Q12:process matchP end
endspecification
```

definition Campbell_Lauer_solution
The Periodic Vector Firing Sequences of the Adequate Smokers

Here also there are no potentially dangerous triples so we may
restrict our considerations to maximally concurrent simulations alone.
solution vector firing sequence svfs1:

```
P1  :    .       .       .       .       .       .       .
P2  :    .paperV.paperP.         .       .       .       .
P3  :    .       .       .matchV.matchP.         .       .
P4  :    .       .       .       .       .smokertV.smokertP.
P5  :    .       .       .       .       .       .       .
P6  :    .       .       .       .       .       .       .
P7  :  sP.       .       .       .       .       .      .sV
P8  :    .       .paperP.         .matchP.smokertV.       .
Q1  :  sP.paperV.         .matchV.         .       .       .
Q2  :    .       .       .       .       .       .       .
Q3  :    .       .       .       .       .       .       .
Q4  :    .       .       .       .       .       .smokertP.sV
Q5  :    .       .       .       .       .       .       .
Q6  :    .       .       .       .       .       .       .
Q7  :    .       .       .       .       .smokertV.       .
Q8  :    .       .       .       .       .       .       .
Q9  :    .       .       .       .       .       .       .
Q10 :    .       .       .       .       .       .       .
Q11 :    .       .paperP.         .       .       .       .
Q12 :    .       .       .       .matchP.         .       .
```
solution vector firing sequence svfs2:

```
P1  :    .tobaccoV.tobaccoP.       .       .       .       .
P2  :    .       .       .paperV.paperP.         .       .
P3  :    .       .       .       .       .       .       .
P4  :    .       .       .       .       .       .       .
P5  :    .       .       .       .       .       .       .
P6  :    .       .       .       .       .smokermV.smokermP.
P7  :  sP.       .       .       .       .       .      .sV
P8  :    .       .tobaccoP.         .paperP.smokermV.       .
Q1  :    .       .       .       .       .       .       .
Q2  :  sP.tobaccoV.         .paperV.         .       .       .
Q3  :    .       .       .       .       .       .       .
Q4  :    .       .       .       .       .       .       .
Q5  :    .       .       .       .       .       .       .
Q6  :    .       .       .       .       .       .smokermP.sV
Q7  :    .       .       .       .       .       .       .
Q8  :    .       .       .       .       .smokermV.       .
Q9  :    .       .       .       .       .       .       .
Q10 :    .       .tobaccoP.         .       .       .       .
Q11 :    .       .       .paperP.         .       .       .
Q12 :    .       .       .       .       .       .       .
```

solution vector firing sequence svfs3:

```
P1  :   .   .tobaccoV.    .tobaccoP.         .        .
P2  :   .    .        .        .         .        .
P3  :   .matchV.      .matchP.            .        .
P4  :   .    .        .        .        .        .
P5  :   .    .        .        .   .smokerpV.smokerpP.
P6  :   .    .        .        .        .        .
P7  :   sP.  .        .        .        .        .sV
P8  :   .    .   .matchP.tobaccoP.smokerpV.        .
Q1  :   .    .   .        .        .        .
Q2  :   .    .   .        .        .        .
Q3  :   sP.matchV.tobaccoV.     .        .        .
Q4  :   .    .   .        .        .        .
Q5  :   .    .   .        .        .   .smokerpP.sV
Q6  :   .    .   .        .        .        .
Q7  :   .    .   .        .        .        .
Q8  :   .    .   .        .        .        .
Q9  :   .    .   .        .   .smokerpV.         .
Q10 :   .    .   .   .tobaccoP.         .        .
Q11 :   .    .   .        .        .        .
Q12 :   .    .   .matchP.         .        .        .
```

By the theorem we have that these are the only vector firing sequences
one need consider since all others can be obtained as prefixes of
multiples of these three.

enddefinition

dossier   Parnas_unproblematic_smokers

description Parnas_description

Simulation of a six branch case statement using a semaphore array,
assignment and simple arithmetic operations yield a solution.

enddescription

specification Parnas_program

```
Rtobacco            Rpaper              Rmatch          the agent
rt:P(s)             rp:P(s)             rm:P(s)
V(paper)                V(tobacco)          V(match)
V(match)                V(match)            V(paper)
goto rt                 goto rp             goto rm

bt:P(smokert)       bp:P(smokerp)       bm:P(smokerm)
   V(s)                 V(s)                V(s)
   goto bt              goto bp             goto bm

at:P(S[6])          ap:P(S[5])          am:P(S[3])   the smokers
   t:=0                 t:=0                t:=0
   **                   **                  **
   V(smokert)           V(smokerp)          V(smokerm)
   goto at              goto ap             goto am
```

```
dt:P(tobacco)      dp:P(paper)          dm:P(match)   the pushers
   P(mutex)           P(mutex)             P(mutex)
   t:=t+1             t:=t+2               t:=t+4
   V(S[t])            V(S[t])              V(S[t])
   V(mutex)           V(mutex)             V(mutex)
   goto dt            goto dp              goto dm

d1:P(S[1])         d2:P(S[2])           d3:P(S[4])
   goto d1            goto d2              goto d3
```

-- initially: s=mutex=1
   t=tobacco=paper=match=smokert=smokerp=smokerm=0
   semaphore array S[1..6]=0
** stands for some operation performed by the process

endspecification

definition Parnas_Habermann_definition

Here one can insert the five page proof by Nico Habermann [12].

enddefinition

enddossier

verification abstraction correctness2

The problem statement from the outer verification of correctness is inherited at this point, but in addition we are required not to use conditional statements. Obviously Parnas_
program contains no such conditional statements.

Note: The problem could be seen as implementing the abstract
specification into the concrete one using no conditional
statements.

Here we again need to show that the given specifications
are in some more abstract sense equivalent to the specification Parnas_program. Applying the translation of abstrac-
tion_correctness1 we obtain the intermediary implementation_
specification below. That leaves the translation of the
effects of the assignment statements on the variable t. t is
always set to zero before new ingredients are supplied. So
the effect of the increments of the three pusher processes
can only be:

   t=1, if Q10 is first;
after which
   t=3, if Q11 is next;
or
   t=5, if Q12 is next;
   t=2, if Q11 is first; etc.

replacing these constants for t in the intermediary and

adding the path P15 which expresses the feedback the various
increments have on t, results in the Janicki Parnas solution.
Similar indications of abstraction correctness can be
given for the other two specifications.

        intermediary implementation_specification

        P1:path tobaccoV;tobaccoP end
        P2:path paperV;paperP end
        P3:path matchV;matchP end
        P4:path smokertV;smokertP end
        P5:path smokerpV;smokerpP end
        P6:path smokermV;smokermP end
        P7:path sP;sV end
        P8:path mutexP;mutexV end
        P9:path S[1]V;S[1]P end
        P10:path S[2]V;S[2]P end
        P11:path S[3]V;S[3]P end
        P12:path S[4]V;S[4]P end
        P13:path S[5]V;S[5]P end
        P14:path S[6]V;S[6]P end
        Q1:process sP;paperV;matchV end
        Q2:process sP;tobaccoV;paperV end
        Q3:process sP;matchV;tobaccoV end
        Q4:process smokertP;sV end
        Q5:process smokerpP;sV end
        Q6:process smokermP;sV end
        Q7:process S[6]P;t:=0;smokertV end
        Q8:process S[3]P;t:=0;smokermV end
        Q9:process S[5]P;t:=0;smokerpV end
        Q10:process tobaccoP;mutexP;t:=t+1;S[t]V;mutexV end
        Q11:process paperP;mutexP;t:=t+2;S[t]V;mutexV end
        Q12:process matchP;mutexP;t:=t+4;S[t]V;mutexV end
        Q13:process S[1]P end
        Q14:process S[2]P end
        Q15:process S[4]P end

        endintermediary

        endverification

    enddossier

    verification correctness_of_solution

Examination of the definition indicates that. there are six
distinct, that is nonequivalent, behaviours of the problematic
smokers. Three of them lead to deadlock and three of them do
not.
    Problem: Devise a strategy which will preserve the extend-
able behaviours of the problematic smokers but eliminate thei:
deadlocking behaviours.
    Consideration of the vector firing sequences of the

Campbell_Lauer_solution shows that if we ignore:

1) the fact that smokers no longer receive the signals about the arrivals of ingredients on the table directly;
2) the firing sequences of the feedback path P8, and the pusher processes Q10-Q12;

we get exactly the periodic vector firing sequences of the problematic smokers.

Abstraction correctness for both Patil_problem and Parnas_ solution implies applied COSY verification of the two "programs".

endverification

enddossier

ACKNOWLEDGEMENTS

I would like to thank Brian Randell and Elizabeth Barraclough for their helpful discussions with me concerning the dossier concept. Brian Hamshere and John Cotronis [13] must addition-ally be given credit for having done considerable preparatory work involving the Textform system used to produce this paper and particularly the treatment of the formal notations by means of Textform. Furthermore, Brian Hamshere is responsible for the production of the BCS environment without which much of the contents of the paper could not have been produced as readily. Richard Janicki should be thanked for his inspiring and clarifying influence during the formulation of the ideas presented here. In particular, the formal definition of BCS and the theorem about the full characterisation of a COSY specification by maximally concurrent simulation is due to him. Finally, John Cotronis was involved in development of the formulation and proofs of the Lemma and Fact about con-current simulation in BCS.

The work reported was supported from grants from the Science and Engineering Council of Great Britain.

REFERENCES

1. Best, E. (1979). Adequacy of path programs. *In* "Net Theory and Applications". Proc. Advanced Course on General Net Theory of Processes and Systems, Hamburg (Ed. W. Brauer). Also (1980) *In* "Lecture Notes in Computer Science", 84, Springer Verlag.
2. Best, E. (1982). Adequacy properties of path programs. *In* "Theoretical Computer Science", 18, pp.149-171, North Holland Publishing Co.
3. Lauer, P.E. and Janicki, R. (1982). The role of maximally

146   P.E. LAUER

concurrent simulation in the computer based analysis of
distributed systems. Report ASM/96, Computing Laboratory,
University of Newcastle-upon-Tyne.
4. Shields, M.W. and Lauer, P.E. (1978). On the abstract
specification and formal analysis of synchronization
properties of concurrent systems. *In* "Proc. of Int. Conf.
on Mathematical Studies of Information Processing", Kyoto.
Also (1979) *In* "Lecture Notes in Computer Science" 75,
pp.1-32, Springer Verlag.
5. Shields, M.W. (1979). Adequate Path Expressions. *In* "Proc.
Symposium on the Semantics of Concurrent Computation",
Evian-les-Bains. Also *In* "Lecture Notes in Computer
Science", 70, Springer Verlag.
6. Shields, M.W. and Lauer, P.E. (1980a). Verifying concurren
system specifications in COSY. *In* "Proc. 8th Symposium on
Mathematical Foundations of Computer Science", Poland.
Also *In* "Lecture Notes in Computer Science" 88, pp.576-
586, Springer Verlag.
7. Shields, M.W. and Lauer, P.E. (1980b). Programming and
Verifying Concurrent Systems in COSY. Technical Report
No. 155, Computing Laboratory, University of Newcastle-
upon-Tyne.
8. Lauer, P.E. (1981). Synchronization of concurrent processes without globality assumptions. SIGPLAN Notices,
Vol.16, No.9. An expanded version is included *In* "1 New
Advances in Distributed Computing Systems", pp.341-365,
Reidel Pub. Co., NATO Advanced Study Institute Series
C80.
9. Lauer, P.E. and Hamshere, B. (1981). A computer based
environment for the design and analysis of highly parallel
and distributed computing systems, ASM/88, Computing
Laboratory, University of Newcastle-upon-Tyne.
10. Lauer, P.E., Best, E. and Shields, M.W. (1977). On the
problem of achieving adequacy of concurrent programs.
Computing Laboratory, University of Newcastle-upon-Tyne,
Technical Report Series No.103. Also *In* "Proc. IFIP TC-2
Working Conference on the formal Description of Programming Concepts", St Andrews, Canada. North-Holland
Publishing Co.
11. Patil, S.S. (1971). Limitations and capabilities of
Dijkstra's semaphore primitives for co-ordination among
processes. Computation Structures Group Memo 57, Project
Mac, Massachusetts Institute of Technology.
12. Habermann, N. (1973). On a solution and a generalization
of the cigarette smokers problem. Carnegie Mellon
University. Computer Science.
13. Cotronis, J.Y. (1982). Programming and verification of

asynchronous systems. Ph.D Thesis, Computing Laboratory,
University of Newcastle-upon-Tyne.
14. Lauer, P.E. and Shields, M.W. (1981a). Interpreted COSY
programs: programming and verification. *In* "Proc. 2nd
International Conference on Distributed Computing Systems"
Paris. IEEE Computer Society Press (Ed. E. Gelenbe).
15. Lauer, P.E. and Shields, M.W. (1981b). COSY: An Environment for development and analysis of concurrent and
distributed systems. *In* "Proc. of Symposium on Software
Engineering Environments", Lahnstein. (Ed. H. Hunke)
North-Holland Publishing Co.

FURTHER READING

Lauer, P.E. and Campbell, R.H. (1975). Formal semantics for
a class of high level primitives for co-ordinating con-
current processes. *Acta Informatica* 5, 247-332.
Lauer, P.E. and Shields, M.W. (1978). Abstract specification
of resource accessing disciplines: adequacy, starvation,
priority and interrupts. SIGPLAN Notices, Vol.13, No.12.
Lauer, P.E., Shields, M.W. and Best, E. (1979a). The design
and certification of asynchronous systems of processes.
Advanced Course on Abstract Software Specification,
Lyngby, Denmark. Also *In* "Lecture Notes in Computer
Science" 86, Springer Verlag.
Lauer, P.E., Shields, M.W. and Best, E. (1979b). Formal
Theory of the Basic COSY Notation. The Computing Laboratory,
University of Newcastle-upon-Tyne. Technical Report Series
No.143.
Lauer, P.E., Torrigiani, P.R. and Devillers, R. (1982). A
COSY banker: specification of highly parallel and distri-
buted resource management. *In* "Proc. 4th Int. Symposium
on Programming", Paris. Also (1980) *In* "Lecture Notes in
Computer Science", 83 (Ed. B. Robinet), Springer Verlag.
Lauer, P.E., Torrigiani, P.R. and Shields, M.W. (1979). COSY:
A system specification language based on paths and pro-
cesses. *Acta Informatica* 12.
Parnas, D.L. (1975). On a solution of the cigarette smoker's
problem (without conditional statements). *CACM* 18, 3.
Shields, M.W. (1981). On the non-sequential behaviour of a
class of systems satisfying a generalised free-choice
property. Technical Report CRS 92-81, Computer Science
Dept, University of Edinburgh.
Shields, M.W. and Lauer, P.E. (1979). A formal semantics for
concurrent systems. *In* "Proc. 6th Int. Colloq. for Automata,
Languages and Programming", Graz. Also *In* "Lecture Notes
in Computer Science" 71, pp.569-584, Springer Verlag.

Co-operation Schemes for Parallel Programming

Jean-Pierre Banatre

1. ABOUT PROGRAM CONSTRUCTION

The task of constructing a program solution to a given problem is a far from simple one. Four stages are usually put forward as fundamental in the process of program construction:

a) Specification
b) Expression using a predefined computation model
c) Deduction of a program
d) Refinement till a runnable program is produced.

This paper addresses stages (b) and (c). The main design principles we propose in order to find a parallel solution to a given problem P can be sketched as follows:

1) Decomposition of P into subproblems. Let $p_1,\ldots,p_n$ be these subproblems.
2) Analysis of logical dependencies between p_i's.
3) Expression of p_i's and of their logical dependencies into a programming notation.
4) Delay as long as possible implementation choices.

It should be clear from (1) and (2) that our approach favours clear characterization of logical dependencies and their direct expression in the program. By "direct", we mean that these dependencies should not rely on existing data structures in order to be "emulated", but rather that specific control structures should be invented when needed.

This paper is concerned with the presentation of some co-operation schemes and of their use in the construction of parallel programs. Section 2 presents a data-driven

Distributed Computing Systems
ISBN 0-12-543970-9

co-operation scheme and overviews some of its potential applications. A co-operation scheme based on proximity relationships is described in Section 3. Section 4 gives some insights
into recursive parallel structures currently under investigation and imagines some further developments for the work
presented in the paper.

2. A DATA-DRIVEN CO-OPERATION SCHEME

2.1. The Co-operation Scheme

Consider a system of processes $(p, c_1, \ldots, c_n)$ co-operating in
the following fashion: p produces an information v which is
broadcast to every c_i. However it may happen that:

1) some c_i's request for v before it is actually produced by
    p. In this case, these c_i's will be interrupted till v
    is produced;
2) some c_i's request v after it has been produced; in this
    situation they can access v without any restriction.

This co-operation scheme may be summarized in Figure 1.

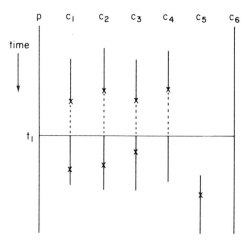

FIG. 1

x Represents access to the value v which should be produced by p. Actually p produces this value at time t_1. Processes $c_1 \ldots c_4$ want to access the value v before its production so they get interrupted till t_1. At time t_1, these
processes are resumed in parallel. Processes c_5 and c_6 which

access v after t_1 are not interrupted.

2.2. Programming Notation

The tools used for expressing the above co-operation scheme
are based upon the notion of event and that of process. These
notions have been described elsewhere [1]. The following
quotation from [1, p.35] briefly summarizes this work:

the processing of an entity E (is considered) as a
process P which may possibly find itself waiting for
information I. I will be called an event. Processes
will wait or not on an event depending on the availability of the information it represents. The knowledge
of I eventually implies the resumption of all processes
waiting for I.

Primitives have been provided for event handling. Among them,
the primitive gets value provides an event with a value and
releases all processes waiting for this value. The activation
of parallel processes is denoted activate(<process body>).
The following program fragment demonstrates the use of these
primitives:

    begin

1)   event int x ;
      .
      .
2)   activate(...x...) ; ##process p_1##
      .
      .
3)   x gets value 3 ;
      .
      .
4)   activate(...x...) ; ##process p_2##
      end

The following actions are taken:

1) An event x whose value is of type integer is declared.
2) A process p_1 using x is activated. This process is suspended if no value has yet been given to x when the process wants to use it.
3) The value 3 is assigned to the event x. Process p_1 is
   resumed, if it was suspended.
4) A new process p_2 is activated. It will not be suspended
   when using x, as x has been given a value.

2.3. Using Events and Processes

Consider a sequential program which uses a value v read from a peripheral device. The read operation may take several forms depending on the underlying system. It may consist of, for example:

1) an actual read command,
2) a buffer to buffer transfer.

Anyway, as far as the user program is concerned, v will end up with its value. v Can be represented as an event declared as <u>event type</u> v (<u>type</u> is the type of the read value). The read operation has the following structure:

<u>activate</u> (#determination of the value to be assigned to v#
          v <u>gets value</u> #the read value#
          ...
)

The sequential program using v, has the following structure:

<u>activate</u> (...
          v
          ...
)

This process will be interrupted when accessing v if the read process (which runs concurrently with it) has not yet delivered the expected value.

This simple example illustrates the basic co-operation scheme. Much more elaborated examples have been dealt with while producing an ALGOL 68 compiler; they are reported in [1].

2.4. Dealing with Dynamic Information Structures

Such information structures are assumed to have the following properties:

1) the number of their elements (cardinality) is *a priori* unknown,
2) they contain elements with similar logical properties, consequently the same processing is applied to each element,
3) elements of such information structures are generated dynamically - they may be considered as events,
4) processing of element i is independent from processing of element j (j $\neq$ i).

Due to these properties one may represent creation and use of such structures using the following co-operation scheme.

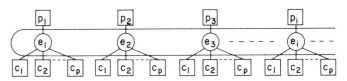

FIG. 2 *Co-operating scheme*

2.4.1. Associated co-operation scheme. This co-operation scheme can be illustrated in Figure 2. Elements e_i of the dynamic information structure are generated by a process p_i and are broadcast to consumer processes $c_1 \ldots c_i$. Co-operation between p_i and c_i follows the same scheme as that presented in Section 2.1. Every newly generated value (e_{k+1}) gives birth to a new bunch of processes $c_1 \ldots c_p$ dealing with e_{k+1}. Similarly, the activation of a new process c_{p+1} implies the creation of as many instances of c_{p+1} as there are elements in the dynamic information structure.

2.4.2. Programming notation. Dynamic information structures are composed of elements which may be unknown at a given time of the computation. As such these elements are events and the global information structure can be seen as a variable-sized set of events. So we can define a dynamic information structure x of elements of type m as vse m x (vse for variable-sized set of events).
Generation of a new element in the collection is done via the following primitive:

one of x gets value v, meaning that a new element of the vse x has just got its value. Completion of the vse is signified by the primitive close (e.g. close x).

Processes dealing with each element of the vse (c_i's on the figure) are generated via a special control structure acting as a process generator. It has the following structure:

for all evt of x

      begin

            <process text>

      end

and can be readily interpreted as

```
      begin
     ⌠ ##for all components of vse id which possess a value##
  I  ⌡   activate(<instruction sequence>),
     ⌠do
     |   wait(##generation of a new component or occurrence
     |         of close primitive##) ;
     |   if #occurrence of close primitive##
  II ⌡      then ##exit do loop##
     |      else activate(<instruction sequence>)
     |   fi
     ⌡od
      end
```

Here Part I expresses the concurrent activation of processes related to events of the vse whose value is known at
the time of activation of the process generator, and Part II
expresses this activation for components whose value becomes
available after activation of the process generator.

Further information on these constructs may be found in
[2].

2.4.3. Using this co-operation scheme. Various examples of
dynamic information structure possessing properties of vse's
may be exhibited. A complete example dealing with compile
time symbol resolution is described in [2]. Let us deal with
a simpler example. Assume that a sequence of identifiers is
generated dynamically and that we want to print all identifiers except one - say y.

The sequence of identifiers may be represented by a vse,
declared as vse string id. The process generating elements
of id can be described quite informally as:

(P1)   do

            read (next entity from the source text, say z) ;

            case z in

               (identifier z) : one of id gets value z,

               (end of the text) : close id ; exit loop

        od

The process generator allowing the printing of elements of
id (except y's) has the following structure:

(P2)   for all evt of id
       begin
  I {   if this elt ≠ y
              then print (this elt)
          fi
       end

Example: Assume that the list of identifiers is:

GEORGE, ANDREW, JOHN, PETER, MIKE, ANDREW, JOHN #

being the end symbol. We want to print all names except
ANDREW. Process P1 when activated will generate the sequence
of names, process P2 will generate an instance of process
executing I above for each name. Thus printing elements
different from y. Here y = ANDREW.
We can figure out the functioning in Figure 3.

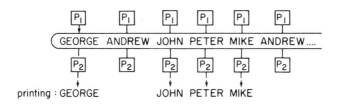

FIG. 3   *A simple example.*

3. PROCESS COMMUNICATING ACCORDING A PROXIMITY RELATIONSHIP

This section proposes a new scheme for process co-operation.
Apart from the co-operation scheme, considerations about the
termination of programs using it are developed.

3.1. A Scheme for Process Co-operation

Consider a system S of processes $p_1,\ldots,p_n$. Each p_i is provided with a "weight" w_i.

Co-operation law. Two processes p_i and p_j of S may communicate if a given predefined binary relationship $R(w_i,w_j)$ holds.
When communication is possible, processes p_i and p_j exchange
their weights i.e. p_i receives w_j and p_j receives w_i.
     Two processes p_i and p_j such that $R(w_i,w_j)$ holds are said
to be "neighbours", otherwise they are isolated. Of course
this neighbourhood relationship is dynamic since after

co-operation, processes p_i and p_j may change their respective
weights in such a way that $R(w_i, w_j)$ does not hold anymore
(but $R(w_i, w_k)$ and $R(w_j, w_r)$ may hold ...).

Steady state. The overall system S is steady when all its
component processes are isolated.

3.2. A Possible Programming Notation.

Weights are tuples which type may be defined as (type 1,
type 2, ..., type n). So all elements of a weight are not
necessarily of the same type. Components of a weight may be
selected by functions such as **1, 2, 3** ... which deliver the
first, second, third ... element of a tuple.
  Processes have the following structure:

$$\underline{process}\ p(weight) \equiv f(w, \overline{w})$$

  The function f describing processing performed by p, uses
as parameters the weight of p and the weight of a process q
allowed to communicate with p (i.e. before execution of
$f(w, \overline{w})$, $R(w, \overline{w})$ holds).

3.3. Programming of an Example

Consider the problem of sorting n (different) names into
alphabetical order. For example, the names may be:

  GEORGE, ANDREW, JOHN, PETER, MIKE

  A process will be attached to each name. The weight associated to this process will be a couple (name, position), position being initially set up to n (number of names to be
sorted). So the above system of processes may be described as:

  (GEORGE,5) (ANDREW,5) (JOHN,5) (PETER,5) (MIKE,5)

  Consider the relationship $R(w, \overline{w}) \equiv 2(w) = 2(\overline{w})$, i.e.
processes possessing the same position may exchange their
weights. Imagine now, that texts of processes be defined as:

  $\underline{process}$ p (name, position) $\equiv$

    $\underline{if}\ 1(w) < 1(\overline{w})\ \underline{then}\ 2(w)\ -:= 1\ \underline{fi}$

  Then the evolution of the system of processes may be
shown as follows:

(GEORGE,5)	(ANDREW,5)	(JOHN,5)	(PETER,5)	(MIKE,5)
(GEORGE,5)	(ANDREW,4)	(JOHN,5)	(PETER,5)	(MIKE,4)
(GEORGE,5)	(ANDREW,3)	(JOHN,4)	(PETER,5)	(MIKE,4)
(GEORGE,4)	(ANDREW,3)	(JOHN,3)	(PETER,5)	(MIKE,4)
(GEORGE,3)	(ANDREW,2)	(JOHN,3)	(PETER,5)	(MIKE,4)
(GEORGE,2)	(ANDREW,2)	(JOHN,3)	(PETER,5)	(MIKE,4)
(GEORGE,2)	(ANDREW,1)	(JOHN,3)	(PETER,5)	(MIKE,4)

Two communicating processes are linked by a horizontal line.
Of course this is one among the possible paths leading to
the solution. This algorithm is non-deterministic as it does
not indicate how co-operating couples are selected.

When the system reaches its steady state, second field of
weight w_i of process p_i represents the alphabetical position
of the name.
Remark: If the names are not assumed to be different, the
condition $R(w,\bar{w})$ is $2(w) = 2(\bar{w}) \wedge 1(w) \neq 1(\bar{w})$.

3.4. Termination Aspects

A usual tool for proving the termination of programs is the
well-founded set: a set of elements and an ordering $>$ defined
on these elements, such that there can be non-infinite de-
scending sequences of elements. The idea for proving termination of a process is to find a termination function that
maps process variables into a well-founded set: the value of
the termination function being successively decreased throughout the computation. Natural numbers under the $\geq$ ordering are
often used for proving termination of loops [3]. In [4] multiset ordering is shown to be well-founded and used for proving
termination of production systems. Multisets are like-sets,
but may contain multiple occurrences of identical elements.
Consider two multisets of natural numbers M_1 and M_2, the
relationship $M_1 \gg M_2$ holds if M_2 can be obtained from M_1 by
replacing one or more elements of M_1 by any finite sequence
of natural numbers, each of which being smaller than the
replaced one (more details in [4]).

Our idea consists of applying this multiset ordering for
proving termination of parallel programs built according to
our co-operation scheme. To each process p_i is associated a
termination function f_i which maps the weight into the set of
natural numbers under the usual ordering. So w_i will be mapped
successively into the following values $\{w_{i1}, w_{i2}, \ldots, w_{ik}, \ldots\}$

such that, $\forall u,v \ u>v \Rightarrow w_{iu}>w_{iv}$. Assume now, that every process p_i is provided with such a function, then the initial state of the global processing (involving $p_1,\ldots,p_n$) will be mapped into the multiset $\{w_{11},w_{12},\ldots,w_{1n}\}=W_1$, any subsequent state $\{w_{i1},w_{i2},\ldots,w_{in}\}=W_i$ will be such that $W_i<<W_1$ and any state derived from W_i be such that $W_j<<W_i$. Thus we have a simple means for proving termination of parallel programs built according to our scheme.

Example: In the above example, every execution of the code of a process p_i will result in the decreasing of its position $(2(w))$ by 1. The function f_i which may be associated to p_i may be: $f_i : w \longrightarrow \mathbb{N}$ such that $f_i(w) = 2(w)$. This is a decreasing function. The initial configuration of the system may be represented $W_1 = \{5,5,5,5,5\}$ and any configuration W_j derived from W_1 will be such that $W_j<<W_1$ and $\forall W_k$ derived from W_j, $W_k<<W_j$. Configurations W_i have a lower bound $W_{1k} = \{1,2,3,4,5\}$. Termination proof is then straightforward.

3.5. Discussion

An interesting feature of the co-operation scheme is that it is associated with a programming methodology: well-founded set + monotony of the termination function $\Rightarrow$ termination. This is very interesting for the construction of programs with "good" properties and follows ideas already put forward in the domain of sequential programming.
    Many open problems remain to be solved and are presently studied:

1) R is a global condition, is it possible to split it up and distribute it over processes p_i's?
2) Correctness.
3) Characterization of an acceptable initialization state. Actually one may imagine starting from a stable state which is not a solution of the problem ...
4) Implementation of this co-operation scheme.

    The above tools have been applied to the programming of problems other than the one above. In particular, we have built a parallel text formatter.

4. FURTHER RESEARCH AND DEVELOPMENTS

Apart from the co-operation schemes presented above, we are presently involved in the study of the recursive composition of parallel activities. This study stems from the following considerations:

1) It is possible to "nest" a parallel clause within a

block

$\underline{\text{begin}}$ B $\underline{\text{parbegin}}$ S_1, S_2, ..., S_n $\underline{\text{parend}}$ E $\underline{\text{end}}$

which may be pictured as:

$$\underline{\quad\overset{S_1}{\quad}\quad}$$

$$\underline{\quad B \quad} \qquad \underline{\quad\overset{S_2}{\quad}\quad} \qquad \underline{\quad E \quad}$$

$$\underline{\quad\underset{S_n}{\quad}\quad}$$

S_i's are nested within the block $\underline{\text{begin}}$ B; E $\underline{\text{end}}$.

2) The question now is: why the dual form is not permitted?,
   i.e. nesting a block within a parallel clause, thus
   giving the following picture

$$\underline{\quad BS_1 \quad} \qquad\qquad \underline{\quad ES_1 \quad}$$

$$\underline{\quad BS_2 \quad} \qquad \underline{\quad B \quad} \qquad \underline{\quad ES_2 \quad}$$

$$\underline{\quad \underset{n}{BS} \quad} \qquad\qquad \underline{\quad \underset{n}{ES} \quad}$$

where BS_i stands for Beginning of S_i and ES_i for End of
S_i. B stands for Block. Of course instead of nesting a
simple block, one could nest a parallel clause.

This composition scheme has been studied along three
directions:

1) a generalized recursion scheme. Actually, common recursion generates dynamically nested blocks, the proposed
   scheme would generate nested parallel clauses, thus
   would allow to take advantage of both recursion and
   parallelism;
2) a high level synchronization mechanism. Synchronization
   operations offered by this co-operation scheme remain as
   simple as those provided by parallel clauses. Their power
   is due to the fact that, unlike parallel clauses, interruption of a process (via nesting) does not imply
   termination of that process;
3) a powerful control structure. The above co-operation
   scheme has been studied as a means of programming multi-

pass algorithms which are used in order to evaluate
attributes attached to the nodes of a tree. Each intermediate pass delivers a special "decorated" tree to the
subsequent pass. Using the above control structure, these
intermediate data structures need not be constructed [5].

Other investigations are still needed, in particular the
implementation of such control structures has not yet been
undertaken.

This paper has presented co-operation schemes which have
been studied or are currently investigated. These co-operation
schemes have been used for the solution of many non-numerical
problems mainly in the compilation field. Solutions to arti-
ficial intelligence problems (e.g. tree traversal) are investigated using the two last co-operation schemes.

REFERENCES

1. Banâtre, J-P., Routeau, J-P. and Trilling, L. (1979). An
   event-driven compiling technique. *Comm. ACM* 22, No. 1.
2. André, F., Banâtre, J-P. and Routeau, J-P. (1981). A
   multiprocessing approach to compile-time symbol reso-
   lutions. *ACM-Toplas* 3, 11-23.
3. Dijkstra, E.W. (1976). "A Discipline of Programming".
   Prentice Hall.
4. Dershowitz, N. and Manna, Z. (1979). Proving termination
   with multiset ordering. *CACM* 22, 465-476.
5. Banâtre, J-P. and Trilling, L. (1981). A Generalization of
   Collateral Clauses and its Application to the Programming
   of Multi-pass Algorithms. Research Report, IRISA.

Part 2

Programming Languages for Distributed Processes

Pascal-m: a Language for Loosely Coupled Distributed Systems

Samson Abramsky and Richard Bornat

1. INTRODUCTION

The ever-falling cost of hardware has made it possible to envisage networks of powerful personal computers which could
provide most of the facilities of present-day timesharing
systems, with much improved response, and with greatly improved user/computer interfaces. Such a network is one kind
of "distributed" computer system, often called an "information
network". Other kinds of distributed system include those
designed to implement parallel algorithms (e.g. processor
arrays, networks of load-sharing machines). Our interest is
in information networks and our language design is directed
to their special problems. The range of applications for such
systems, in factory, home, school and office, could vastly
exceed the scope of present-day systems. Software technology
has lagged behind, however, and we lack systematic and reliable methods for constructing programs which will run on
such a network. Indeed, constructing the operating system for
even a conventional single-machine timesharing service is
still something of a black art.

Our aim is to develop a methodology for programming distributed systems, based around a small, powerful, coherent set
of concepts. The basic operation in our methodology is synchronised message-passing; the active components of a system
which initiate these operations are processes. The interfaces
between processes, through which messages are passed, are
mailboxes. Both mailboxes and processes are organised into
groups called modules which allow us to describe the initial
interconnection of processes and to control the lifetime of

Distributed Computing Systems
ISBN 0-12-543970-9

mailboxes. Associating types with mailboxes and the messages
they may transmit allows us to extend conventional forms of
type-security across the entire system. Permitting the transmission of mailbox-identifying values allows us to specify
dynamically extensible patterns of interconnection.

This methodology provides us with a tool for the design
and specification of systems of communicating processes -
admittedly a restricted tool: our methodology at present gives
us no way to describe the behaviour of processes as they communicate over their interface mailboxes other than in the sequential code of a process. The methodology extends to the
connection of a system of processes to the outside world: we
regard external devices (discs, keyboards, screens, etc.) as
processes executing in external machines, communicating
through special interface mailboxes. We intend also (see
Section 5) to use the same methodology to describe the interconnection of processes in different workstations of a network.

Within such a methodology there are at least two distinct
ways in which implementation of a practical system might proceed, in order to ensure that the execution obeys the constraints on the use of interfaces which are prescribed in the
design. Either the executing system might check its own operation so as to prohibit impermissible activities, or it might
be programmed in a language which makes it impossible to describe those impermissible activities. The restrictions in
our methodology are based on conventional notions of scope
and type-security: this makes it possible to use conventional
compilation techniques to construct a system which obeys the
constraints with the minimum of run-time type checking. Hence
we base our experiments with the methodology on a language
designed for the purpose.

Our language is based on Pascal because it is reasonably
type-secure (and, it should be admitted, partly by historical
accident - there was a modifiable Pascal compiler available
on our existing computer system). We extend Pascal's type-
checking to encompass type-checking of values sent and receive
in messages and its scope mechanisms to control the visibility
of mailboxes within processes. The design of the language owes
much to other languages based on synchronised message-passing
between communicating sequential processes - in particular,
to LIMP [1] and CSP [2].

Our implementation so far has demonstrated several multi-
process simple operating systems (up to about 100 processes)
on a single-processor workstation, controlling keyboard,
screen, disc and timer devices. One particular demonstration
system contains a simple editor, two games programs, a visible
clock and a "reminder" (timed wake-up) process. It is describe
further in Section 4. This implementation is currently being

extended to allow communication between the machines of a
multiprocessor workstation and between workstations in a network of Pascal-m systems (see Sections 5 and 6).

2. THE PASCAL-M LANGUAGE

The design of Pascal-m concentrates on the problems of non-
determinism and system extensibility. The original motivation
for its design arose out of research on human/computer interfaces [3,4,5,6] which showed that the pattern of interaction
between human and machine can usefully be described as a non-
deterministic pattern of human interactions with multiple con-
currently-executing machine activities. Although certain kinds
of interaction can be described in terms of a fixed collection
of possible activities with a fixed interconnection network,
others seem to require dynamic modification of the pattern of
interconnections and still others require a system which can
take in definitions of new kinds of activities and incorporate
them into itself.

A computer system able to respond to non-deterministic
interactions could be programmed most simply, it would seem,
in a language capable of describing the non-deterministic
interaction of a number of concurrent processes. One or more
processes per visible activity could handle interaction with
the non-deterministic demands of the system-user, plus invisible "server" processes responding to the demands of those
processes. And if the system-user is able to modify the interconnection of activities, to introduce novel types of process
and to connect them into the existing system, the language in
which it is described must give special attention to those
possibilities.

Pascal-m can be described in two parts: the language of
modules and the language of processes. A Pascal-m process is
analogous to a conventional Pascal program, except that it
communicates with its environment by sending and receiving
messages rather than by file input/output. Non-determinism
within a process is catered for by the **select** statement, a
form of guarded command. The inter-process channels of communication are called **mailboxes,** and the language of modules
allows processes and mailboxes to be organised into groups
with control of the visibility of mailboxes both outside the
group and within the processes of the group.

A mailbox is an abstraction of an inter-process interface,
behind which the details of the implementation of an activity
can be hidden. A single mailbox can be used to connect any
number of senders and receivers in a non-deterministic
fashion. Each mailbox has a type, used by the compiler to
control the types of messages which may be sent through it,

and a unique system-wide identification. A mailbox identification is a first-class value which can be assigned to a variable, in particular by receiving it in a message. This last
enables us to describe dynamic modification of the pattern of
interconnection of processes: for example we can program
"directory" processes, which put a user-process in touch with
one of a number of server-processes.

Extensibility of a Pascal-m system can be one of three
kinds. First it is possible to modify the interconnection of
an existing collection of processes, by sending and receiving
mailbox identifications in messages: i.e. a fixed collection
of processes with variable interconnections. This form of
extensibility is already implemented and demonstrated in the
system discussed in Section 4.

The second form of extensibility is dynamic process invocation. It is possible, within a pre-compiled collection of
process-types, to execute precompiled invocations of new
process instances. Each new instance has access to those mailboxes given as arguments in its invocation, and can use these
(if necessary) to extend its connection with other existing
processes. This second form is also implemented and demonstrated.

The limit of Pascal-m extensibility is reached when a user
can specify new process instances which are to be introduced
into a running system, including instances of processes of
novel type. This kind of extensibility arises naturally in
program-development systems, for example, and the main implementation problem is to ensure that overall type-security is
preserved.

The module-level language may be regarded as a design and
configuration language aimed at programming-in-the-large. The
process-level language is used to describe the actual implementation of the required system behaviour. At the top level
a system description is a sequence of type definitions, mailbox declarations and module and process instance invocations.
The intended interpretation is that the definitions and invocations are executed sequentially so that new definition and
new invocation is in principle always possible. This means
that a system could be made type-extensible by the inclusion
of an "eternal compiler" process. Such a process would start
with a description of the definitions, declarations and invocations which gave rise to the system, then proceed to process
subsequent definitions and declarations to ensure that they
fit into that system. Each definition and declaration which
was successfully processed would be executed, and would extend
the running system. Some of the difficulties of type-extensib
systems and the eternal compiler are described in Section 6.

The flavour of the language is best conveyed by examples.

We give several extended examples in Section 3 and devote the
rest of this section to an outline of the main features of
the language.

2.1. Mailbox Identification and Mailbox Types

Mailboxes are objects like conventional Pascal variables –
they have an extent and a scope. However, the declaration of
mailboxes is confined to the language of modules and at the
process level only mailbox identifications are manipulated.
A mailbox identification is a value, with no peculiar restrictions on its use: however there are no operations which produce such a value and hence they can only be assigned to a
variable of the correct type, delivered as the result of a
function of the correct type, or sent in a message through a
mailbox of the correct type.

The identification of a mailbox capable of transmitting
values of type <t> has type **mailbox of** <t> (**mailbox of** is a
type-constructor in Pascal-m, similar to **record**, **array** and
set of in Pascal). A variable capable of holding a mailbox
identification can be declared, for example

var x: mailbox of integer

Note that this declaration does not create a mailbox – rather
it creates an uninitialised Pascal variable which can contain
a mailbox-identification of the correct type.

Processes initially acquire mailbox identifications as
arguments or as imports from their environment or by declaring
mailboxes in their outermost block; subsequently they may acquire additional mailbox identifications by receiving them in
messages from other processes.

A mailbox identification is used in a **send**, **receive** or
select statement. The compiler can check that the type of the
value being sent, or the type of the variable accepting the
value received, matches the message type of the identification. That type is known either because the identification
is an argument or an import to the process, or because it is
held in a variable of type **mailbox of** <t>.

2.2. Send, Receive and Select Statements

The message-sending operations of Pascal-m involve the sending and receiving of values through mailboxes. Messages are
transmitted purely by value: pointers are prohibited in
messages. Thus there is no possibility of shared storage in
Pascal-m, and processes which wish to have a private dialogue
must do so by initially transmitting mailbox identifications.

The simplest message operations are the **send** and **receive**
statements. The syntax is

send <expression> to <mailbox-expression>
receive <variable> from <mailbox-expression>

A <mailbox-expression> must evaluate to a mailbox identification. The type of the <expression> in the send (the
<variable> in the receive) must match the message type of the
identification. This can easily be checked by a conventional
compiler.

Message-sending is synchronised - a process attempting to
send a value through a mailbox suspends execution until there
is a matching receiver: symmetrically a receiver suspends
execution until there is a matching sender. Mailboxes may be
removed from the system, under circumstances discussed below:
if communication is attempted with a send or a receive statement through a removed mailbox the communication fails and the
process aborts execution.

The effect of message transmission between a paired sender
and receiver is that of a distributed assignment: the value of
the <expression> of the sender is assigned to the <variable>
of the receiver.

A process may simultaneously attempt to communicate over
several mailboxes using the **select** statement, whose syntax is

    select <guard>: <statement>
          {; <guard>: <statement> }
    end

A <guard> always contains a **send** or **receive** element specifying a communication through some mailbox, but may optionally
be prefixed with a Boolean expression which prevents the
attempt at communication whenever it is **false**.

<guard> ::= <message guard>|
          if <Boolean expression> then <guard>

<message guard> ::= send <expression> to <mailbox-expression>|
          receive <variable> from <mailbox-expressic

The execution of a **select** statement proceeds in several stages
first, the Boolean expressions are evaluated to discover which
message guards are enabled; second, communication is attempted
simultaneously through all the mailboxes specified in the enabled guards - if there is no complementary communication
offered at any of these mailboxes then the process suspends
execution. When one of the attempted communications succeeds
(whether immediately or by the attempt of another process to
make the complementary communication) the other attempts made
in the **select** statement are instantaneously withdrawn. Finall·
the statement labelled by the successful communication is
executed.

Execution of a **select** statement will fail if there are no

enabled guards; or if all attempted communications refer to
removed mailboxes. We have recently introduced a **fail** statement, and corresponding **fail** guard, which causes no interprocess communication but can be used to detect the removal
of a mailbox. It is intended to assist with process garbage-
collection and is particularly useful to enable server processes to detect when their ill-disciplined users terminate
abnormally. In either case the process will abort execution.

There is a corresponding **repselect** statement, whose syntax
is almost identical to the **select** and whose semantics are that
it repeatedly executes until there are no enabled guards or
until all attempts at communication fail.

2.3. Type-Security

It should be clear that no run-time type-checking is required
when messages are sent, even when the operation is via a
mailbox identification received from elsewhere. The compiler
can check that each message operation is through a mailbox of
the correct type, or via an identification stored in a variable of the correct type. Then if only identifications of the
correct type are assigned to mailbox variables the type-
security of the system is assured.

Pascal has notorious black-spots in its type-checking, to
do with procedures and functions passed as actual parameters
and with variant records: it is our intention eventually to
erase these deficiencies, perhaps in the manner suggested by
the Ada definition [7].

2.4. Processes, Mailboxes and Modules

The second part of the Pascal-m language has to do with the
creation of process instances and the control of visibility
of mailboxes in their environment. The fundamental notion is
that of a module, which consists of a number of mailboxes,
processes and (sub-) modules packaged together. A module may
export any of its mailboxes - optionally either to all processes and modules in its immediate environment, or only to
particular named modules and processes in that environment.
It may also import mailboxes declared in its immediate environment or exported from other modules in that environment.
Control over imports and exports allows us to restrict the
initial connection between modules, and hence between the
processes which they contain.

The language allows us to declare module and process types
as well as module and process instances. An instance is
created by specifying a type and arguments, rather as in a
procedure call. The arguments, like values passed in a message, may not be pointers or values containing pointers:

typically they are mailboxes and constants. The mailbox-
arguments of an instance describe interconnections which
differ between instances of the same type, while imports and
exports describe interconnections which are common between
every instance of a particular type.

Processes are the building blocks of the system. They may
import mailboxes and they are allowed to declare new mailboxes
in their outermost block, but they are not allowed to export
any of these private mailboxes. A process must therefore send
the identification of its own private mailboxes to other processes before they can be useful for communication.

2.5. Mailbox Removal

The design of the language at the module level, which is
described fully in [8] is intended both to control process
interconnection and to allow simple process, module and mailbox garbage collection. Each mailbox belongs to the module or
process in which it is declared: when that module or process
is terminated the mailbox is automatically removed and any
attempt to communicate through it must fail. A process terminates in the manner of a normal Pascal program and as soon
as it does so its mailboxes are removed. A module terminates
when all its constituent modules and processes have terminated.
It follows that mailboxes declared at the outer (system) level
exist for as long as the system does, and that imported mailboxes exist for at least as long as the module or process
which imports them.

3. EXAMPLES

This section gives some extended examples of the use of the
language.

3.1. Producer-Consumer Example

Firstly, we consider the familiar "producer"-"consumer"
pattern illustrated in Figure 1. The Pascal-m text declares
a type, a mailbox and two process-types, then creates two
process instances, connected by their common mailbox argument.
The declaration of each process type gives the type of the
argument mailbox with, as is often the case in practice,
restrictions on the use to which that argument may be put in
the text of the process - the producer can only send, the
consumer can only receive. In any sensible program the consumer process at least could be expected to make some additional communication through some other mailboxes, but that
connection is omitted for the sake of simplicity.

Suppose now that the producer and consumer have different

```
type mt = mailbox of t;

mailbox M: mt;

process producer(X: mt as send);
  begin .... send e to X .... end;

process consumer (Y: mt as receive);
  begin .... receive v from Y .... end;

instance p = producer(M); c = consumer(M);
```

FIG. 1 *Producer-consumer connection*

response latency in some particular case - perhaps the producer generates data in separate grouped bursts, whereas the
consumer can accept it only at regular intervals. It would be
possible to re-program producer and/or consumer to cope with
the problem but, in general, this is an unattractive solution
because the same type of producer process might be connected
to one of several types of consumers (and vice-versa). The
most attractive solution, we feel, is to insert a buffer process between producer and consumer, as illustrated in Figure
2. Here the same producer process as in Figure 1 sends its
data to mailbox P, the same consumer process receives its
data from mailbox C. The buffer process between them receives
from P and sends to C. It executes a **repselect** statement which
never terminates, offering to receive from the producer whenever there is room in the buffer array, and simultaneously to
send to the consumer whenever there is something in the buffer
array. The buffer process is otherwise very like a conventional Pascal program, using a vector to store data which the
producer is sending faster than the consumer can momentarily
receive.

Programmed in this way, any number of identical buffer
processes can be inserted between producer and consumer -
Figure 3 shows how two consecutive buffers can be used should
you wish to do such a thing. The mailbox to which the producer
sends is indeed a kind of abstract interface and the designers
of the producer and consumer processes need take no notice of
the inclusion of a buffer process which might intervene between them. Because the data is sent to a mailbox, not to a
particular process, buffering can be decided upon when the
process network is configured.

3.2. Mailbox Identifications in Messages

The fact that a mailbox identification may be sent as a
message (or as part of a larger message) allows the interconnection of processes to be altered dynamically. Consider

```
const Tmax = ...

mailbox P, C: mt;

process producer(X: mt as send);
  begin ... send data to X ... end;

process buffer(U: mt as receive; V: mt as send);
  type Tindex=1..Tmax;
  var T: array[Tindex] of t;
      nextin, nextout: Tindex;
      count: 0..Tmax;

  begin count:=0; nextin:=1; nextout:=1;
    repselect
      if count<Tmax then receive T[nextin] from U:
        begin nextin:=(nextin mod Tmax)+1; count:=count+1 end;

      if count<>0 then send T[nextout] to V:
        begin nextout:=(nextout mod Tmax)+1; count:=count-1 end
      end {repselect}
    end; {buffer}

process consumer(Y: mt as receive);
  begin ... receive V from Y ... end;

instance p = producer(P); b = buffer(P,C); c = consumer(C);
```

FIG. 2 *Producer-buffer-consumer*

```
mailbox P, B, C: mt;

instance p = producer(P);
         b1 = buffer(P,B); b2 = buffer(B,C);
         c = consumer(C);
```

FIG. 3 *Producer-buffer-buffer-consumer*

the problem of a display which shows a number of independent "windows" each of which is controlled by a virtual-terminal process. Application processes each require to be able to communicate with an individual virtual terminal. It is an additional advantage if processes can be designed so that we can be sure that only one application process is capable of communicating with each virtual-terminal process.

The initial implementation of Pascal-m (see Section 4) performs this feat using a memory-mapped display. There is a single "screen-manager" process, which maintains a character array containing an image of the screen, and a number of virtual-terminal processes which maintain smaller arrays representing individual "windows" on the screen. Application

```
type mchar = mailbox of char; mreply = mailbox of mchar;
    mrequest = mailbox of mreply; mscreen = mailbox of screen;

mailbox R: mrequest; manager: mscreen;

process application(...);
    import R: mrequest as send;
    mailbox reply: mreply;
    var terminal: mchar;
 begin send reply to R; receive terminal from reply;
    ..... send characters to terminal ....
 end; {application}

instance a1=application(...); a2=application(...);

process instance termcreate;
 import R: mrequest as receive;
 var U: mreply;
 begin repeat
          receive U from R; instance terminal(U);
        until false;
 end; {termcreate}

process terminal(X: mreply as send);
    import manager: mscreen;
    mailbox input: mchar;
    var S: screen; modified: boolean; c: char;
 begin send input to X; modified:=false; ...
    repselect
      receive c from input:
        begin ... alter S ... modified:=true end;

      if modified then send S to manager:
        modified:=false
    end
 end; {terminal}
```

FIG. 4 *Use of reply mailboxes to connect user and server*

processes initially need know of only the mailbox which allows
them to apply for access to a virtual terminal: Figure 4 shows
a simplified version of the mechanism used in the demonstration
system. A mailbox of type "mchar" is a mailbox through which
characters can be transmitted; a mailbox of type "mreply" is
one through which the identification of mailboxes of type
"mchar" can be transmitted; a mailbox of type "mrequest" is
one through which the identification of a mailbox of type
"mreply" can be transmitted.

   Each application process obtains a virtual terminal by
sending a message which consists only of its private "mreply"
mailbox to the "termcreate" process. The "termcreate" process

creates an instance of a terminal process, giving it the
user's "mreply" mailbox as argument. The newly-created terminal process then sends its private "mchar" mailbox via its
argument - i.e. direct to the application process which requested its creation. It then receives characters from the
application process, updates its image of its particular
virtual screen and sends it to the screen manager (not shown
here).

Note that the virtual-terminal, which is a kind of server,
can also be viewed as a kind of buffer between the application
process and the screen manager process. The use of a bidirectional **repselect** allows the virtual-terminal process to
accept characters from the application process, even though
the screen manager may not yet have accepted the latest
version of the screen image.

This example demonstrates the programming possibilities
opened up by the use of mailbox identifications as assignable
values. Initially the application and termcreate process share
knowledge of a single mailbox; the application process uses
this to communicate with termcreate and is then put in exclusive touch with a virtual terminal process. The text of
the termcreate process makes it clear that it makes no use
whatever of the identification of the "mreply" mailbox it is
sent, other than to provide it as argument to the newly-
created virtual-terminal process. Other forms of extensibilit
including the possibility of introducing novel processes to
the system through an "eternal compiler", are discussed in
Section 6.

3.3. Non-Deterministic Sender-Receiver Pairing

The separation of mailboxes from processes allows us to intro
duce non-determinism in message destinations. If there are
several potential receivers from a mailbox then a sender can
have no influence over which of them happens to receive a
message sent to that mailbox. Conversely, a single receiver
cannot control which of several potential senders will be
successful in sending a message to it.

One application of this principle is in the disc-driver
module of the demonstration system. To reduce latency of disc
response, the disc-driver module contains a number of disc
buffer processes, each of which receives requests from users
through a single disc-transfer-request mailbox. (The emphasis
on buffering in the examples of this section reflects our
early concerns with the programming of a particular system of
communicating processes. The problems of latency are, however
more fundamental and would occur in many different kinds of
system.) Each buffer communicates with the disc driver to se

```
type mdrq: mailbox of discrequest;
     block: array[...]of char;
     mblock: mailbox of block;
module disc;
   export DR: mdrq as send;
   mailbox DR: mdrq as receive;

   process discbuffer;
      import DR: mdrq as receive;
      mailbox data: mblock;
      var r, r1: discrequest; B: block;
   begin
      repeat
         receive r from DR; ...
         case r.info.direction of
           read:
              begin ... send information to driver ...
                 receive B from data; send B to r.data
              end;
           write:
              begin receive B from r.data;
                 ... send information to driver ...
                 send B to data
              end
         end
      until false
   end; {discbuffer process}
   ....
   instance d1=discbuffer; d2=discbuffer; ...
   ....
end{disc module}
```

FIG. 5 *Multiple receivers from a single mailbox*

control information, and with the user to transfer data. It
is then possible for the stages of several transfers to be
concurrent - one buffer may be transferring data to or from
a user process whilst others are organising transfers or
transferring data to or from the disc. In principle it would
even be possible to dynamically reduce or increase the number
of disc buffers in a running system, without disturbance to
the processes using the disc module except for the effect of
increasing or reducing response latency. Non-deterministic
pairing of senders and receivers thus allows multiple servers
to share the service load between themselves, without need of
any explicit request-distribution activity.

Figure 5 shows a simplified example of the disc-buffer
interface. Note that the **instance** invocation statements allow

the creation of as many buffers as prove necessary or convenient, and that users send their requests to a single disc-
request mailbox. Note also that this mailbox is exported from
the "disc" module yet separately declared for use inside it.
This double declaration allows us to impose separate restrictions on the use made of the mailbox identification inside
and outside its declaring module.

4. AN INITIAL IMPLEMENTATION

The initial implementation of Pascal-m runs on an Intel 8086.
We use a cross-compiler and loader programs, running on a
DEC PDP-11 under the UNIX operating system, to create the
binary image of a system which is downline-loaded into the
8086. Our demonstration hardware at present comprises 8086-
based workstations, each with memory-mapped character display
and 20 Mbyte Winchester disc. The demonstration system described in this section contains a minimum of about 10, and
a maximum of some hundreds of potentially concurrently executing processes designed to provide an example human/compute
interface.

The kernel of the system is written in 8086 assembly code.
It provides support for inter-process message transmission
and converts the interrupt-and-I/O register interface of the
peripheral devices (screen, disc, keyboard, etc.) into a
process-device and device-process message-sending interface.
Currently it occupies about 8 kbytes of 8086 code. In certain
future implementations (on the PERQ, for example) the kernel
will be written as far as possible in microcode. The assembly
code kernel runs at a message rate of about 1000 inter-proces
messages per second: we hope that a microcoded kernel would
improve this by a factor of ten.

The kernel schedules processes using a system of round-
robin queues at eight different priorities. Despite its simplicity this mechanism works well, and processes at the lowes
level of priority run reasonably smoothly. There is also a
simple message-priority mechanism, which ensures that an offe
of communication is not indefinitely overlooked.

4.1. Offers and Mailboxes

The Pascal-m message-sending constructs each compile into
code which pushes data for the attempted communications
(several in general for a guarded command, just one for a
single send or receive statement) on the stack, and then
executes a "message" virtual machine instruction which cause
entry into the kernel. The kernel manipulates a number of
objects in its address space, which is distinct from that of
any process. These objects, or descriptors, include one for

each process and mailbox, and also one for each pending offer
of communication. Thus the kernal introduces a fine structure
into message sending, invisible to a Pascal-m process.

The message instruction causes the kernel to check through
the mailboxes whose identifications are given in the stacked
request, finding first whether any of them has a queue of
complementary offers: if so the communication can proceed
immediately; if there are none, the kernel queues each of the
process's offers on the mailbox to which it refers. At the
same time offers are also cross-threaded into another list,
connecting them to their originating process. Finally the
process is suspended and another selected for execution.

If a matching offer of communication is found on any of
the mailboxes, the corresponding process's offers are all instantaneously withdrawn - this is the reason for the cross-
threading of the offer list of a suspended process - and the
message data is copied directly from the data space of the
sending process to that of the receiver. Finally the matching
process is made runnable, and a process selected for execution.
In the case that there is more than one potentially successful
offer, the kernel has a simple message scheduling mechanism,
discussed below.

The description above shows that the operation of message-
sending can be split into several stages - offer, acceptance,
transfer, completion - but it simplifies what actually happens
in one important respect. Since the kernel runs non-interrup-
tibly, it suggests that the entire activity of sending a
message, from acceptance through data transfer to completion,
is an indivisible kernel operation. As the contents of a
message can be large - any arbitrary Pascal data value, e.g.
a large array - this could reduce the interrupt latency of
the system to an unacceptable extent.

A technique is used, therefore, which turns out to have
quite general application. This is to run the kernel code
which copies the message data inside one of the two processes
involved, as if that process was executing normally. That is,
its state is overwritten so that its code segment becomes
that of the kernel, and its program counter is set to the copy
routine within the kernel, while its data space combines those
of both processes involved in the message. While this so-
called "devil" process is running, the kernel treats it like
any other, and it is interruptible. When the copy routine
finishes, it returns control directly within the kernel, which
restores the process's original state, and then (indivisibly)
completes the message operation as described above.

The crucial point is that each such operation concerns a
fixed number (two) of processes exclusively, and moreover the
processes involved cannot engage in any other activity while

the operation is being performed, so the fact that the operation is interruptible in itself poses no danger. A number of
lengthy operations, particularly module and process creation
are also handled by "devil" processes in this way.

4.2. Scheduling of Process Executions and Message Passing

A large system of processes requires a scheduling mechanism
if execution is to be shared fairly. There must also be some
mechanism to ensure that a process which repeatedly executes
a guarded command does not forever ignore offers of communication on some of the mailboxes which it accesses. Both of
these problems are solved in our initial system by use of a
simple priority mechanism. Processes are assigned a static
priority as part of the process type or process invocation
statement.

At any instant the kernel maintains a number of queues of
processes which are ready for execution. On every entry to
the kernel the previously-executing process is noted; on exit
it is moved to the back of its queue (if it is still runnable)
and the kernel executes the first process from the highest-
priority non-empty queue. Entries to the kernel are frequent -
one each time a process offers communication, one on each processor interrupt - so re-scheduling is very frequent indeed.
In practice this simple round-robin scheduling mechanism gives
impressively smooth results.

A different scheduling problem arises when a process executes a guarded command and more than one of its offers might
immediately succeed. If we adopted a static priority mechanism - e.g. textual ordering within the guarded command - then
it is possible that a process might never respond to one of
the potentially succeeding offers, no matter how many times
it executes the guarded command. To avoid this we attach
priorities to pending offers: the initial priority is computed
from that of the offering process, and its priority is incremented each time it might succeed but is overlooked in favour
of another offer. Coupled with the tactic that offers from
external devices are assigned infinite priority, this mechanism provides a measure of fairness between the offers of
equal-priority processes which to date has proved fully adequate, ensuring that urgent messages are processed with little
delay and that even low-priority-process offers are not indefinitely overlooked.

4.3. Processes in an Early Demonstration System

The demonstration system consists initially of 12 processes.
A screen-manager displays the output of up to about 30
virtual-terminal processes: initially there are two of them,

each displaying a menu of options. One of the menu-windows is
connected to a shell process which allows the user to choose
between six fixed invocations, each of which will create an
instance of a particular kind of process. The other window is
connected to a so-called root process, which displays names
of those activities already activated – initially it contains
the single entry "shell". There is also a terminal creator
which handles the creation and deletion of various types of
virtual terminal processes in conjunction with the root process. In addition to these six (screen manager, two menu-
window processes, shell, root and terminal creator) the system
initially contains a number of processes dedicated to communication with external devices: a keyboard driver, a clock
driver, a disc driver and two disc buffers together with a
disc waggler process which meaninglessly reads and writes data
in a portion of the disc so as to exercise our scheduler algorithms (and, at one time, our confidence in our disc interface processes!).

The shell menu window displays five lines which read
respectively: clock, reminder, chess, hanoi, editor. If the
user selects any of these the shell process will invoke a
process or module of the appropriate type: the action of the
process will initially be to acquire an interface to a virtual-
terminal process, via the terminal create process, to register
its existence with the root (which will enter it in the root
menu window), and then to communicate with the user via its
own virtual terminal. User input is directed to a particular
virtual terminal either by selecting its line in the root
menu or by moving a special "screen cursor" over the window
and depressing a special "window select" key.

Each clock process displays a real-time clock, which can
be made to bounce around the screen at intervals and/or to
chime a bell on the quarter hour. Each reminder process can
be given a clock-time and a message, which it will then display, with suitable audible warning, at the appropriate moment. The chess process displays a board and plays a rather
poor game; the hanoi process displays a five-ring tower-of-
hanoi and plays the game (perfectly) at regular intervals.
The editor process communicates with the disc via a file process and a cache process, which then communicates with the
disc buffers: it provides a window on to an area of the disc
which enables text to be typed in rather as to a conventional
VDU screen editor.

For various reasons the size of the root window is limited
to ten entries: when it is completely filled the system consists of about 30 processes. Some other extant demonstrations
have no such restriction, and can include hundreds of processes.

At the centre of the system the screen-manager process creates, places and moves windows on the screen and accepts updates from the various virtual-terminal processes. Each update contains a complete image of the virtual-terminal display. Windows can be overlaid and moved around in real time ("dragged" across the screen).

The current system runs in real-time with acceptable response, despite the fact that it is interpreter-based (our compiler generates a form of em-1 [9] which is interpreted by an assembly-coded interpreter). It can accept keyboard interrupts at the maximum rate generated by our keyboard (20 per second); each such interrupt causes at least a message from the keyboard device to the keyboard driver, a message from the driver to the currently-selected virtual-terminal process, a message from the virtual terminal to the screen manager and a final message from screen manager to screen. The illusion of simultaneity is almost always effectively preserved. Window movement is not so satisfactory. When the scree manager is constructing a screen image almost all other processing stops: so, for example, the clock windows may seem to jump several seconds and the game windows just stop.

4.4. Future Implementations

A UNIX-like filing system has recently been implemented in Pascal-m [10]: we intend to use it to support our current cross-compilation system and so to build up a self-supporting system on an 8086 workstation. Various screen manager mechanisms have been built and used, as part of a parallel project on human-computer interfaces [4]: those based on colour terminals are particularly satisfying. The next section describes the basis of work towards a distributed implementation which will use several 8086 workstations connected over a Cambridge Ring [11,12]: each workstation, in turn, will contain two or more processors each running a separate Pascal-m system. Inter machine communication within a single workstation and inter-workstation communication across the ring will use the same linguistic mechanisms as communications within a single-machine Pascal-m system.

5. MESSAGE-SENDING ACROSS A NETWORK

In this section, we are concerned with how the implementation of a Pascal-m can be extended to a network of machines. There are two aspects of this question: the first concerns the high level issues of naming, which inevitably involve questions of the user view of the distributed system. The second concerns the distributed implementation of the basic mechanisms of synchronised message sending over mailboxes. Here the main

issue is whether such an implementation can be made acceptably
simple, efficient and reliable. This section concentrates on
describing our proposed implementation.

Our approach is directed towards the implementation of a
network of powerful workstations. But we wish to make it easy
to define the boundaries of a particular workstation in a
number of ways without altering the interface of the services
accessible from that station. A shared filestore, for example,
should be accessible using the same kind of mailbox as a local
filestore. Hence we can identify certain main principles:

1) Each module (and hence all processes and mailboxes within
   it) is located at the node where it was created. Processes
   and mailboxes do not travel around the network: only
   messages do.
2) Message sending is transparent as regards the locations
   of the mailboxes and processes involved.

Of course it is very likely that in most implementations
message sending across a network will turn out to be very
much more expensive (in computational effort or in processing
delay, or both) than local message sending, and that program-
mers will therefore avoid it as far as possible. Nevertheless
we do not make any linguistic restriction on the way that
message interaction can take place with a distant process or
via a distant mailbox.

5.1. Truthful Networks

The outcome of a local message operation is either successful
completion, or failure. The only way in which failure arises
in the purely local case is by mailboxes being removed, because
of termination of their enclosing module. In the distributed
case, the causes of failure are extended, because of the
possibilities of network failure and remote node failure, but
its semantics remain unchanged. It is left to the applications
programmer to introduce the appropriate recovery actions in
response to such failure; we regard it as quite inappropriate
to include such actions at the most basic level of interprocess communication.

We believe that it is essential to implement the underlying
mechanisms of remote communication in such a way that the
message constructs may have a tractably simple and regular
semantics. This sets a standard for reliability of the communications subsystem - it must be truthful. On any request
to perform a transmission it must do so returning one of two
possible results, corresponding to success or failure, and
must report success if and only if it has performed a successful transmission, and failure otherwise. Our initial studies

of remote communicatiou mechanisms have indicated that the
truthfulness requirement can be met with acceptable efficiency
[13]. In the remainder of this section we will study the design
for our initial protocol [14].

5.2. The Pascal-m Network Protocol

The distributed implementation is based on the local one; we
consider a network of machines, each running a Pascal-m system with a kernel, as described in the previous section. These
kernels communicate with each other to achieve communication
between remote processes. Each mailbox identification indicate
a machine within the network, and identifies the mailbox withi
that machine. Therefore any kernel, on inspecting an attempted
communication made by a process, can detect whether it is via
a local or a remote mailbox.

In the case that it is via a local mailbox, the kernel's
action will be as discussed above: in the case of a remote
mailbox, there must be some inter-machine communication. Our
mechanism relies on the unique identification of offers to
communicate within the network: in order to preserve the
possibility of atomic creation, acceptance and withdrawal of
offers within each machine, our mechanism depends on the
creation of pairs of offers, one in the machine which originates the offer to communicate and one in the mailbox-machine
which contains the mailbox over which communication is attempted. In addition the existence of a unique offer within
each participating machine makes it simple to identify the
particular transaction at any stage of message-passing
protocol.

The offer-matching mechanism discussed in the previous
section has a particular advantage: if anything goes wrong
during a message-passing operation it is always possible to
re-execute the "message" virtual-machine instruction, so that
all a process's offers to communicate are re-established.
Therefore it is possible to recover from distant machine
breakdown at any stage of protocol negotiation, even when a
process has accepted an offer and become committed to it by
withdrawing all its parallel offers of communication.

The protocol transmissions (we use the term "transmission"
to denote those protocol-messages which are passed during the
activity which in total comprises a single Pascal-m "message"
communication) start with the detection of an offer to communicate via a remote mailbox. First the kernel creates a
surrogate offer descriptor for the attempted communication
within its own machine, connected to the originating process
but to no mailbox, and then sends a **request** protocol transmission to the remote machine quoting the mailbox and the

surrogate offer identification. The intention is that the
remote machine will create a distant offer, connected to the
mailbox but to no process, which will eventually be matched
with some other offer of communication over the same mailbox.
However the surrogate offer may be withdrawn if it is made
within a guarded command and one of the parallel offers of
communication made within the same command succeeds: in this
case it is not necessary for the process-machine to inform
the mailbox-machine of that event. It will be possible in
practice to include advisory messages which inform remote
machines of the withdrawal of offers, in order to increase
the efficiency of network communications, but it is not
essential to do so.

One possible response to a **request** is a **deny,** if the remote
mailbox does not exist or goes out of existence before the
distant offer is matched. If the surrogate offer is still
outstanding then the corresponding attempt at communication
will fail in the same way as an attempt to communicate via a
non-existent local mailbox. If the surrogate offer has already
been withdrawn, the deny can be ignored.

If the request is addressed to a mailbox on which there is
already a complementary local offer then all the offers made
in parallel with the matched offer will be withdrawn and the
mailbox-machine will respond with **accept:** it will also send an
accept when a distant offer has been placed on a mailbox and
a local process makes a matching offer. In either case the
local process in the mailbox-machine is immediately committed
to the remote communication with the originating machine: it
can make no parallel offers and the mailbox-machine will not
lightly renege on its acceptance.

On receiving an **accept** the originating machine may reply
with a **reject,** if the surrogate offer has been withdrawn, and
the mailbox-machine must then release its local process from
its commitment by re-executing its "message" instruction. If
the surrogate is still outstanding, however, then the parallel
offers of the process in the originating machine will be withdrawn, so that both processes will now be committed to the
communication. If the original offer was to send then the
originating kernel will respond with a **transfer** transmission,
containing the actual message data: if the offer was to
receive then its response will be an **acknowledge,** to which
the mailbox-machine will in turn reply with a **transfer** of the
message data.

The minimum set of protocol mini-messages proposed for the
distributed implementation is therefore:

1) **request** – place a "distant" offer on a mailbox (quoting
   distant mailbox and surrogate offer identifications);

2) **deny** - distant mailbox has been removed (quoting surrogate offer identification);
3) **accept** - matching offer found on distant mailbox (quoting surrogate and distant offer identifications);
4) **acknowledge** - response to accept, requesting data transfer (quoting surrogate and distant offer identifications);
5) **transfer** - response to accept or acknowledge, includes Pascal-m message data (quoting distant or surrogate offer identification);
6) **reject** - surrogate offer has been withdrawn (quoting distant offer identification).

The protocol relies on an ability to identify offers, mailboxes and processes uniquely within a system. At present this is done with an address, which identifies a descriptor, and a version number within the descriptor. Each time a descriptor is returned to the free pool (when a mailbox is removed, an offer withdrawn, a process terminated ...) the version number is incremented. Hence an identification which includes an outdated version number can be detected.

The protocol is effectively idempotent in that no confusion is caused by a protocol message which is multiply received. This means that we can use re-transmission techniques to increase the reliability of a network carrying Pascal-m messages Details are given in [13].

5.3. The Way-Station Problem

The mechanism sketched above is adequate when one of the paired processes is in the same machine as the mailbox. Since mailbox identifications can be transmitted in messages, it is quite possible that sending process, receiving process and mailbox could all be in separate machines.

In such a case the problem is excised by the mailbox-machine kernel, which finds a match between two distant offers. It is necessary to allow a "buck-passing" transmission in the protocol, so that the mailbox-machine can inform one or other (or both) of the remote machines that their offer has been accepted by a third party. Completion of the transfer (or failure of it) is then a matter of negotiation between those machines, without the involvement of the mailbox-machine kernel.

5.4. Reliability, Truthfulness, Deadlock and Livelock

Present-day networks are notoriously non-reliable: that is, there is a finite and not entirely insignificant probability that the network will signal success when it should have signalled failure, and vice-versa. In the absence of such non-reliable performance, our protocol will not deadlock.

It appears that present-day networks, although not truthful, can in practice be made transmission-truthful - that is,
they may signal failure when in fact there has been a success
but will never signal success when there has been a failure.
Since our protocol is idempotent [13] we can re-transmit protocol transmissions whenever there appears to have been a
failure.

If a machine breaks down after receiving a protocol message,
then the originating machine might wait for ever for a reply.
We expect to use timeouts at the lowest level to ensure that
no machine waits for ever: since our protocol messages are
idempotent, we can re-transmit them after a timeout and failure (probably, repeated failure) will signal that the receiving machine has broken down. It is then possible, at any
stage of the protocol, for a process which is committed to
communication over a distant mailbox to abandon it and to re-
execute its "message" instruction: hence we can eliminate
deadlock due to distant-machine breakdown.

We do not believe that the problem of non-reliable networks will prove long-lived in practice, or that any magical
protocol will be devised which will permit reliable synchronisation at a distance over an unreliable network. Suitable
multi-transmission mechanisms can reduce the probability of
error in sensibly-designed networks to any finite level [13],
and we believe that the pressure of user demand will force
the development of more reliable networks in any case.

We believe that our protocol is free from deadlock. We
know, however, that there are logical difficulties which can
lead in certain unlikely circumstances, indefinitely prolonged,
to the individual starvation of one or more processes making
or accepting offers across the network. A full treatment is
given in [15]. We intend to experiment with an implementation
of the protocol as described, while continuing to pursue the
search for logical improvements.

6. FUTURE WORK

The existing implementation of Pascal-m allows dynamic extension of process interconnection, by transmission of mailbox identifications between processes, and extension of the
process population by dynamic process invocation. Work is
underway on the first distributed implementation, using a
Cambridge Ring to connect several similar workstations, and
on use of the protocol to implement multi-processor workstations. Future developments in the language and its implementation must face the problems of type-extensibility in a
single system, in a network of systems and across generations
of short-lived system instances.

6.1. Semi-Extensible and Type-Extensible Systems of Processes

The current demonstration system is initialised to contain a
number of module- and process-image-templates from which any
number of modules and processes may be created. The pre-
compiled **instance** declarations in modules create an initial
population of processes: **instance** statements executed by processes add to that population dynamically.

Such a system might be called semi-extensible: the number
of processes is extensible, but not their types. Nevertheless
we can do quite a lot with such a system. We can, for example,
implement a simple UNIX-like "shell" program, which can create
instances of compilation processes, editor processes and so
on. A more genuinely extensible system would permit the user
to request new instances of existing process or mailbox types,
to describe instances connected into the system in novel ways
and to introduce new types of process, module or mailbox. To
be type-secure it is essential that each new addition to the
system conforms to the type definitions of the existing system - i.e. that each new instance is given arguments of the
appropriate type, that the import and export specifications
of each new module or process type are valid in the present
state of the system.

Such a mechanism could be provided by a compiler which
runs as part of the system, which is initially provided with
a description of the system as booted, and which possesses the
identifications of certain mailboxes enabling it to create
mailboxes, instantiate processes from type-templates held on
disc (say) and so on. In effect such an "eternal compiler" is
merely serialising the declarations, invocations and definitions which make up a system, checking each one for consistency with those which precede it.

6.2. Type "Any"

Problems begin to arise when we consider a filestore in a
type-extensible system. We wouldn't be satisfied with charac-
ter-files, or even with a filing system which has only a fixed
variety of file-types. We would like to be able to store typed
values in typed files, without having processes which break
type-security (say by some use of variant records). The
question then arises, could we write a directory process which
gives access to a collection of typed files, when the types of
the files may be defined long after the directory process itself? Clearly it would be unacceptable to have to rewrite the
filing system each time we extended the library of file types

To help with this problem Cook [16] proposes a form of
run-time type-checking, using a universal type **any** which is
capable of holding a value of any other type. There is a

special **wrap** operation, which generates a type **any** value, and
a corresponding **unwrap** operation which retrieves the value. A
value may only be retrieved as the same type which was wrapped
or the process aborts: thus a wrapped integer value can only
be unwrapped into an integer. For convenience it is possible
to specify the size of a type **any** value. Thus "any(512)"
describes a value exactly 512 bytes long: such values might
be used by a disc buffering system, and could accept values
of any type small enough to fit into 512 bytes together with
the necessary wrap/unwrap information. Also "any(mailbox of
integer)" describes a value whose size is just large enough
to hold a mailbox identification together with wrap/unwrap
information.

This form of run-time type-checking will allow us to write
a directory process in a type-extensible system - and, of
course, a simpler directory process in a semi-extensible system. The simplest directory process might be given a name (a
text string) and reply with a type **any** value, which contains
a mailbox identification. The requesting process must successfully unwrap the mailbox identification into a variable of
the correct type, or face the consequences. The directory can
receive a single type of reply mailbox (**mailbox of any**) and
can perform without any run-time type-checking.

6.3. Scope and Extent across System Boundaries

Interesting problems will arise when a network of type-
extensible systems can be constructed. It would be unacceptable to limit messages over the network to be of a type determined at network construction time, so some mechanism must
be devised which will allow the eternal compilers of different
systems to update their knowledge of network-wide types, in
order to permit communication. Some form of "type-server" in
the network would seem to be inevitable.

An exactly similar problem arises when using a filestore
which persists across the lifetime of several Pascal-m systems.
The justification for the existence of filestores is that they
provide repositories of information which are longer-lasting
than operating system instances. If operating systems were as
reliable as disc surfaces, we wouldn't need filestores. If an
executing Pascal-m system creates files which contain values
of novel type and then ceases to exist, there must be some
mechanism provided to enable a later Pascal-m system to access
that information - i.e. some way in which the compiler or a
similar process can discover how those values are declared
and represented.

At present mailboxes are an attribute of a system instance:
if the instance breaks down, all its mailboxes automatically

disappear. In a multi-system network this might be unacceptable: if mailboxes are used as unforgeable tickets then it
would be better if they lived longer than the systems which
originate them. This would also mean that they could sensibly
be stored in filing systems.

The problems of scope and extent of types and mailboxes in
a multi-system network, or in a filing system which is to be
used by many generations of systems, are difficult and will
demand much future research.

ACKNOWLEDGEMENT

The authors wish to acknowledge the support of the United
Kingdom Science and Engineering Research Council.

REFERENCES

Note: "Queen Mary College Computer Systems Laboratory Report
Number nnn" is abbreviated to "QMC CSL Report nnn".

1. Hunt, J.G. (1979). A Methodology for Interprocess Communication Using Typed Channels. Ph.D. Thesis, University
   of London.
2. Hoare, C.A.R. (1978). Communicating sequential processes.
   Comm. ACM 21, 666-677.
3. Coulouris, G.F. (1982). Designing software for the office
   of the future. *Behaviour and Information Technology* 1,
   No.1.
4. "Distributed Systems Requirements for Effective Man-
   Machine Interaction". United Kingdom Science and Engineering Research Council Grant Number GR/A 46132.
5. Lamming, M.G. (1978). The Arguments for an Entirely Pro-
   cess-based Programming Environment. QMC CSL Report 206.
6. Lamming, M.G. (1980). An office information design study.
   In "Proc. IEE Conf. on Office Automation", London.
7. United States Department of Defense (1980). "Reference
   Manual for the Ada Programming Language".
8. Bornat, R. (1980). Formal Description of Pascal-m. QMC
   CSL Report 274.
9. Tannenbaum, A.S., Stevenson, J.W. and van Staveren, H.
   (1979). Description of an Experimental Machine Architecture. Vrije University, Amsterdam, Netherlands.
10. Abramsky, S. (1981). A Pascal-m Filing System. QMC CSL
    Report 298.
11. Needham, R.M. (1980). System aspects of the Cambridge
    Ring. *ACM Operating Systems Review* 13, No.11.
12. Wilkes, M.V. and Wheeler, D.J. (1979). The Cambridge
    Digital Communication Ring. *In* "Proc. Local Area Communi-
    cation Networks Symposium", Mitre Corp. and National

Bureau of Standards, Boston, USA.
13. Bornat, R. (1982). The Thirty-Year Truthfulness Problem".
    QMC CSL Report 304.
14. Abramsky, S. (1980). A Network-Independent Implementation
    Scheme for Remote Communication in Pascal-m. QMC CSL
    Report 275.
15. Abramsky, S. and Bornat, R. (1982). Livelock in the
    Pascal-m Protocol. QMC CSL Report 324.
16. Cook, S. (1981). ANY: a New Primitive Type for Pascal-m.
    QMC CSL Report 299.

Distributed Path Pascal

Roy H. Campbell

1. INTRODUCTION

The ability to separate the implementation concerns of programs for distributed systems aids the production of high quality, low cost software. Data structures, synchronization, procedures, machine dependencies, processes, and the distribution of tasks to networked computers are all examples of concerns that, when separated, enhance modularity, improve readability, and facilitate modifiability and verification. The ability to specify these concerns orthogonally through logically independent programming language features encourages implementation of software through techniques of successive refinement. Path Expressions improve the reliable, economic design and construction of communicating concurrent software by clearly specifying synchronization and structure of the shared data's description. Distributed Path Pascal augments Pascal with a small number of extensions for Path Expressions, encapsulated data types, and processes. This paper extends previous documentation of Path Pascal [1] by describing features for distributed programming and introducing a technique to verify synchronization and deadlock properties of Path Pascal programs.

Path Expressions were introduced as a technique for specifying process synchronization [2] and a number of authors discussed such techniques further [3,4,5,6,7,8]. Others introduced models of system behavior based on similar notations to Paths [9,10] and developed a variation on the Path Expression idea [11]. Lauer and Shields also designed a specification language based on Path Expression notation [12].

Distributed Computing Systems
ISBN 0-12-543970-9

1.1. Path Pascal

Path Pascal is based on the P4 subset of Pascal [13]. The Path
Pascal compiler is written in Pascal P4 and accepts any Pascal
P4 program that does not use Path Pascal reserved words as
identifiers. An encapsulation mechanism (see Section 2), Open
Path Expressions [8] (see Section 3) and a process mechanism
(see Section 4) augment Pascal. Open Path Expressions, when
integrated with the encapsulation mechanism to enforce a
strict discipline upon the programmer, describe synchronization of access to shared data objects. All access to encapsulated data is through "operations" contained in the object
and is synchronized by Open Paths. A process invoking such
operations may execute the operation only if permitted by the
Open Path Expression associated with the shared data object.
Supporting synchronization of resources with an encapsulation
mechanism that isolates the implementation of the resource
from its use provides the modularity and resulting reliability
[14] that is required in large systems of interacting processes.

1.2. Distributed Path Pascal

The ability to communicate between processors implies the
possibility that connected systems with fewer (or less idle)
resources can utilize those systems with more (or more available) resources. Redundancy increases reliability, speed and
availability while reducing costs. Communicating processors
can allow concurrent access to some resources, decentralization of authority, and increased isolation (hence protection)
of data. Finally, distributed systems sometimes provide more
economical growth steps than upgrades to centralized systems.
    Requirements for languages for distributed processing
mirror those required for uniprocessing:

- Modularity
- Ability to construct hierarchical systems
- Abstract expressiveness, expressive power, richness
- Clarity, ease of use
- Efficiency
- Parallelism, extent of concurrency
- Ease of implementation
- Ability to modularize for distribution
- Co-operation, synchronization
- Provability
- Separation of dependencies, synchronization, data
  structures, & code
- Orthogonal, nonoverlapping specifications

• Direct relationship between program & algorithm
  complexity
• Non-data dependent declarations

It is difficult to formulate absolute measuring scales for
each of these criteria. While no one language can excel at all
of them, some can satisfy them all adequately and be outstanding in a few categories [15]. Path Pascal added only a
few extensions to Pascal; Distributed Path Pascal extends the
semantics of the object and introduces a mechanism and standard procedure for binding network resources to running programs.

1.3. Contents

The following sections describe Distributed Path Pascal in
more detail. Section 2, Section 3 and Section 4 describe Path
Pascal's encapsulation, Open Path Expressions, and processes,
respectively. Section 5 introduces Distributed Path Pascal
extensions. Section 6 explains a technique for verifying the
properties of Path Expressions and Path Pascal programs. Moti-
vations for the design of Path Pascal are discussed further
in [1,15,16,17,18]. The Pascal Report [27] contains a description of Pascal. Appendix A lists a summary of the additional
Path Pascal syntax. Appendix B describes the semantics of
Open Path Expressions in terms of P and V operations. Appendix
C contains several sample programs.

2. DATA ENCAPSULATION

2.1. Introduction to Objects

Encapsulating the data and definitions of operations on that
data ensures that only intended accesses and changes are made
to an information structure and provides a uniform interface
to that data. The addition of a synchronization mechanism to
data encapsulation allows protection from asynchronous access.
In Path Pascal, an encapsulation mechanism called an object
specifies access, transformation, and synchronization. Other
parts of the Pascal program access an object's data only by
explicit declaration of entry types and invocation of entry
operations. Objects are an extension of the Pascal structured
type facility.

2.2. Object Declaration

Each object begins with the declarator object, then specifies
the synchronization for the object via a Path Expression (see
Section 3), followed by const declarations if needed, type
declarations if needed, var declarations if needed, the

routines of the object (routines can be an initialization
block, procedures, functions, processes, or exported procedures, processes, and functions) in appropriate order for
scope consideration, and finally an end token. The const,
type, var, and routine specifications are expressed as in
standard Pascal and have the same actions.

The object defines a block which follows the scope of
standard Pascal though exported procedures, functions, processes, and types have the additional attribute of appearing
as defined in the scope containing the object. Only exported
types, procedures, processes and functions are available to
enclosing scopes for examination and manipulation of encapsulated data.

Object types may be declared with explicit names in a type
statement or implicitly (along with instantiation) using the
var statement. The var statement can instantiate any number
of objects declared with explicit typenames. Once instantiate
each object has its own copies of storage, the object's operations, and synchronization information.

Structures and other objects may contain nested objects.
Recursive object instantiations, however, are flagged as
errors during compilation.

Var statements can also specify pointers to objects in a
manner similar to declarations of pointers to other data
types. The standard procedure 'new', with a pointer argument,
creates dynamic instances of objects. Pointers to objects
permit the construction of encapsulated and recursive data
structures.

2.3. Operations

Functions, processes and procedures whose names are exported
from an object are known as "operations". They are differenti
ated from internal procedures, processes and functions by pre
fixing their declaration by the token entry. Operations, like
all routines within an object, can invoke other operations
and routines within the object (as long as scope considerations are satisfied). Synchronization is applied as usual for
invoked operations.

Operations within an object are invoked as standard procedures. Outside the object, however, the name of the object
instantiation (or a dereferenced pointer to the object's
instantiation) and a period must precede the name of the
operation to be invoked. Operations may be invoked recursivel
even though a deadlock might eventually result.

2.4. Exported Types

An object may export names of types in addition to names of

functions, processes and procedures. Variables may then be
declared to be of such types, though no examination of the
internal structure or representation of the type is possible.
A type to be exported has the keyword entry between the "="
and normal type declaration. It is impossible to export simple
types. Variables of exported types may be defined both inside
and outside an object. They may be passed as arguments into
and out of objects but may not be examined or manipulated outside the object, since their structure is unknown.

2.5. Path Declaration

The object's Path Expression specifies the synchronization
constraints of the object's operations. The Path Expression
mentions each operation's name at least once in the Path
Expression. Section 3 discusses Path Expressions in detail.

2.6. Initialization Block

The initialization part of an object is an optional block of
code executed upon instantiation of the object. The initialization block may contain labels, constants, types, variables
and routines just like any other block; standard scope rules
apply. A single initialization block may appear anywhere
within an object's routine declarations.

An initialization block declaration contains token init
followed by a semicolon and the tokens begin and end surrounding the block (of declarations and code) to be executed
when the object is created. The use within an init block of
variables and routines global to the object is discouraged.
The init blocks of object variables nested within other
objects are executed before the blocks of the surrounding
objects.

2.7. Implementation Details

Assignments between variables containing objects are dis-
allowed. Object variables or structured variables containing
objects are always passed as reference parameters to routines.

2.8. Examples

The example below shows the declaration of a typical object
type, its instantiation, and two invocations:

```
const   nbuf = 5;
type
      bufrange = 1..5;            (* 5 = nbuf *)
      ring = object

         path nbuf:(1:(put); 1:(get)) end;

         var buffer: array[bufrange] of item;
             inp, outp:  bufrange;

         entry procedure put(x: item);
            begin
                 inp := (inp mod nbuf) + 1;
                 buffer[inp] := x
            end;

         entry function get:(var x : item);
            begin
                 outp := (outp mod nbuf) + 1;
                 x := buffer[outp]
            end;

         init; begin
                 inp := nbuf;
                 outp := nbuf
            end;
      end;

var buf: ring;          (* declaration of a ring                    *)
    bufptr: ^ring;      (* declaration of a pointer to a ring       *)
    x: item;
...
    buf.get(x);         (* gets item ´x´ from ring ´buf´            *)
    new(bufptr);        (* dynamically creates a new ring           *)
    bufptr^.put(x);     (* puts item ´x´ in new ring                *)
```

The initialization block sets the pointers to appropriate
values for standard ring buffering. The operation 'put' is
called to deposit characters within the buffer, 'get'
retrieves them. The Path Expression eliminates need for any
further synchronization specification.

2.9. Syntax

Appendix A contains a Backus Naur Form specification for the
syntax of objects.

3. PATH EXPRESSIONS

3.1. Introduction to Path Expressions

An Open Path Expression specifies the synchronization constraints for a possibly concurrent set of process, procedure,
and function executions within objects. This static description allows code to be written without any explicit reference
to synchronization primitives. Each object contains one Path
Expression to specify the allowed orders of sequential and
concurrent execution of the object's entry operations. Since
only the entry operations can be accessed from outside the
object, the Path Expression constrains data access to safe
sequences.

Normally, the order of invocation of procedures is unknown
until the invocation occurs since processes can execute asynchronously. Path Expressions allow three distinct kinds of
constraints to be specified: sequencing (denoted by ';'),
resource restriction (denoted by 'n:( )'), and resource derestriction (denoted by '[ ]'). Combinations of these provide
complex synchronization constraints.

A Path with no synchronization information consists of a
comma separated list of operation names surrounded by path
and end. The Path below:

    path name1, name2, name3 end

imposes no restriction on the order of invocation of the
operations and no restriction on the number of concurrent
executions of 'name1', 'name2', and 'name3'.

The sequencing mechanism constrains the order of procedure
executions. The order is specified by a semi-colon separated
list. In the example below:

    path first; second; third end

one execution of operation 'first' must complete before each
execution of 'second' may begin, and one execution of 'second'
must complete before each execution of 'third' can begin. Of
course, the execution of a 'third' or 'second' in no way inhibits the initiation of 'first'; several operations may be
executing concurrently.

Limited resources (e.g., line printers) occasionally make
it desirable to limit the number of concurrent executions of
an operation. The resource restriction specification allows
concurrent execution of operations to proceed until the restriction limit is reached. Restrictions are denoted by surrounding the expression to be restricted by parentheses and
preceding it with the integer restriction limit and a colon.
The restriction below:

path 2:(ttyhandler) end

allows only two invocations of 'ttyhandler' to proceed concurrently. Any invocation of 'ttyhandler' will wait until less
than two executions are active before it begins execution. The
number preceding the colon in a restriction can be thought of
as the number of resources for which the operation competes.
A critical section, in which only a single resource is to be
shared, is specified in the example below:

path 1:(routine1, routine2, routine3) end.

Only one of the three operations can be active at a time. Re-
strictors may be positive integers or positive constants.
    For some applications it is convenient to process all calls
to an operation once that operation's execution has begun.
Such a situation might occur when a large spooler is brought
into memory to process I/O requests. The specifier denoting
"derestriction" of a list of operations is shown by surrounding the list in square brackets. The Path below:

path setup; [spooler] end

requires 'setup' to be executed before each sequence of calls
to 'spooler'. Once 'spooler' has begun execution, its invocations proceed until all executions have terminated. After-
wards, 'setup' must again complete before any 'spooler' can
begin.
    Each of the forms above (without path and end) can be con-
sidered to be a subexpression of a Path. Combinations of sub-
expressions (with the optional use of parentheses for clarity)
yield complex Paths. Normally, the sequencing operator (";")
has higher precedence than the alternation operator (","). An
operation name repeated within a Path causes synchronization
constraints for each occurrence of the operation to be applied
in order from left to right.

3.2. Examples of Open Paths

1) path a end;
    Routine 'a' can execute at any time and any number of
    'a's can execute concurrently. No synchronization is
    specified.
2) path a, b, c end;
    Routines 'a', 'b', and 'c' can execute at any time. Any
    number of each one can execute concurrently. No synchroni-
    zation is specified.
3) path a; b end;
    Routine 'a' can be executed at any time, but 'b' can only
    begin if the number of 'b's that have begun execution is
    less than the number of 'a's that have completed.

4) path 1:(a) end;
    Routine 'a' must be executed sequentially ('a' is a
    critical section).
5) path 2:(a) end;
    At most two executions of routine 'a' can proceed con-
    currently.
6) path 1:(a), b end;
    Multiple invocations of routine 'a' proceed in sequential
    execution. No restriction is placed on routine 'b'.
7) path 1:(a), 1:(b) end;
    Both 'a' and 'b' are critical sections. A maximum of one
    'a' and one 'b' can execute concurrently.
8) path 6:(5:(a), 4:(b)) end;
    As many as five invocations of 'a' and four of 'b' can
    proceed concurrently as long as the limit of six total
    executions is not exceeded.
9) path 5:(a; b) end;
    No more than five executions of routine 'a' and routine
    'b' can be proceeding concurrently. Each execution of
    'b' must be preceded by an execution completion of 'a'.
10) path 1:([a], [b]) end;
    Routines 'a' and 'b' operate in mutual exclusion.
    Either proceeds as long as requests for its execution
    exist. When the executing routine's request list is
    exhausted, either routine may start again.

3.3. Syntax

Appendix A contains a Backus Naur Form specification for the
syntax of Open Paths.

4. PROCESSES

A process is a program structuring unit which has an independent execution sequence associated with it. Processes can
communicate and are co-ordinated by performing operations on
shared variables. In Path Pascal, the declaration of a process is separated from its activation. A process may be declared in any block and activations of the process may be
created from any body of code with a scope that includes the
declaration.
    Processes are declared in a manner similar to standard
Pascal procedures. They may possess parameters (passed by
value or sometimes by reference) and may also have a size
attribute. The optional size attribute is an estimate of the
process's storage requirements.

4.1. Instantiation

An instance of a process is dynamically created by invoking
the process name in the same manner as a procedure invocation.
The creating process does not wait for the created process to
terminate and continues its own execution. Each process created receives a run-time heap and stack from the heap of the
process which is performing the creation. The optional size
attribute specifies the number of words allocated. No mechanism is provided to abnormally terminate a process; termination
occurs only when a process reaches the end of its code body.
Processes may themselves spawn processes.

4.2. Process Lifetimes

The lifetime of a block which contains a process declaration
is at least as long as the lifetime of any activation of that
process. The exit from a block is delayed until all processes
instantiated from process declarations within the block
terminate.

4.3. Parameter Restriction

The scope of an actual parameter passed by reference to a
process must contain the scope of the process's declaration
(so that storage for the parameter will exist as long as the
process does).

4.4. Time, Delays and Simulation

The procedure 'delay' suspends a process for a fixed time
interval. Its integer argument specifies how long the process
is to be delayed (in time units). The parameterless integer
function 'time' returns the number of time units elapsed since
execution of the program began. The procedure 'await' delays
execution until the system time exceeds the value of its
integer argument. The Path Pascal system includes a simulation
mode option for executing Path Pascal programs. In this mode,
an event driven clock simulates 'delay', 'await' and 'time'.
Thus, real-time system designers may analyse programs by
simulation before attempting installation.

4.5. Interrupt Processes

Path Pascal provides interrupt processes for programming input and output devices. The doio statement [19] appears only
within interrupt processes and suspends process execution
while input or output is being performed.
      Interrupt process declarations prefix a normal process
declaration by the token interrupt and a priority and

interrupt vector is specified (enclosed within square
brackets) after the name of the process.
A sample output driver for a PDP-11 exemplifies interrupt
processes and is shown below:

interrupt process print [priority = 4; vector = #64] (buf: buffer);

```
var
    i: integer;
    pts[#177564]: bits;    (* printer status word *)
    ptb[#177566]: char;    (* printer buffer word *)

begin
    i := 0;
    repeat
        i := i + 1;
        pts := [6];          (* enable printer interrupt *)
        ptb := buf [i];      (* send char to printer *)
        doio;                (* wait for interrupt *)
        pts := pts - [6];    (* disable interrupt *)
    until ((i >= linesize) or (buf [i] = cr))
end;
```

An extension of the var declaration allows access to absolute
memory locations. Square brackets surround a variable's
address (expressed in octal if preceded by the '#' token).
The address follows the variable's name in its var declaration.
The bracketed parameters specify the priority of the process and the location of its interrupt vector. In the example
above, the vector is location octal 64 (decimal 52) and the
priority of the process is 4. (On the PDP-11, the processor's
priority is set to the priority of the process it is running.
Interrupts from devices can only affect the process when the
process priority is less than the priority of the interrupting
device. Other processes normally run with a processor priority
of 0.)
Interrupt processes are created in exactly the same manner
as other processes. Running duplicate interrupt processes or
terminating an interrupt process while an interrupt is pending is discouraged.

5. REMOTE OBJECTS AND DISTRIBUTED SYSTEMS

5.1. Motivation

Many computer networks are constructed to share a limited
number of expensive or protected resources (e.g., printers,
fast or large disks, private data bases, specialized processors) among many computer systems. These resources are

accessed via a communications network and protocol. Messages
with protocol information and data are transmitted between
communicating processes on both the computer requesting access
to a resource and the computer that has the resource.
Efficiency requires that all resources are accessed by a
common protocol as the coding of new protocols and message
formats is a tedious and error prone task. However, specific
user and system programs and network resources may require
tailored high level protocols to co-operate. The remote procedure call offers pleasing properties [20]: the notation is
clear and precise, and protocols are automatic. Most implementations of remote procedures, however, do not allow access
to distributed data. Several authors [21,22,23] embed shared
abstract data types in their languages. These implementations
do not include full concurrency, dynamically installed and
bound resources, and often require extensive modification of
an existing language or development of a new language. Distributed Path Pascal introduces a shared encapsulated data type
called a remote object to mitigate these problems and enhance
the users' ability to utilize resources on a network.

5.2. Definition

A Path Pascal remote object specifies synchronization for,
access to, and transformation on encapsulated data that is
located on a computer in a communications network. Although
similar to the Path Pascal object, its variables and code may
be instantiated on remote machines. Validated Path Pascal programs executing on any networked host may invoke the entry
routines of an instance of a remote object using the standard
Path Pascal entry routine call mechanism. Thus, in use, remote
objects can be indistinguishable from normal Path Pascal
objects. An import mechanism is provided to establish the
network address of a remote object using a network oriented
identification scheme. Application programs may explicitly or
implicitly import remote objects required for their execution.

5.3. Properties

Path Pascal remote objects share most properties of normal
Path Pascal objects including those concerned with correctness. Each remote object encapsulates its data (or resources)
while providing a well defined interface between its data
access routines and scopes outside the object. Remote objects
are separately compiled and installed. Many different processes can attempt to access a remote object; Path Expressions
protect execution sequences to ensure proper synchronization.
Most remote objects are "passive": that is, they usually have
no locus of control within their scopes. An invocation of a

remote object entry routine transfers a process's loci of control across the network and into the remote object.

5.4. Program Viewpoint

Any validated program in the network may access an installed remote object. The designer of a remote object programs the Path Expressions, entry routines, and internal routines of the object as a shared network resource and may be unaware of the network software that will eventually use the remote object.

An installer creates a "remote object" on a particular machine using the compiled remote object code. The installer may be the designer, an operator, a user, or even a Distributed Path Pascal program executing a system call. Installation includes the allocation of memory and data space, initialization of the synchronization, execution of the object's initialization procedure "init", and provision of a network-wide identifier for that object's instance.

A program invokes the entry routines of an imported instance of a remote object using the standard Path Pascal entry routine call which consists of the name of the instance prefixed to a period, the routine name, and the parameter list. Program declarations or statements activate the import mechanism implicitly or explicitly. The mechanism then binds the local name that refers to the external remote object to its network counterpart. To the user, calls to remote object entry routines behave like normal entry routine calls and result in a transfer of control (and parameters) to some other context. Just as with normal entry routines, control eventually returns and the user's program continues. Thus, operations on encapsulated data and resources are kept independent of implementation details (locations, availability and protocols) concerning network communication.

5.5. Network Overview

Machines on the network may each contain objects and programs. Programs are normally "active" and contain a thread of control within their locus. They are "loaded" by the operating system and finally "exit" when completed. On the other hand, remote objects are normally passive and have no thread of control within them. They are instantiated or deleted by local or remote users with appropriate access authority.

Programs may pass a thread of control (corresponding to a process) to an object's entry routine and it will normally be returned on completion of that routine. The exchange of threads of control among the machines provides a logical accounting mechanism for managing control and data flow dependencies among distributed system components and supports error reporting. A call to an entry process increases the total number of threads of control. A process completing its activity reduces the number of control threads.

The network and CPU support provided to Distributed Path Pascal is assumed to be reliable. Thus, transmission and remote machine failures must either be made fault tolerant at the network support level or Distributed Path Pascal programs may abort.

5.6. Remote Objects

Each remote object begins with the object's name (type) and the declarator remote object. If the object is a network resource that must be imported, the keyword external follows. The remainder of an external object declaration specifies the object's skeletal type and consists of the entry routine names and formal parameters that are required for manipulating the remote instance. If, instead, the remote object specifies an implementation for an installable remote object, the declarator is immediately followed by the remaining components of a normal object declaration including Path Expression, entry routines, internal routines, initialization block, and encapsulated data. Specifications for installable remote objects must be declared at the outer scope of a program. Since remote objects are normally separately compiled, remote objects not only isolate their data from other routines but also are isolated themselves from accessing data or routines outside their scope (except other remote objects).

Example of a Remote Object

```
type lpr_typ = remote object

          path 1 : (print , status) end;

          type item = line_image;
               ring = ... (* see type ring in section 2.8 *)

          var buffer : ring;

          entry procedure print(line : line_image);
               begin buffer.put(line) end;

          entry function status : lpr_status_typ;
               begin status := lpr_device_status end;
```

```
process driver;

    var line : line_image;

    begin
       while true do
          if lpr_device_status = running then
             begin buffer.get(line); write(lineprinter,line) end
          else delay(poll_time);
    end;

    init; begin driver; end;

end;
```

The system call "install" instantiates a remote object on a
particular machine. The parameters of an install specify a
network identifier and an object identifier pair to specify
the new resource's name and a code file containing the compiled object.

```
install('dcsvaxb','printer1 ','server.o ');
                     (*server.o is codefile *)
```

Using conventions for standard Pascal user types, declare
external remote object types with explicit names in a type
statement or implicitly using the var statement.

Examples of External Remote Object Types

```
type
     lpr_typ = remote object external
                     entry procedure print(line : line_image);
                     entry function status: lpr_status_typ;
                     end;

     lpr_ptr = ^ lpr_typ;

     server = remote object external
                     entry function acquire : lpr_ptr;
                     entry procedure release(var r : lpr_ptr);
                     end;
```

User programs import an external remote object in three ways:

  • statically at block entry time as an implicitly named
    network resource,
  • statically at block entry time as an explicitly named
    network resource,
  • dynamically using an import statement and as an
    explicitly named network resource.

Network resources are identified in a Path Pascal program
using a string of characters conforming to the following
Backus Naur Form specification:

```
<resource_identifier>  ::= <network_identifier> <object_identifier>
<network_identifier>   ::= <identifier> ":"  |  "*" ":"  | ":"  |
<object_identifier>    ::= <identifier>
```

Each resource identifier consists of a network and object
identifier pair. A '*' matches every network identifier in
the network. A blank or empty network identifier uses a de-
fault local network identifier stored on the local system.
The resource identifier is the logical address of an instance
of a remote object within the network. This logical address
may not be unique and may map to different physical machines
and different physical addresses within a machine every time
the importation mechanism binds it.

External remote object variables specify a resource identifier by encoding the identifier as a string constant and
embedding it between square brackets placed after the variable
identifier in the declaration of the variable.

Example of Network Identifiers

```
var   local_lpr    [´room199:lpr ´] ,   (* lpr in room199 *)
      any_lpr      [´*:lpr ´] ,         (* any network lpr *)
      default_lpr  [´qume ´] : lpr_typ;(* the default qume *)
```

An external remote object identifier is implicitly defined by
a declaration without the square brackets.

```
var   lpr001 : lpr_typ;        (* implicitly defines  ´*:lpr001´ *)
```

On block entry, the import mechanism binds each external remote object variable to an instance in the network. This
binding does not change for the lifetime of the block. Re-
entry to a block may result in a different network resource
being selected by the import mechanism. A descriptor that
uniquely defines the remote object is stored as the external
variable's physical network address.

The "import" standard procedure uses external remote object
pointers to import explicitly named network resources dynamically. Its arguments are a specific resource identifier and
a remote object pointer.

Example of Import

```
var   pool_lpr : lpr_ptr; (* must be imported *)

...   import (´microlab:lpr´, pool_lpr);
      if pool_lpr = nil then (* resource is not in the current *)
                             (* network configuration          *)
         import(´*:lpr´, pool_lpr); (* find any printer *)
```

Import creates a network descriptor for the remote object and
returns a reference to the descriptor in the pointer variable.
If the import mechanism fails to find the remote object, it
returns a nil pointer value.

Remote entry routine calls have identical syntax to normal
object entry routine calls.

Example of Remote Entry Routine Calls

        local_lpr.print(test_string_of_chars);
        pool_lpr^.print(test_string_of_chars);

The parameter lists are slightly constrained: remote object
routines may not have normal object, object pointer, and
meaningful record pointer parameters. However, remote object
routines may have remote object and remote object pointer
parameters.

Example Use of a Remote Lineprinter

var owner_lineprinters[´uiucdcs:lprserver´] : server;
    spool : local_print_queue;
...
    repeat
        pool_lpr := owner_lineprinters.acquire;
        if pool_lpr = nil then
            begin
                writeln(console,´error: line printers all down ´);
                delay(average_repair_time);
            end;
    until (pool_lpr <> nil);

    (* the server gave me one and he will ensure *)
    (* that he will not give it to someone else   *)
    (* until I return it   *)

    repeat
            spool.fetch_a_line(line_image);
            pool_lpr^.print(line_image);
    until not lines_to_print;

    (* give the line_printer back *)
    owner_lineprinters.release(pool_lpr);

The requirement that the distributed system share resources
requires care to avoid errors arising from aliasing. Aliasing
can arise through resource identifiers, remote object pointer
variables, and remote objects transmitted as var parameters.
A program may detect aliasing of dynamically bound remote objects by comparing remote object pointer values. Management
of resource identifiers is a research topic not dealt with in

this discussion of Distributed Path Pascal: the language is
designed to be independent of many network naming issues.

5.7. Further Considerations

The lifetime of an instance of a remote object exceeds that
of the program that invokes its routines. Binding of a program to a remote object occurs when the program imports the
object. The import mechanism broadcasts a query over the network (or searches a local table of resource names and locations) to find an active object. The import mechanism may in
the future include a protection scheme to ensure that particular users or programs only have access to a limited set
of resources. If an active remote object is not found, the
import mechanism returns a nil pointer and descriptor that
ensures the program will fail if it attempts to invoke the
routines of that object. When a "generic" object is specified,
any of a number of machines may be eligible. One is chosen at
random (usually the first) and bound to the local object
reference.

A remote procedure call to an active object by a Path
Pascal process generates a system call. Copies of the routine
arguments and the values of any formal var (or reference)
parameters are encoded into a message. The message includes
an encryption of the size, type, and kind (actual or formal)
of each parameter along with the destination and source
physical network address. The system suspends the Path Pascal
process and stores its process descriptor in a message reply
table. The message is enqueued for dispatching by the network
communications system. Execution continues in other Path
Pascal processes which are not suspended or blocked while the
remote routine call occurs.

On receipt of a valid request for a remote object routine
call, the network communications software places the message
in a queue for the Path Pascal system. The system removes and
decodes the message. A server process is either created or
selected from a pool of suspended servers, an environment for
the routine call is constructed from the arguments, and the
server process is activated to execute the routine. Concurren
remote object routine calls may result in several active
servers. The remote object Path Expression synchronizes the
server processes as they execute the routines.

After the call, modified var parameters and any function
values are returned in a similar manner. The server process
is suspended, a reply message is constructed and enqueued for
transmission, and any storage associated with the remote procedure environment is released. On receiving a reply message
from the network communications software, the Path Pascal

system copies altered variables and function values back to
the suspended process's environment and the process is activated.

Remote process calls differ from procedures or functions
by replying to the requesting message as soon as the remote
process has been instantiated.

A remote object can be deactivated. If a program has imported a physical network address for that remote object, it
may make a routine call. Revoking a remote object after
binding causes invocations of its entry routines to fail.

5.8. Implementation Overview

The Distributed Path Pascal compiler and run-time system [15]
are implemented under Berkeley UNIX (trademark of Western
Electric). A network simulator provides a star-like network
of up to fourteen simulated machines each of which executes
an interpreter. The UNIX timesharing system allocates timeslices to each of the simulated machines which in turn allows
each interpreter to allocate timeslices to Path Pascal processes. The run-time system consists of a portable interpreter
written in Pascal that reads messages from an input 'pipe'
and writes messages to an output 'pipe'. These 'pipes' maintain the interpreter's independence from any network implementation details. Each output 'pipe' from an interpreter enters
a switchboard process. The switchboard copies incoming messages into the destination interpreter's input 'pipe'. The
switchboard supports the import mechanism by broadcasting
import messages to all machines.

6. CORRECTNESS CONSIDERATIONS

Open Path Expressions impose static synchronization constraints
upon execution of an object's operations. Abstractions of the
Path Expression correspond to invariants on the number of
operations of the synchronized abstract data type. Invariants
aid both the design and understanding of Path Pascal programs.
This chapter introduces the invariants corresponding to Open
Path Expressions constructed from the sequence, resource
restriction, resource derestriction, and selector synchronization schemes. These invariants support specification of the
abstract data type, provide pre- and post-conditions for
operations, and allow construction of intermediate assertions.

Guttag characterizes the notion of an abstract data type
[24] as a set of axioms both upon the sequence of operations
defined for the abstract data type and the resulting values
of those operation's arguments. Path Expressions specify constraints on the sequence of operations on an abstract data
type termed the "object". The COSY system developed by Lauer

and Shields [12] uses Path Expressions to allow abstract
specification of concurrent systems. These abstractions are
described by sets of interconnected state machines that correspond to each COSY Path Expression. Open Path Expressions
impose implementation restrictions upon sequences of actions
to manage resource constraints. For example, a Path Expression
for a finite stack may specify that a limited number of 'push'
operations can precede a 'pop'. Flon and Habermann discuss
the derivation of invariants for Path Expressions [6] and how
they might be used in correctness proofs. Andler devised a
Predicate Path Expression [7] that encouraged verification.
Gerber [25] introduced a Path Expression notation for specifying invariants in terms of procedure counters.

  Open Path Expressions have two separate forms of invariants
one type for sequencing of actions and the other for use of
resources internally within the object. The derivation of
these invariants yields understanding of the synchronization
specified by Open Path Expressions and allows verification
of the correct implementation of Path Pascal objects. First,
this section introduces functions upon which the invariants
are based, some simple invariant relations that allow construction of invariants for Open Path Expressions, and
examples of their use. Second, it examines Open Path Expressions which include repeated routine names and provides
a method for deadlock analysis. Last, an example of the invariant technique applied to a Path Pascal object shows the
technique's use for the verification of synchronization constraints for shared data types.

6.1. Path Expression Invariants

Two positive integer functions aid this discussion. Let the
letters "P" and "Q" represent Path Expression phrases, "n"
represent an integer constant, and "id" represent a routine
identifier.

Definition 1:

  s(id) is the number of executions of routine "id" that
  have started since program execution began.

  c(id) is the number of executions of routine "id" that
  have completed since program execution began.

  (A process executing routine "id" cannot both start and
  complete the routine simultaneously.)

```
s(P; Q)   = s(P)
s(P, Q)   = s(P) + s(Q)
s(n: (P)) = s(P)
s([P])    = e(P) + if (s(P) = c(P)) then 0 else 1

c(P; Q)   = c(Q)
c(P, Q)   = c(P) + c(Q)
c(n: (P)) = c(P)
c([P])    = e(P)
```

where e(P) is the number of intervals in which:

$$s(P) = c(P)$$

since program execution began. (Thus, e(P) represents the number of completed synchronization phrases "[P]".)

Initial Conditions: Prior to program execution the values of s(id), c(id), and e(id) are:

$$s(id) = c(id) = e(id) = 0.$$

Example 1:

For A, B, C as various Path Expression phrases:

```
s(A; B)            = s(A)
c(A, B)            = c(A) + c(B)
s(A; (B, C))       = s(A)
s(1: (A; B), C)    = s(A) + s(C)
c(1: (A; (B, C)))  = c(B) + c(C)
c(1: ( [A]; [B] )) = e(B)
s(1: ( [A]; B ))   = e(A) +
                   if (s(A) = c(A)) then 0 else 1
```

Invariants involving these functions describe the static synchronization constraints imposed by Open Path Expressions. The following relations are invariant for routines synchronized by Path Expressions. The letters "P" and "Q" denote Path Expression Phrases:

```
Axiom 1: {identity}    path ... P     ... end -> s(P)   >= c(P)
Axiom 2: {sequence}    path ... P; Q  ... end -> c(P)   >= s(Q)
Axiom 3: {restriction} path ... n:(P) ... end -> c(P)+n >= s(P)
```

Corollary 1: Blocking:

```
c(P) >= s(P) ->                                         {identity}
    s(P)  = c(P) ->
    routines in P are blocked.
```

Path Expressions composed of parentheses, sequences, and other constructs are treated as expected and have invariants determined by evaluating the parentheses and expressions in order of their nesting and precedence.

Example 2: Associativity:

```
path A; (B; C) end ->                              {sequence}
     c(A) >= s(B; C) /\ c(B) >= s(C) ->            {defn of;}
     c(A) >= s(B)    /\ c(B) >= s(C) ->            {identity}
     c(A) >= c(B)    /\ c(B) >= s(C) ->
     c(A) >= s(C).
```

Example 3: Parentheses, Sequencing, and Selection:

```
path A; (B, C) end ->                              {sequence}
     c(A) >= s(B, C) ->                            {defn of,}
     c(A) >= s(B) + s(C).


path (A, B); C end ->                              {sequence}
     c(A, B)    >= s(C) ->                         {defn of,}
     c(A) + c(B) >= s(C).
```

Example 4: A critical section constructed from a resource restriction:

```
path 1: (A, B) end ->                              {restriction}
     c(A, B) + 1    >= s(A, B) ->                  {defn of,}
     c(A) + c(B) + 1 >= s(A) + s(B).
```

Example 5: An alternating sequence of operations:

```
path 1: (A; B) end ->                   {restriction /\ sequence}
     c(A; B) + 1 >= s(A; B) /\ c(A) >= s(B) ->     {defn of;}
     c(B) + 1    >= s(A)    /\ c(A) >= s(B) ->     {identity}
     c(B) + 1 >= s(A) >= c(A) >= s(B) >= c(B) ->   {identity}
     (the operations alternate)
     c(B) + 1 >= s(B) /\ c(A) + 1 >= s(A) ->
     A and B are critical sections.
```

Example 6: The Resource Derestriction and the Readers and Writers:

```
    path 1: ([R], W) end ->                        {restriction}
         c([R], W) + 1    >= s([R], W) ->          {defn of,}
         c([R]) + c(W) + 1 >= s([R]) + s(W)        {derestriction}
         e(R) + c(W) + 1   >=
         e(R) + (if (s(R) = c(R)) then 0 else 1) + s(W) ->
(i)      c(W) + 1 >= (if (s(R) = c(R)) then 0 else 1) + s(W).

Case 1: (i) /\ s(R) > c(R) ->                      {reads in progress}
         c(W) + 1 >= 1 + s(W) ->
         c(W) >= s(W) ->                           {blocking}
         no ⌐W⌐s may occur if ⌐R⌐s are executing.

Case 2: (i) /\ s(R) = c(R) ->                      {no reads}
         c(W) + 1 >= 0 + s(W) ->                   {blocking}
         ⌐W⌐s execute in mutual exclusion.
```

Lemma 1: (i) /\ s(W) > c(W) ->   {writes in progress}
         s(W) + 1 > (if (s(R) = c(R)) then 0 else 1) + s(W) ->
         1 > if (s(R) = c(R)) then 0 else 1 ->
         s(R) = c(R) ->   {blocking}
         no ´R´s may occur if ´W´ is executing.

6.2. Repeated Routine Names and Deadlocks

The functions and invariants apply to synchronization schemes
in which repeated routine names occur within an Open Path
Expression and allow deadlock detection. (If repeated names
do not occur in a Path Expression, then the Path Expression
cannot express the synchronization required to create a deadlock by itself. A proof of this property is a good exercise
with the functions and invariant relations.)

Example 7: Applications of definitions to Repeated Names:

        s(A, A)   = s(A) + s(A)
        s(A; A)   = s(A)
        c(A, (B; A)) = c(A) + c(B; A) = c(A) + c(A)
        c((A; B), (A; C), (A; D)) = c(B) + c(C) + c(D)

Example 8: Repeated Name within a Path Expression:

path A, A end ->   {identity}
    s(A, A) >= c(A, A) ->   {defn of,}
    s(A) + s(A) >= c(A) + c(A).

Example 9: A Simple Deadlock

    path 1: (A, A) end ->   {restriction}
        c(A, A) + 1 >= s(A, A) ->   {defn of,}
        c(A) + c(A) + 1 >= s(A) + s(A) ->   {identity}
        c(A) + 0.5 >= s(A) >= c(A).

    c(A) = 0 ->   {initial condition}
        0.5 >= s(A) ->
        the routine A is always blocked.

Similarly, the Path Expression:

    path A; A end ->   {sequence} /\ {identity}
        c(A) >= s(A) /\ s(A) >= c(A) ->   {blocking}
        s(A) = c(A) ->   {initial condition}
        the routine A is always blocked.

Example 10: A two-routine deadlocked Path Expression:

    path (A; B), (B; A) end ->   {sequence}
        c(A) >= s(B) /\ c(B) >= s(A) /\   {identity}
        s(A) >= c(A) /\ s(B) >= c(B) ->
        s(A) >= s(B) /\ s(B) >= s(A) /\ c(A) >= s(B) /\ s(B) >= c(A)
            /\ c(A) >= c(B) /\ c(B) >= c(A) ->
        s(A) = s(B) = c(A) = c(B) ->   {blocking}
        the routines A, B, or C are always blocked.

Example 11: In which one routine of a Path Expression is
permanently blocked.

```
    path 1: ((A, B); C), 1: (A; (B, C)) end ->        {restriction} /\ {sequence}
          c((A, B); C) + 1 >= s((A, B); C) /\ c(A) >= s(B, C) ->      {by defn}
(i)       c(C) + 1 >= s(A) + s(B) /\ c(A) >= s(B) + s(C) ->           {identity}
          c(C) + 1 >= 2 * s(B) + s(C) >= 2 * s(B) + c(C) ->
          0.5 >= s(B) -> 0 = s(B) ->
          routine B is always blocked.
```

(If B blocks, the other routines also block. The benefit of further
analysis is dubious. It is unlikely that a Path Expression which permanently
blocks a routine's execution is satisfactory.)

Suppose B is never invoked:

```
    s(B) = 0 /\ (i) ->                                            {identity}
    c(C) + 1 >= s(A) >= c(A) >= s(C) >= c(C) ->
    A and C executions alternate and are mutually exclusive.
```

6.3. Example: Correctness of a Circular Buffer

A circular buffer with 'bmax' elements will exemplify the use
of Path Expression invariants for informal correctness arguments about Path Pascal objects. The buffer allows storage of
up to 'bmax' messages and permits concurrent retrieval and
storage of different messages.

The circular buffer object is implemented as an abstract
data type with the operations 'enqueue' and 'dequeue' which
are synchronized to operate correctly when the buffer is
shared. The processes sharing the buffer may deadlock; this
is of no concern to the correctness of the buffer and the
integrity of its contents. This section shows a Path Expression for the circular buffer, describes the buffer's implementation and verifies properties of the implementation.

6.3.1. Derivation of circular buffer synchronization

1) The circular buffer is of finite capacity. A total of
    'bmax' buffers are shared. This is an implementation
    restriction and requires a resource restriction.

    path bmax : (... dequeue ... enqueue ...) end

2) A dequeue cannot start until its corresponding enqueue
    has completed.

    path bmax : (... enqueue ...; ... dequeue ...) end

3) Processes executing enqueue share a data structure
    (pointer) that indicates the front of the queue. This is
    another resource restriction.

    path bmax : (1 : (enqueue); ... dequeue ...)) end

4) Dequeues share a data structure (pointer) that indicates the back of the queue.

path bmax : (1 : (enqueue); 1 : (dequeue)) end

6.3.2. A circular buffer implementation. The circular buffer object and Path Expression in Path Pascal follows:

```
object
      path bmax : ( 1 : (put); 1 : (get) ) end;

      var
          ring : array [1..bmax] of message;
          front, back : 1..bmax;
      entry procedure put(newitem : message);
      begin
          ring[front] := newitem; (*L1*)
          front := (front mod bmax) + 1;
      end;
      entry function get : message;
      begin
          get := ring[back]; (*L2*)
          back := (back mod bmax ) + 1;
      end;
      init;
      begin front := 1; back := 1 end;
end
```

The synchronization of the circular buffer is specified statically in this example and does not depend upon the values of variables or flags and dynamic control flow of the program. Furthermore, the synchronization does not unnecessarily constrain the execution of the operations nor does the implementation include any redundant variables or code.

6.3.3. Informal arguments about correctness. The circular buffer requires examination of one major assertion:

• No two processes may execute the get and put routines so that they assign and read the same message concurrently.

Within the circular buffer, processes access messages on lines commented (*L1*) and (*L2*). The discussion utilizes assertions at L1 and L2 and is simplified because only the variable 'ring' is shared between put and get.

The following are invariants derived from the axioms and Open Path Expression of the example:

(1)	c(get) + bmax >= s(put)	{restriction}
(2)	c(put) >= s(get)	{sequence}
(3)	c(put) + 1 >= s(put)	{restriction}
(4)	c(get) + 1 >= s(get)	{restriction}

The following are pre- and post-conditions for 'put' and 'get' on the variables 'back' and 'front' and the number of executions of these procedures:

(5)	front = c(put) mod bmax + 1
(6)	back = c(get) mod bmax + 1

Path Pascal initializes the object before any operations may be invoked and hence initially these pre-conditions for 'put' and 'get' are true. Put is executed in mutual exclusion (invariant (3)) and get is also executed in mutual exclusion (invariant (4)). Updating the variables 'back' and 'front' is interference-free [26] as they are referenced in only one of the routines. An inductive argument on executions of these procedures validates the above post-conditions.

The pre-conditions for 'put' and 'get' are also pre-conditions for statements (*L1*) and (*L2*) respectively since no assignment occurs to 'front' and 'back' in 'put' and 'get' and neither c(put) nor c(get) change. A complete correctness argument should involve both a complete specification of the buffer and an analysis of the values stored in the array. This is omitted.

6.3.4. Reading and writing to the same message. Processes could fail if they write to and read from the same message slot in the array ring at statements (*L1*) and (*L2*), i.e.:

front = back. (at L1 and L2)

A process executing procedure put at L1 and another process executing get at L2 requires:

s(put) > c(put)	/\ s(get) > c(get) ->	{invariant 3}
s(put) = c(put) + 1	/\ s(get) > c(get) ->	{invariant 4}
s(put) = c(put) + 1	/\ s(get) = c(get) + 1 ->	{invariant 1}
c(get) + bmax >= c(put) + 1	/\ s(get) = c(get) + 1 ->	
c(get) + bmax > c(put)	/\ s(get) = c(get) + 1 ->	{invariant 2}
c(get) + bmax > c(put)	/\ c(put) > c(get) ->	
c(get) + bmax > c(put) > c(get) ->		
bmax > c(put) - c(get) > 0 ->		{pre-conditions 5, 6}

bmax > front - 1 - (back - 1) + k * bmax > 0 /\ integer k /\ k >= 0 ->
bmax > front - back + k * bmax > 0 ->
front <> back for all k ->
processes do not read and write the same message concurrently.

6.4. Discussion

Open Path Expressions define invariants that support Path

Pascal program design and verification. The derivation of invariants and proof of properties about the routines synchronized by Open Path Expressions appears to be amenable to automatic theorem proving programs. However, despite this support,
in general it remains difficult to verify Path Pascal programs
because of the difficulty of formally specifying the results
of routines and because of other semantic considerations.

7. SUMMARY

The Distributed Path Pascal programming language extends
Pascal P4 to include concurrent processes, Path Expressions,
objects, and remote objects for distributed computing. The
Distributed Path Pascal compiler is written in Pascal P4 and
is self-compiling. The compiler produces intermediate code
(an extended P-Code) for interpretive execution or assembly
into machine instructions. The language supports system simulation, distributed applications, and operating system construction.
      We believe that the careful selection of extensions in
Distributed Path Pascal has led to a lean and elegant set of
features which span the criteria for synchronization in systems programming. More ambitious synchronization schemes can
be devised which permit the expression of very complicated
ordering constraints such as those found in schedulers; however, such mechanisms lead to synchronization features that
include computational capability and have sophisticated implementation requirements. By keeping the Path Expression
notation of Path Pascal simple and embedding it in a simple
but general encapsulation and abstraction mechanism, complex
synchronization is described using all the features of the
language. The static synchronization constraints imposed by
Path Expressions provide invariants useful in program correctness proofs. Likewise, the extension of the encapsulation
mechanism to distributed systems provides a simple but general
method of allocating software tasks to a network of machines.
Our intent is the provision of simple language mechanisms
which can be combined to synthesize complex synchronization
schemes in an elegant manner rather than the provision of an
all purpose synchronization mechanism.

ACKNOWLEDGEMENTS

Funded in part by NASA Grant NSG1471, NSF Grant MCS 77-09128,
and the Science and Engineering Council of Great Britain.

REFERENCES

1. Campbell, R.H. and Kolstad, R.B. (1980). An overview of
   Path Pascal's design and Path Pascal user manual. SIGPLAN
   Vol.15, No.9, pp.13-24.
2. Campbell, R.H. and Habermann, A.N. (1974). The specification of process synchronization by Path Expressions.
   In "Lecture Notes in Computer Science" (Eds G. Goos and
   J. Hartmanis), Vol.16, pp.89-102, Springer-Verlag.
3. Habermann, A.N. (1975). Path Expressions. Dept of Computer
   Science Technical Report. Carnegie-Mellon University,
   Pittsburgh, USA.
4. Lauer, P.E. and Campbell, R.H. (1975). Formal semantics
   of a class of high level primitives for co-ordinating
   concurrent processes. *Acta Informatica* 5, 297-332.
5. Habermann, A.N. (1976). "Introduction to Operating System
   Design". Science Research Associates, 89 pp.
6. Flon, L. and Habermann, A.N. (1976). Towards the construction of verifiable software systems. SIGPLAN Notices Vol.
   8, No.2.
7. Andler, S. (1979). Predicate Path Expressions. 6th Annual
   ACM Symposium on Principles of Programming Languages,
   San Antonio, Texas. pp.226-236.
8. Campbell, R.H. (1976). Path Expressions: A technique for
   specifying process synchronization. Ph.D. Thesis, University of Newcastle-upon-Tyne. Also: Dept of Computer
   Science, Technical Report. UIUCDCS-R-77-863, University
   of Illinois, Urbana-Champaign, USA.
9. Shaw, A.C. (1978). Software descriptions with flow expressions. *IEEE TSE* 4, 242-254.
10. Riddle, W.E. (1976). Software System Modelling and
    Analysis. RSSM/25, Technical Report, Dept of Computer
    and Communication Sciences, University of Michigan.
11. ONERA CERT (1978). Parallelism, control and synchroni-
    zation expression in a single assignment language.
    SIGPLAN Notices Vol.13, No.1.
12. Lauer, P.E. and Shields, M.W. (1978). Abstract specifi-
    cation of resource accessing disciplines: adequacy,
    starvation, priority and interrupts. SIGPLAN Notices,
    Vol.13, No.12, pp.41-59.
13. Ammann, U., Nori, K. and Jacobi, C. (1976). "The Portable
    Pascal Compiler". Institut Für Informatik, EIDG, Tech-
    nische Hochschule CH-8096, Zurich.
14. Parnas, D.L. (1972). On the criteria to be used in decom-
    posing systems into modules. *Comm. ACM* 15, 1053-1058.
15. Kolstad, R.B. (1982). Distributed Path Pascal. Ph.D.
    Thesis, University of Illinois, Urbana, USA.
16. Miller, T.J. (1978). An implementation of Path Expressions

in Pascal, M.S. Thesis, University of Illinois, Urbana, USA.

17. Campbell, R.H. and Kolstad, R.B. (1979). Path Expressions in Pascal. Fourth Int. Conf. on Software Engineering, Munich.

18. Campbell, R.H. and Kolstad, R.B. (1979). Practical applications of Path Expressions to systems programming. ACM 79, Detroit.

19. Wirth, N. (1977). Modula: a language for modular multiprogramming. *Software-Practice and Experience* 7, 3-84.

20. Peterson, J.L. (1979). Notes on a workshop on distributed computing. *Operating Systems Review* 13, 18-30.

21. Liskov, B. and Scheifler, R. (1982). Guardians and actions: linguistic support for robust, distributed programs. *In* "Proc. 9th ACM Principles of Programming Languages Conference", pp.7-19. Albuquerque, New Mexico.

22. Cook, R.P. (1979). *MOD - A language for distributed processing. *In* "Proc. Int. Conf. on Distributed Operating Systems", (IEEE CH1445-6/79/0000-233), pp.233-241.

23. Andrews, G.R. (1979). Synchronizing Resources. Technical Report TR 79-20, University of Arizona.

24. Guttag, J.V., Horowitz, E. and Musser, D. (1978). The design of data type specifications. *In* "Current Trends in Programming Methodology", Vol.4, "Data Structuring", pp.60-79, Prentice-Hall, Englewood Cliffs, New Jersey.

25. Gerber, A.J. (1977). Process synchronization by counter variables. *Operating Systems Review* 11, 6-17.

26. Owicki, S. and Gries, D. (1976). Verifying properties of parallel programs: an axiomatic approach. *Comm. ACM* 19, 279-285.

27. Jensen, K. and Wirth, N. (1975). "Pascal User Manual and Report". Springer-Verlag, New York.

APPENDIX A
PATH PASCAL SYNTAX

The following Backus-Naur form (BNF) grammar summarizes the syntax of Path Pascal. This list of rules contains both standard Pascal [Ammann, et al., 76] and the Path Pascal additions. The following symbols are meta-symbols belonging to the BNF formalism and are not symbols of the language Path Pascal:

| ::=   { }   ""

The curly braces denote the possible repetition of the enclosed symbols zero or more times. Double quotes enclose terminal symbols.

A.1 Object Syntax

Backus Naur Form for object specifications is shown below:

```
obj_type        ::=  <obj_hd> <path_decl_part> <const_defn_part>
                     <obj_typdef_pt> <var_decl_part> <operation_part> "end" |
                     <obj_hd> "external" <operation_part> "end"

obj_hd          ::=  "object" |
                     "remote" "object"

obj_typdef_pt   ::=  <obj_type_defn> { ";" <obj_type_defn> } |
                     <empty>

obj_type_defn   ::=  <type_defn> |
                     <ident> "=" "entry" <type>

operation_part  ::=  { <routine> ";" } |
                     { <routine> ";" } "init" ";" <block> { <routine> ";" }

routine         ::=  <pp_or_f_decl> |
                     <opn_decl>

pp_or_f_decl    ::=  <proc_decl> |
                     <func_decl> |
                     <procs_decl> |
                     <intrp_decl>

opn_decl        ::=  "entry" <pp_or_f_decl>
```

A.2 Open Path Expression Syntax

The BNF syntax for Open Paths is shown below:

```
path_decl       ::=  "path" <list> "end"

list            ::=  <sequence> { "," <sequence> }

sequence        ::=  <item> { ";" <item> }

item            ::=  <bound> ":" "(" <list> ")" |
                     "[" <list> "]" |
                     "(" <list> ")" |
                     <ident>

bound           ::=  <unsgnd_int> |
                     <const>
```

APPENDIX B
SEMANTICE AND REDUCTION ALGORITHM FOR OPEN PATHS

Open Path semantics are described below in terms of P and V operations on counting semaphores in the prologues and epilogues of the procedures, functions, and processes. The following recursive algorithm [Campbell, 77] will translate Open Paths into this P and V implementation. In general, the Path Expression to be translated will be surrounded by two strings of generated synchronization operations which are on its left and right (L and R respectively.) Each translation rule operates on a string of the form "L M R" which represents the left, middle, and right parts of the string. The translation rule chosen to operate on M corresponds to the production rule which recognizes M (see Appendix A). The translated string consists of one or two strings of similar form and initialization code denoted by "⌈sx := y⌉".

The algorithm is initialized when Path <list> End is transformed into R=null, M=<list>, L=null. The left column of the table below shows M (assumed to be surrounded by L and R); the right columns show the new translated L, M, and R.

If an operation_id occurs more than once, the extra synchronization is embedded within the previous synchronization. Additional synchronization code L´ and R´ is embedded as shown below:

    begin; L; L´; operation; R´; R end .

TRANSFORMATION TABLE

M	new L	new M	new R	and	new L	new M	new R	init
<seq>,<list>	L	<seq>	R	|	L	<list>	R	
<item>;<seq>	L	<item>	V(s1)	|	P(s1)	<seq>	R	[s1:=0]
n:(<list>)	P(s2) L	<list>	R V(s2)	|				⌈s2:=n⌉
⌈<list>⌉	PP(c,s,L)	<list>	VV(c,s,R)	|				⌈s:=1, c:=0⌉
(<list>)	L	<list>	R	|				
<oper´n_id>	begin;L;operation;R end			(algorithm terminates)				

where PP(c,s,L) represents: and VV(c, s, R) represents:

    P(s);   P(s);
    c := c + 1;   c := c - 1;
    IF c=1 THEN L;   IF c=1 THEN R;
    V(s)   V(s)

APPENDIX C
PROGRAMMING EXAMPLES

C.1 DINING PHILOSOPHERS

The well known problem of the dining philosophers involves a set of five philosophers whose activities in life are eating and thinking. Each philosopher thinks for a while, eats, thinks, eats and so on. The philosophers share a unique dining arrangement: though two utensils are required for a philosopher to eat, the five dining places are located around a circular table with only one utensil on the right of each dining place. Therefore, the philosophers must share utensils. The problem involves the scheduling of the philosophers so that no philosopher attempts to begin eating when his utensils are not available. The Path Pascal solution to this problem is different from many in that no explicit queues are needed.

A quick solution to the five philosophers is to make pairs of philosophers share the same resource in a scheme such as:

```
table: object
   path
      1: (eat1, eat2),
      1: (eat2, eat3),
      1: (eat3, eat4),
      1: (eat4, eat5),
      1: (eat5, eat1)   end;

   entry procedure eat1; begin ... end;
   entry procedure eat2; begin ... end;
   entry procedure eat3; begin ... end;
   entry procedure eat4; begin ... end;
   entry procedure eat5; begin ... end;
end;
```

This scheme provides the desired constraints and is deadlock free. The solution is not parameterized for arbitrary numbers of philosophers.

An alternative solution allows the parameterization of the number of philosophers. Each philosopher is a process attempting to use the 'fork' objects. Paths synchronize access and prevent deadlocks from occurring. Note that only simple synchronization statements are given (e.g., only four philosophers eating at a time, only one using each fork). The rest of the program specifies the logic of thinking and eating.

```
const   nphilosophers = 5;
        maxindex = 4;        (* nphilosophers - 1 *)

type    diner = 0..maxindex;

var i: integer;
    table: object
path maxindex:(starteating; stopeating) end;
var fork: array [diner] of
       object
             path 1:(pickup; putdown) end;
             entry procedure pickup;  begin end;
             entry procedure putdown;  begin end;
       end;
```

APPENDIX C (continued)

```
entry procedure starteating(no: diner);
    begin
        fork[no].pickup;
        fork[(no+1) mod nphilosophers].pickup
    end;

entry procedure stopeating(no: diner);
    begin
        fork[no].putdown;
        fork[(no+1) mod nphilosophers].putdown;
    end;
end;          (* table *)

process philosopher(mynum: diner);
    begin
        repeat
            delay(ran(seed));
            table.starteating(mynum);
            delay(ran(seed));
            table.stopeating(mynum);
        until false;
    end;

begin
    for i:= 0 to maxindex do philosopher(i)
end.
```

MASCOT and Multiprocessor Systems

Ken Jackson

1. INTRODUCTION

The paper starts with a general introduction which aims to
identify the characteristics of MASCOT, why they are there
etc. and identifies why MASCOT is different from other
approaches.

We then introduce an example of a MASCOT kernel written in
a version of Pascal which has been specially extended to support the style of modularity introduced by MASCOT. Using the
same notation a simple example system is introduced and described.

Having set this framework, it is then possible to discuss
the results of a research contract which Systems Designers
Limited (SDL) has recently completed for the Ministry of
Defence Royal Signals and Radar Establishment (RSRE) into the
application of MASCOT to multiprocessor systems. Again the
extended Pascal notation is used to illustrate the discussion.

2. MASCOT

2.1. Background

The only actions any computer system can perform consist of
taking in information, transforming information and outputting
information. This action can be represented diagrammatically
by the data flow graph of Figure 1, in which rectangles are
used to denote information sources or sinks and a circle is
used to represent the active process of transforming information. This simplistic model of a computer system, while
accurate, is not particularly valuable or helpful because it

Distributed Computing Systems
ISBN 0-12-543970-9

FIG. 1

makes all systems look identical.

Real systems differ from this simple model in many respects they usually have to handle many sources of information and many sinks for information, plus they have to perform many distinct functions. Also it is usually impossible to predict or define the order in which a set of functions will need to be performed, indeed there will usually not be a unique solution to the ordering and frequently the need for functions to be performed will be deduced in real time as part of the operation of the system.

The consequence of all of these factors is that a more sophisticated model for describing the behaviour of a system is required. Phillips [1] realised this problem in 1965 when he was attempting to design the computer control system for an automatic adaptive radar system. His solution was the invention he called Network Diagrams which show (see Fig. 2) data flowing from a set of data sources to a set of data sinks (shown as crosshatched rectangles) via a network of internal functions (circles) and data boxes (i.e. repositories for data in transit between functions or needed for reference by severa functions).

Network diagrams proved an invaluable aid in the design and documentation of real time systems and their use is now incorporated into Ministry of Defence documentation standards. Their chief value is that they present a picture of a system. This is important because it enables any group of people involved with a system to visualise, in a consistent manner, something which is otherwise totally intangible. The other major benefit of network diagrams is that they provide a means of decomposing a system into a set of components with a well-defined set of interactions. They therefore represented a major breakthrough into structured design, modular software and provided a basis for managing the development of computer-based systems.

2.2. The Requirement for MASCOT

Network diagrams were purely a design aid and provided no help or discipline during the subsequent programming stages.

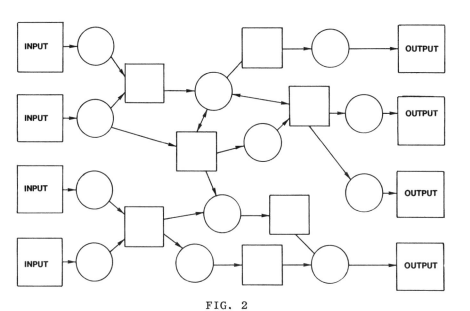

FIG. 2

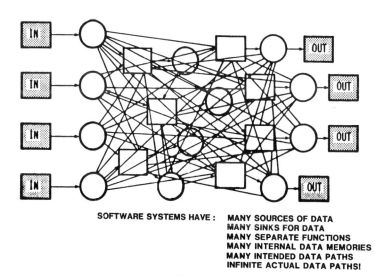

SOFTWARE SYSTEMS HAVE :   MANY SOURCES OF DATA
MANY SINKS FOR DATA
MANY SEPARATE FUNCTIONS
MANY INTERNAL DATA MEMORIES
MANY INTENDED DATA PATHS
INFINITE ACTUAL DATA PATHS!

FIG. 3

As a result the limited interactions between components intended by the designer and expressed in the network diagram
could be totally undermined by the possible interactions allowed by the programming language used for implementation
(see Fig. 3). Many languages now recognise this need to control interaction but most widely available languages do not
(e.g. FORTRAN, COBOL, C), even the widely publicised US
Department of Defense new language Ada does not insist upon
this control!

Thus one of the starting points for MASCOT was to provide
a programming system linked to a network design representation which enforced the diagram representation in the way the
software was constructed and executed, and also provided comprehensive aids for testing.

The other main starting point of MASCOT was the wish to
create a small set of necessary and sufficient scheduling and
synchronisation facilities to enable a set of co-operating
parallel processes to be set up and reliably executed in
accordance with the designers' intentions. This was felt to be
necessary because of the widely divergent sets of facilities
offered by the purveyors of real time operating systems.

2.3. What is MASCOT?

MASCOT is an acronym standing for "A Modular Approach to
Software Construction, Operation and Test". It provides:

1) A formalism for expressing the software structure of a
   real-time (parallel processing) system which:
   a. can be represented diagrammatically;
   b. is independent of the computer configuration;
   c. is independent of the programming language used.
2) A methodology based on the formalism for design, implementation, testing and documentation which is applicable
   during all stages of a computer-based system life cycle
   from design onwards into maintenance during operational
   use of that system.
3) A small kernel to provide a run-time (executive level)
   set of facilities which supports the formalism and provides scheduling and synchronisation. This kernel can be
   (and has been):
   a. implemented directly on bare machine(s) to provide a
      vendor independent executive which is compact and
      efficient for operational use - especially for micro-
      computers;
   b. implemented on top of a host operating system to pro-
      vide a convenient checkout environment prior to down-
      line loading into real targets;
   c. totally integrated into an existing operating system,

as has been done on UNIX (*) as part of the ANGUS
system [2].
(It is also important to provide software construction
facilities related to MASCOT. The combination of MASCOT
construction plus a kernel is known as a MASCOT machine
[3]. Some of the construction facilities are alluded to
in the next section.)

2.4. MASCOT Formalism

2.4.1. ACP diagrams. The MASCOT formalism is most easily described in terms of the diagram notation used to describe
systems produced using MASCOT. However, it must be emphasised
that one of the unique features of MASCOT is that the modularity of the design level formalism is not only identifiable
in the executing software, but also used in the construction
and testing of the system.

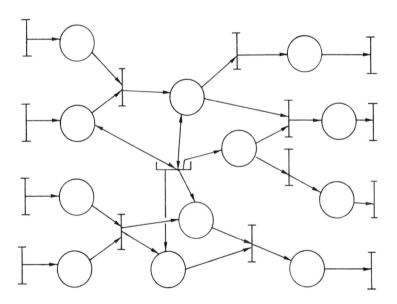

FIG. 4 *A simple activity channel pool (ACP) diagram.*

The MASCOT diagram notation, derived from Phillips' network diagram notation, is called the ACP diagram (see Fig. 4)
because it represents the major MASCOT software components

(*) UNIX is a trademark of Bell Labs

namely: Activities, Channels and Pools.

An Activity is a process which can execute conceptually in parallel with all other activities and is represented as a circle with its name inside it. Channels and Pools are the two classes of Intercommunication Data Area (IDA) which provide the sole means by which one Activity may communicate with another. Channels which are used to represent data flow between producers and consumers, are represented by the letter 'I' symbol which reinforces the producer/consumer relationship by exhibiting two interfaces. By convention the Activities which write to the Channel are connected to one side of the symbol and all readers are connected to the other side. The direction of data flow is indicated by the arrow head. Pools, which are used to hold non-transient data that may be referenced from more than one Activity, are represented by a square off letter 'U'. Again this symbol aims to reinforce the idea of data accumulation in a Pool as opposed to data flow in the Channel.

2.4.2. Construction: templates and instances. Although the ACP diagram can be considered to be a useful development of the Phillips network diagram, merely changing the shape of some of the symbols cannot achieve the objective of enforcing the designers' intention on to the operational software. In order to achieve this requirement, software is constructed by MASCOT in a special and unusual way.

Once the ACP diagram has been determined by analysing the data flow and parallel processing constraints of the system, each component, in turn, is examined. Each component is potentially different: i.e. each Channel and each Pool can have individual characteristics, each Activity can have a requirement for a unique data processing algorithm. However, it may be found that some components have identical characteristics. In the latter case the idea of a template which defines a component having the required characteristics which may then be instantiated several times is not unusual. In MASCOT this concept of a template to define the characteristics of a required component, and then the creation of instances of that template as required by the particular system being constructed is used for all components. Further, having created instances of the required components, the process of connecting together the components to create the required network is clearly recognisable and a vitally important stage of software construction. This stage is called FORMing. It enables a very large number of possible networks to be constructed from a given set of components and reinforces the concepts of functional modularity and re-usable software.

In order to achieve this capability and enforce the

designers' intentions, it is vitally important that components
which should not fit together are not fitted together. This
implies that the FORM facility must have some understanding
of how components can fit together. This is achieved by each
Channel and Pool template having a unique type indicator, and
by the Activity template having a definition of the number
and type (and their order) of the Channel and Pool instances
to which it must be connected to form a legal network. Thus
the FORM facility will only produce legal networks and any
Activity cannot distinguish any one network from any other.
This means that Activities may not directly refer to other
Activities; they may only communicate directly with the IDAs
they have been connected to by the FORM facility and thence
to the Activities that happen to be also connected to them.
It also means that an Activity can be realistically tested in
a test environment that it is unable to distinguish from the
real operational environment.

2.4.3. IDAs and access procedures. So far we have stated that
Activities may only communicate via IDAs. However, since
Activities are running conceptually in parallel with each
other, there is an obvious requirement for process synchronisation around IDAs and also much potential for real time bugs.
MASCOT recognises these problems and introduces the concept
of the Access Procedure to solve them.

FIG. 5

Figure 5 shows an ACP fragment representing a producer
Activity communicating via a Channel with a consumer Activity.
Figure 6 shows in more detail exactly how the two Activities
achieve their communication via Access Procedures. (The symbol
of arrow with a "squiggle" in it is Phillips' notation for a
procedure call.)
    Thus each Activity calls the one procedure appropriate to
its requirement. In general, the IDA provides an encapsulated
data area with an interface provided by a set of Access Procedures. Thus the IDA with its Access Procedures provides an
interprocess communication mechanism which:

1)   is designed to meet the needs of a particular system
     requirement i.e. the interprocess communication mechanism

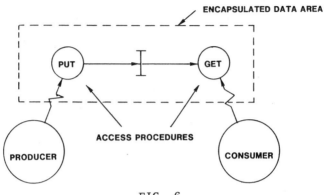

FIG. 6

becomes part of the system design and not (as in a host
of other techniques) a constraint on the system design;
2) hides the internal data structure of the IDA;
3) hides the use of the synchronisation primitives and encapsulates all parallel processing knowledge of the
system;
4) leaves the Activities as single sequential processes free
from any need to know about the existence of other
Activities and hence free to concentrate on the algorithm
they are designed to implement.

In short, the encapsulated data area of the IDA separates the
concerns of real time, synchronisation etc. from straightforward algorithmic concerns. It thus further enhances the
notions of functional modularity and re-usability already well
established in MASCOT by the (design and) construction method.

2.5. MASCOT Kernel

2.5.1. Synchronisation requirement. The major requirement of
the MASCOT kernel is to provide the synchronisation facilities
required by Access Procedures. Since the MASCOT philosophy is
to provide facilities with which the designer/implementor can
create precisely the set of interprocess communication facilities that the system requires, and since the Access Procedure
is the main means by which this is achieved it follows that
the synchronisation facilities provided by the kernel need
not be elaborate and must not pre-empt the designer.
   There are two basic requirements which arise when attempting to synchronise a set of parallel processes:

1) Mutual exclusion.

Mutual exclusion is required when, for any reason, a

process must be sure that no other process can intervene during a critical set of actions. Mutual exclusion allows only one of a set of competing processes to proceed and temporarily holds the competitors until the mutual exclusion requirement no longer exists.

2) Cross stimulation.

Cross stimulation is required where one process needs to be held until signalled by another - examples are: buffer full when writing or buffer empty when reading.

Both of these requirements can be met by standard binary semaphores [4]. However, it is not easily determined from the source text for which purpose a semaphore is currently being used, and worse, it is possible to confuse the two uses with spectacular consequences and without any run-time error being detected.

2.5.2. MASCOT synchronisation. MASCOT synchronisation provides both mutual exclusion and cross stimulation in a far safer and much easier to understand form than the semaphore. The MASCOT synchronisation device is called a "Control Queue" because it is used to control Activities and its use involves the creation of (orderly) queues. There are four primitive operations allowed on Control Queues:

a) JOIN and LEAVE are used when mutual exclusion is required. When an Activity JOINs a Control Queue, it will proceed immediately if no other Activity is currently involved with that Control Queue. In this case the Activity becomes known as the "owner" of that Control Queue. If, when an Activity JOINs a Control Queue, there is already an owner, then the JOINer is held until it works its way to the front of the queue by the action of successive owners LEAVEing the Control Queue when their requirement for mutual exclusion has terminated.

b) WAIT and STIM are used to provide the cross stimulation effect. An Activity may issue a STIM on a Control Queue at any time. The convention is that a STIM is always issued when an Activity completes an action on an IDA which may be of interest to an Activity (if there is one) which might be WAITing in front of the Control Queue for some condition to become true (e.g. buffer not full, buffer not empty). An Activity may only WAIT in front of a Control Queue when it is the owner. The convention is that WAITs are "guarded" by a conditional expression as in the following:

WHILE condition DO WAIT(cq);

Thus the Control Queue mechanism only passes the STIM but it is the Access Procedure's job (by means of the condition) to determine whether he wants to continue processing or not. This is a further example of the separation of concerns in MASCOT:

1) The kernel deals only in synchronisation and understands nothing about the reason for any particular use of the primitives.

2) The use of the primitives and hence the interprocess strategy is firmly in the hands of the Access Procedure writer.

2.5.3. Comparison with semaphores. Finally it is worth noting the following:

a) LEAVE and WAIT are both illegal if called by any Activity other than the current owner. When it is realised that LEAVE corresponds to Dijkstra's 'V' operation and WAIT corresponds to his 'P' operation, it can be seen why semaphores cause problems.

b) STIM is always allowed and a maximum of one STIM is remembered (for consumption by the next WAIT controlled by its guard). When it is realised that STIM corresponds to Dijkstra's 'V' operation, it is clear that this easy and loosely coupled relationship between WAITs and STIMs is completely impossible with semaphores. In particular the semaphore V operation used as a STIM can be confused with the semaphore V operation used as a LEAVE.

3. EXTENDED PASCAL NOTATION (PALE)

The notation described here and used in the rest of the paper has been developed by SDL as part of a Programming Support Environment called "Perspective". Perspective provides a controlled environment primarily for the development of software for embedded microprocessor applications using a host-target approach. Perspective draws on the experience of providing similar facilities for the MOD standard language Coral66 with MASCOT. It has also received significant cross-fertilisation from the USA DOD sponsored language effort for Ada.

3.1. Why Extend Pascal?

The reason for introducing the language extensions to Pascal is simply that, as defined by BSI/ISO, the language is totally unsuitable for developing major commercial or real time projects. This view and the reasons for it are clearly expressed by Wichmann [5]. The major omission from Pascal is any notion of separate compilation or modularity within the language.

The Pascal Language Extensions (PALE) we have introduced have taken some ideas from Ada and some from MASCOT.

3.2. PALE

From Ada comes the notion of separating the specification of an interface from the implementation of the interface. In Ada this notion is introduced by the Package which can have a public specification (i.e. its interface) and a private body (the implementation of the interface). In PALE this very important separation is not only allowed, it is mandatory! PALE introduces two distinct syntactic units for these items:

1) the Interface (to define the externally available characteristics);
2) the Module (to implement exactly one interface).

From MASCOT comes the notion that modularity must be enforced. The concept of universally accessible global data must be totally eliminated. (Note: although this idea is encouraged by Ada supporters, the language itself does not enforce it!) Therefore a further syntactic unit is introduced which is equivalent to the MASCOT notion of an Activity:

3) the Process (defines the algorithm for a parallel process and has a set of parameters which define the interfaces it will use).

Each of the three syntactic units introduced is a separate compilation unit as well as being a modularity unit. This is also derived from MASCOT.

These three units, as defined so far, enable us to represent the software structure we need for MASCOT. The Interface defines the set of Access Procedures provided by an IDA, the Module provides the means of introducing an implementation of an interface, and the Process provides the means of representing the code of an Activity.

3.3. A simple example

Appendix A contains an example of an Interface for a Channel which can be used to pass characters from one Activity to another. It also contains an example of a module which implements this interface, and a Process which uses the interface to provide a duplication function.

Appendix A indicates two other facilities worth mentioning at this point. Firstly, the main body of the module contains the initialisation code for the module. Secondly, it shows that a module has the same capability for using interfaces that a process has. This provides an extra level of modular decomposition over and above that initially suggested by

MASCOT. However it will be shown that exploiting this additional capability can lead to a convenient way of mapping
a MASCOT network on to a multiprocessor hardware configuration.

3.4. A MASCOT Kernel

Appendix B contains an Interface which specifies the MASCOT
kernel interface and a Module which implements the interface.
This is included here primarily for interest. It is hoped
that the implementation is reasonably self-explanatory and
that the comments which have been added to explain the basic
Perspective primitives provide sufficient explanation of them.

4. MULTIPROCESSOR MASCOT STUDY

During the past year SDL has been engaged in a study of the
application of MASCOT to systems which require to be built on
a multiprocessor hardware configuration. The study was funded
by the Ministry of Defence and was performed in conjunction
with RSRE at Malvern. The work of the study can be divided
into two main phases. The first phase looked at how the existing standard of MASCOT could be applied without any en-
hancements to the MASCOT machine and also attempted to provide a method by which software which had previously been
developed to run on a single processor configuration could be
used without change for a multiprocessor application. The
second phase was a more wide-ranging theoretical study which
looked into the possibility of defining extensions to the
MASCOT machine to explicitly handle multiprocessor aspects.
Thus the first phase attempted to identify how or whether the
MASCOT method needed to be constrained in order to cope with
multiprocessor situations, while the second phase aimed to
keep the MASCOT method intact and determine how the MASCOT
machine should be modified as a consequence.

4.1. Porters

The first phase concluded that in any multiprocessor hardware configuration which was going to support a MASCOT network, it was necessary to have a communication medium which
could support the traffic flowing along the many logical paths
between processors. Consequently much of this part of the
study was devoted to defining an appropriate protocol which
could be supported on the extremely wide range of possible
hardware configurations able to be built today. This range
included configurations without any shared store between processors at one end of the spectrum and configurations built
entirely around the concept of shared store (for example,

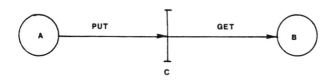

A SIMPLE CHANNEL

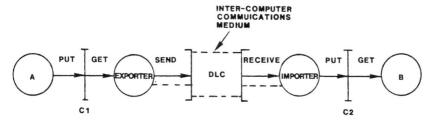

FIG. 7 *Distribution of the simple channel using porters.*

bus systems). Having established that such a communication
mechanism was feasible the study then went on to devise a
method of designing and implementing systems to use such a
communications facility. The concept of "porters" was invented
as a means of satisfying this requirement and the further requirement mentioned above of re-using existing single processor software. The idea is quite simple and is illustrated
in Figure 7. The existing Channel is duplicated so that a
copy appears in each computer. A porter is also introduced
into each computer. These are normal activities which communicate with the duplicated Channel on one side (using the existing Access Procedures) and with the standard communications
mechanism on the other side (using the standard Access Procedures provided for the purpose). Thus the "exporter" takes
data from Channel C1 and passes it to the transmitting port
of the communications IDA. The "importer" performs the inverse
operation and takes the data from the output IDA of the communications medium, reformats it and passes it (using the
previously existing Access Procedure) to the Channel C2. The
logical path between the two Channels C1 and C2 is allocated
a number during the design stage which is passed to the porters as a constant parameter when they are FORMed.
    This approach satisfied the requirement for communication
between a pair of Activities in different computers. It could
also cope quite well with a situation where there were several

writers in one computer communicating with one or more readers
in a different computer. However, it did not provide a general
solution for communication by Channels irrespective of hardware configuration. The situation was worse as far as Pools
were concerned, because the data flow semantics of a Pool are
totally different and one is lead immediately into problems
of multiple copies of data etc.

For these reasons this line of investigation was abandoned.
We will return to discuss an alternative implementation of
the porters concept in the next section, but first we discuss
the second phase of the study.

4.2. Remote Procedure Calls

The second phase of the study started with a review of possible
hardware architectures and looked at how the various components of a MASCOT system could be mapped on to them. The particular MASCOT components considered were:

1) Activity code
2) Access Procedure code
3) MASCOT primitive code
4) MASCOT scheduler code
5) Activity "stack" data (i.e. the Activity's work space
   used by the Activity code and the Access Procedures, and
   in some implementations also by the primitive handler and
   the scheduler)
6) IDA data (exluding Control Queues)
7) Control queues
8) Scheduler data (including Activity descriptors, scheduler
   lists etc.).

In addition the possibility of whether the last three items
were in shared store (and therefore accessible concurrently
by more than one processor) was also considered.

Obviously the combination of all these software options
with all the possible hardware options led to a very large
number of possibilities. Fortunately we were able to see some
simplifications which led to a considerable reduction in
possibilities but without sacrificing any generality. It is
not possible to go into the details here. The reader who is
interested should look in reference [6].

The conclusion of the study was that if an Activity was
considered to consist of a set of co-routines (each one responsible for part of an Activity's execution in a different
computer) of which only one could be executable at any one
time, then there are a number of relatively straightforward
options open. These are discussed briefly below. In all of
these discussions it is a common assumption that the MASCOT

construction mechanism has been extended to allow any System
Element to be positioned within a particular hardware domain.
This, in turn, presupposes that the hardware configuration
has also been described to the MASCOT machine.

4.2.1. Remote Access Procedure calls. When an Activity is
FORMed so that any of the IDAs it references reside in a
different computer to the Activity, then it is possible for
the MASCOT construction mechanism to create a Co-routine of
the Activity in the remote computer. This will be responsible
for calling the normal Access Procedures of that IDA in the
remote computer when the Activity issues a call of that Access
Procedure in its own computer. This presupposes the existence
of a mechanism for transferring a procedure call from one
computer to another. This mechanism is the "remote Access
Procedure call" mechanism. It involves the following steps:

1) gathering the parameters from the calling environment,
2) stopping the calling Activity co-routine,
3) transferring the data of the call to the appropriate co-routine in the computer containing the IDA.
4) setting up the appropriate parameter environment,
5) activating the appropriate co-routine,
6) intercepting the procedure return following its completion,
7) gathering any data to be returned to the caller,
8) stopping the co-routine which has just finished calling the Access Procedure,
9) sending the data back to the calling Activity co-routine,
10) re-establishing the return data in the calling Activity, co-routines' environment,
11) and, finally, allowing the calling Activity co-routines to proceed.

The advantage of this approach is that the existing primitive handlers remain exactly the same, because they do not
have to know about or cope with the multiprocessor aspects.
The mechanisms for calling a remote procedure and returning
from a remote procedure are relatively straightforward assuming that a communication protocol such as that devised in the
first part of the study exists or can be implemented.
Since Access Procedures are always called locally, the
method applies equally well to Pools and Channels and can
cope with any MASCOT network. It should be noted though, that
the designer has the responsibility for deciding how to locate
the components of his network on the hardware configuration in
such a way that the communication overheads which are necessarily involved do not cause any embarrassment. However, it is
right that the designer should be aware of such problems,

because only by being aware can he accomplish his task
properly.

4.2.2. Remote primitive calls. This is one of the proposals
to cope with the shared store situation. The idea is that the
IDA data is in shared store, but that each communicating
Activity will have access to a local copy of the Access Procedure code. Thus there is no need for a remote Access Procedure call. However, it can be shown that a simplification
of the primitive handler can be made if only one processor is
responsible for performing control queue primitives on any
one Control Queue. Therefore, when a Control Queue primitive
is encountered the local primitive handler checks whether it
is responsible for operations on that Control Queue. If so
then it carries on. If not, then it uses the mechanism already
mentioned to call the appropriate primitive in the appropriate
computer. In this case though, the mechanism can be simplified
because the message length is known and there is no need for
return data.

4.2.3. Shared Control Queues. This solution does not require
any remote calling mechanisms, but it does require a hardware
lockout mechanism (semaphore) to protect the Control Queue
from simultaneous access by two or more processors. The problem with this approach is that it is only appropriate to bus
configurations, and it does impose some constraints on the
positioning and manipulation of scheduler lists and Activity
control blocks.

5. PALE AND MULTIPROCESSOR PROBLEMS

In this section we present a representation of some of the
ideas from the multiprocessor study. We have limited this to
the notion of porters and the remote Access Procedure call,
because, when represented in PALE, these two notions do come
remarkably close.

Using the components we introduced earlier and which are
shown in Appendix A, we can use them to produce the network
depicted in Figure 8. If we now choose to put each activity
in a different computer as indicated in Figure 9 by the dotted
line areas, then we need to have a different implementation
of the interface as shown. The new module, instead of using
the MASCOT kernel interface in its implementation, uses an
inter-computer communications interface. This, in turn, uses
the MASCOT kernel.

The interesting question to ask now is this: "Does this
represent an implementation of porters or remote Access
Procedure calling?"

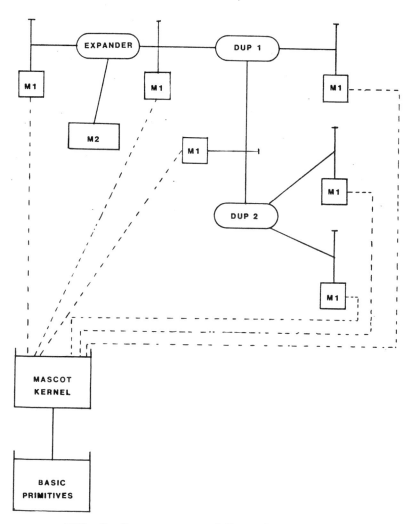

FIG. 8 *Processes, modules, interfaces.*

In fact the answer is "Yes"! It is an implementation of
porters because there are two instances of the channel implemented using the communications subsystem, but it is far more
efficient because there is less context switching. On the
other hand, it can also be argued that this is a representation of remote Access Procedure calling, because it represents
what the underlying mechanisms would have to do. The transmitting side takes the parameter information, formats it for
transmission and could wait for a reply from the receiving

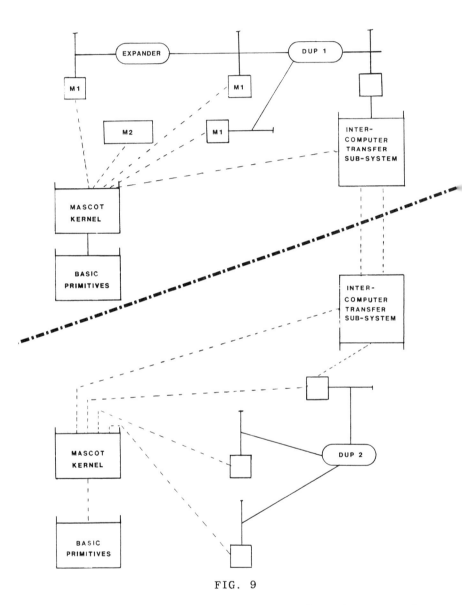

FIG. 9

side before continuing (if it did not wait this would violate
the co-routine semantics). The receiving side takes the information from the communications interface and formats for
the normal Access Procedure call. Thus the question of which
one of the two approaches is implemented by this network come
down to the question of whether the transmitting side waits

for the receiving side to complete before it continues. This
seems like splitting hairs and therefore it is suggested that
the PALE approach gives the designer plenty of scope and freedom to handle multiprocessor systems.

6. CONCLUSION

We have reviewed MASCOT and discussed its application to
multiprocessor systems. It is clear that MASCOT as it is
currently formulated can be used for multiprocessor systems,
because the author knows of such applications of MASCOT. However, these all treat each computer as a separate system.
There are already MASCOT machines which do support multiprocessor applications, but these support only shared store
configurations. The study has suggested two approaches which
can be adopted to cope with non-shared store configurations.
The Pascal language extensions (PALE) developed for Perspective offer an alternative approach which can efficiently
support both of these approaches.

REFERENCES

1. Phillips, C.S.E. (1968). Networks for real-time programming.
   BCS Computer Journal.
2. "Angus-Product Description". Systems Designers Limited,
   1 Pembroke Broadway, Camberley, Surrey, UK.
3. RSRE (1980). "Official Handbook of MASCOT". RSRE, Malvern.
4. Dijkstra, E.W. (1968). Cooperating sequential processes.
   In "Programming Languages", (Ed. F. Genuys). Academic
   Press, New York.
5. Wichmann, B.A. (1982). A comparison of Pascal and Ada.
   BCS Computer Journal 25, No.2.
6. Defence Research Information Centre (1982). Final Report
   of a Study into the Application of MASCOT to Multiprocessor Systems. Defence Research Information Centre,
   St Mary Cray, Kent, UK.

APPENDIX A
INTERFACE, MODULE AND PROCESS EXAMPLES

```
INTERFACE charchan;

    PROCEDURE put (c:CHAR);
    FUNCTION  get : CHAR;
END.


MODULE charchan__body (mk: mascot): charchan;
{This module:
             -   uses the interface "mascot"
                 implements the interface "charchan".}
VAR buffer:CHAR;
    full : BOOLEAN;
    inq,outq:mk.controlq;

    ACCESS PROCEDURE put (c:CHAR);
        BEGIN
            mk.join(inq);
                WHILE full DO mk.wait(inq);
                buffer:= c;
                full := TRUE;
                mk.stim(outq);
            mk.leave(inq)
        END;

    ACCESS FUNCTION get : CHAR;
        BEGIN
            mk.join(outq);
                WHILE not full DO mk.wait(outq);
                get := buffer;
                full := FALSE;
                mk.stim(inq);
            mk.leave(outq)
        END;
BEGIN
    mk.init__cq( inq);
    mk.init__cq(outq),
    full := FALSE;
END.


INTERFACE, MODULE AND PROCESS EXAMPLES.


PROCESS duplicate (in, out1, out2 : charchan);
BEGIN
    DO BEGIN
            c:= in.get;
            out1.put(c);
            out2.put(c);
        END
END.
SYSTEM triplication
    in, out1, out2, out3 : charchan BY charchan_body;
    dupl : duplicate (in, out1, inter);
    dup2 : duplicate (inter, out2, out3);
END.
```

APPENDIX B
MASCOT KERNEL WRITTEN IN EXTENDED PASCAL


```
INTERFACE mascot;
  TYPE CONTROLQ = ^ACTUAL_CONTROL_Q,
       REF_ACT = ^ACTIVITY,
       REF_LIST = ^LIST;

       LIST = RECORD
                 front : REF_ACT,
                 back  : REF_ACT,
              END;

       ACTUAL_CONTROL_Q = RECORD
                            owner         : REF_ACT;
                            waiter        : BOOLEAN;
                            stimmed       : BOOLEAN;
                            pending_list  : REF_LIST,
                            next_controlq : CONTROLQ,
                          END;
       ACTIVITY = RECORD
                    pid        : PROCESS_IDENTITY;
                    owned_cqs  : CONTROLQ;
                    priority   : INTEGER;   { should be process_priority }
                    next_act   : REF_ACT;
                  END;

  PROCEDURE join  (cq:CONTROLQ);
  PROCEDURE leave (cq:CONTROLQ);
  PROCEDURE wait  (cq:CONTROLQ);
  PROCEDURE stim  (cq:CONTROLQ);
  PROCEDURE suspend ;
  PROCEDURE init_cq (VAR cq:CONTROLQ);

END.


MODULE mascot_body : MASCOT;

  CONST num_priority = 4;
        defaultp     = 4;

  VAR current_activity : REF_ACT,
      sched_list       : ARRAY [1..num_priority] OF REF_LIST;

      i                : INTEGER,
      nextp            : PROCESS_IDENTITY;
      new_act          : REF_ACT,

  PROCEDURE add_to_back (act : REF_ACT, list : REF_LIST);
  BEGIN
    IF list^.front = NIL THEN
    BEGIN
      list^.front := act;
      act^.next_act := NIL;
    END
    ELSE
    BEGIN
      list^.back^.next_act := act;
    END;
      list^.back := act;
  END;
```

APPENDIX B (continued)


```
FUNCTION remove_front (list : REF_LIST) : REF_ACT;
BEGIN
  remove_front := list^.front;
  IF list^.front = list^.back
  THEN list^.front := NIL      { not necessary to set list.back to nil }
  ELSE list^.front := list^.front^.next_act
END;

PROCEDURE reschedule;

  VAR i : integer;

BEGIN
  i := 1;
  { allow interrupt in case nothing to do }
  WHILE sched_list[i]^.front = NIL DO
    IF i < num_priority
    THEN i := i+1
    ELSE i := 1;

  { inhibit interrupts }
  current_activity := remove_front (sched_list[i]);
  schedule (current_activity^.pid) { tells Perspective to remember the
                                     state of the current process and
                                     begin execution of the process
                                     whose process id is in the paramete
END;


PROCEDURE EXCEPTION (message : INTEGER);
BEGIN
  write('exception no ');
  writeln(message);
END;


ACCESS PROCEDURE JOIN (cq : CONTROLQ);
BEGIN
  WITH cq^ DO
  BEGIN
    IF owner = NIL THEN
    BEGIN
      owner := current_activity;
      next_controlq := current_activity^.owned_cqs;
      current_activity^.owned_cqs := cq;
    END
    ELSE
    BEGIN
      add_to_back (current_activity, pending_list);
      reschedule
    END
  END
END;
```

APPENDIX B (continued)

```
ACCESS PROCEDURE LEAVE (cq . CONTROLQ);
VAR this_cq : CONTROLQ;

BEGIN
  WITH cq^ DO
  BEGIN
    IF owner <> current_activity
    THEN exception(1)    { leave_not_owner }
    ELSE
    BEGIN
      owner := remove_front (pending_list);
      IF owner <> NIL
      THEN add_to_back (owner,sched_list[owner^.priority]);
      this_cq := current_activity^.owned_cqs;
      IF this_cq <> cq
      THEN WHILE this_cq^.next_controlq <> cq DO
        this_cq := this_cq^.next_controlq;
      this_cq^.next_controlq := cq^.next_controlq
    END
  END
END;


ACCESS PROCEDURE wait (cq : CONTROLQ);
BEGIN
  WITH cq^ DO
  BEGIN
    IF owner <> current_activity
    THEN exception (2)          { wait_not_owner }
    ELSE
    BEGIN
      IF stimmed
      THEN stimmed := false
      ELSE
      BEGIN
        waiter := true;
        reschedule
      END
    END
  END
END;


ACCESS PROCEDURE stim (cq : CONTROLQ);
BEGIN
  WITH cq^ DO
  BEGIN
    IF waiter THEN
    BEGIN
      waiter := false;
      add_to_back (owner, sched_list[owner^.priority]);
    END
    ELSE stimmed := true
  END
END;
```

APPENDIX B (continued)


```
ACCESS PROCEDURE init_cq (VAR cq : CONTROLQ);
BEGIN
  NEW (cq);
  WITH cq^ DO
  BEGIN
    owner := NIL;
    waiter := false;
    stimmed := false;
    pending_list := NIL;
    next_controlq := NIL;
  END
END;


ACCESS PROCEDURE SUSPEND;
BEGIN
  add_to_back (current_activity, sched_list[current_activity^.priority
  reschedule
END;


BEGIN
  FOR i := 1 to num_priority DO
  BEGIN
    NEW (sched_list[i]);
    sched_list[i]^.front := NIL;
  END;

  nextp := next_process; { primitive function to obtain next process
                           from Perspective construction system.
                           Delivers NIL when list exhausted.}
  WHILE nextp <> NIL DO
  BEGIN
    NEW (new_act);
    WITH new_act^ DO
    BEGIN
      pid := nextp;
      owned_cqs := NIL;
      priority := defaultp;
      add_to_back (new_act, sched_list[priority]);
    END;
    nextp := next_process;
  END;
  reschedule; { during initialisation the schedule primitive
                called by this procedure  tells Perspective
                which process must be executed when initialicsation is
                complete }
END.
```

Part 3

Local Area Networks and Distributed Systems

Architecture of the CHORUS Distributed System

Jean-Serge Banino

1. INTRODUCTION

Computing systems design has to face up to technological progress in two fields. First, the large-scale production of
microcomputers has induced penetration of computer science in
wider application domains and also allowed specialization and
autonomy of dedicated equipment. Second, the communication
techniques have become more and more efficient; examples are
the large packet-switching networks, high-bandwidth local networks, and now communications via satellites. Therefore it
has become technologically and economically feasible to design
dedicated applications as a set of specialized computing
equipment interconnected via a communication medium and
organized in such a way that they co-operate. Under this
hypothesis, a large benefit is obtained due to the modularity
of the system, flexibility and probably reduced software development costs. But in order to reach this point in distributed computing systems engineering, one needs to have on
each computer an operating system relying on concepts adequate
to the distributed nature of applications.

The CHORUS project is oriented towards this objective. It
consists of designing a run-time architecture for distributed
systems and building an operating system kernel intended to
support this architecture with the aim to get at the system
level the same degree of flexibility as the hardware architecture. Currently a first version of the system has been
designed and implemented on a network of microcomputers interconnected through a local broadcast network.

In this paper, Section 2 is a description of the main

Distributed Computing Systems
ISBN 0-12-543970-9

features of the CHORUS system architecture. Section 3 presents
examples of CHORUS services, as they are implemented in the
first prototype. In Section 4 will be found considerations on
our current and future work.

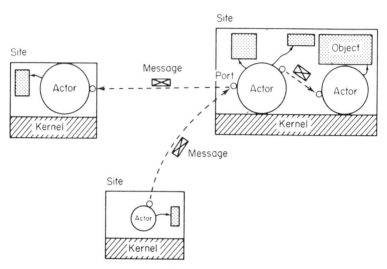

FIG. 1 *Run-time architecture of CHORUS system*

2. THE CHORUS SYSTEM

2.1. Overview of the Architecture

The CHORUS system is designed to support execution of distributed applications. Such an application is seen, at run-time,
as a set of elementary execution granules, called processing
steps. A processing step is sequential. Its action can affect
only local objects, i.e. objects of the site. The execution
environment of a processing step is an actor. An actor is
sequential, i.e. it performs one processing step after the
other. The logical chaining between processing steps is done
with messages: a processing step is triggered within an actor
by reception of a message by this actor. Conversely completion
of a processing step can cause the sending of one or several
messages to actors. Messages are sent and received by actors
through ports. Lastly, an actor can access an object only if
it has got a link to it. The execution of an actor is supported and controlled by the operating system kernel of its
site. In particular controls apply to exchange of messages
and to linkage of actors to objects. Figure 1 is an illustration of this run-time architecture.

Services are implemented within the CHORUS architecture by

actors. For example, system resources (memory, devices, ports,
actors, communication paths, ...) are handled by system actors.
User actors invoke system services by means of system service
calls which can be executed either asynchronously or synchronously. The effect of a system service call is to run, in the
calling actor context, an interface procedure which handles
communications with the service actor(s).

2.2. Basic Concepts in CHORUS

2.2.1. Control of execution. In order to design the CHORUS
architecture we started from the observation of dynamic
aspects in both centralized and decentralized computing systems. A common notion for these two kinds of systems is that
they have to support execution and co-operation of independent processes. In centralized systems the privileged way to
achieve synchronization and communication for processes is
sharing objects. In order to control this kind of interaction,
methods and tools are developed, for example structured programming, functional or data abstraction, proofs and synthesis
of programs. The case of distributed systems is different
since communication by messages is the basic means for co-
operation. In the same way theoretical and practical tools
are defined to control this activity; examples are methods
for specification, validation and synthesis of protocols.
    We found it worthwhile to give to the designer of a distri-
buted application the ability to adopt both points of view,
i.e. processing-driven or communication-driven execution control. Therefore, in CHORUS processing is organized as follows.
    The processing step is the elementary quantum of execution.
It is performed sequentially by an actor which is the local
and sequential active entity. A processing step is triggered
in an actor on reception of a message by this actor. Conversely completion of a processing step may cause the sending
of one or several messages. So, a distributed system is viewed
at run-time, as a network of processing steps connected by
messages (Fig. 2).
    Messages computed during a processing step are emitted
only at the end of the processing step. Therefore, if the
processing step does not complete, no one message is emitted.

2.2.2. The actors - the kernel. The CHORUS architecture is
designed to support implementation of the processing model
described in the previous section.
    The execution environment for a processing step is the
actor. An actor can be viewed, in a first approximation, as
a sequential process. But it is activated on reception of a
message, and at the end of the corresponding processing step

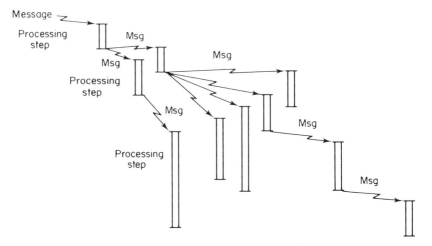

FIG. 2 *Processing steps connected by messages*

can send other messages. Inside the actor, processing steps
are performed one after the other.

The function of the CHORUS kernel is to support execution –
of the processing step, to achieve local transmission of
messages at the end of the processing step, and to select the
next processing step to be triggered, either in the same actor
or in another one. At this level, the kernel can be viewed as
an extended machine. Interrupts are received by the kernel,
which changes them into messages processed by system actors.

For the sake of simplicity and reliability the kernel is
kept minimum and most operating system-oriented functions are
performed by actors. Facilities provided by the kernel are
described as services which can be called upon by actors and
executed at the end of the processing step only. In other
words, the kernel services are called and executed by the
actor in a single, indivisible phase at the end of the processing step.

2.2.3. Ports - communications between actors. Actors communicate by exchanging messages through ports. A message is sent
from one port of the sending actor towards one (or several)
destination port(s) of the receiving actor(s). Ports are bidirectional, i.e. the same port can be used for sending and
for receiving messages as well. This choice results from the
consideration that most communications are bidirectional. In
addition this facilitates loopback with ports sending messages
to themselves which proved to be extremely valuable for tests
and maintenance.

Sending of a message is performed as a service offered by the kernel:

SEND (Source port, destination port(s), message);

The indication of a source port in the SEND primitive has two justifications:

1) it allows to perform appropriate controls on the sent message;
2) it may be used by the receiving actor to identify the source of the message e.g. for a reply.

Actors have a uniform view of communications whether local or remote. They do not need to know where the destination port(s) is located. Ports are identified, at the systems level, by global unique names. The communication with a remote port may involve protocols with the destination site. For handling these protocols, the kernel will call service actors but this is hidden to application actors. The uniform view of all communications between actors is essential for easy reconfigurations of distributed activities.

Execution of a SEND service causes copies of the message to be queued at the receiving port(s) after a variable delay with some probability of success. In the absence of flow control (basic communication facility), overflow of the receiver(s) capacity causes additional message to be discarded.

The SEND service provides a low level of service; a general purpose time-out mechanism will be used in order to cover such cases as loss of a message expected by an actor or failure of a correspondent from which a response is expected:

TIME-OUT (Port, time);

This service means that if no message is received on "Port" during "time" (starting now), the kernel sends an error message on Port. Conversely, if one message is received on "Port" during "time", the time-out is disabled.

A send control procedure associated with each port permits the kernel to check the validity of messages being sent by the actor. Conversely, a receive control procedure associated with each port permits the kernel to check the validity of messages being received by actors. This decomposition of controls on communications into two parts (sending side and receiving side) matches physical distribution and provides each actor with its own autonomous protection. These controls may, for instance, be used to check message-types, passwords and so on.

Ports function only when associated with actors, i.e. a message destined to a port not currently associated with an actor will be lost. One port can be associated with only one

actor at a time, but an actor can have several ports. Establishment and release of an association between a port and an
actor is performed as system services offered by the port
management service implemented into several system actors.
The interface of this service is

        CREATE-PORT (port-name, initial parameters)
        OPEN-PORT (port-name, priority)
        CLOSE-PORT (port-name)
        DESTROY-PORT (port-name)

When execution of the CREATE-PORT service is completed, the
calling actor receives a port-name as a result parameter.
    Dissociation between creation and opening ports allows to
open the same port (i.e. with the same name-port) in two
different actors consequently. This mechanism is provided for
dynamic reconfigurations.
    More generally, the main reason to introduce the concept
of ports is to decouple organization of communication from
organization of processing. A correspondent is primarily interested in the functions being performed behind ports and
not in the way these functions are implemented. Usage of ports
permits for instance to reorganize actors which provide a
function behind a set of ports; actors which use this function
have not to be aware of this reorganization.

2.2.4. **Internal operation of actors.** CHORUS attempts to provide consistent schemes for organizing communications and
processing. Messages which are the basic communication units
are also the basic processing units.
    Actors send messages, receive messages and process messages
as well. For the sake of simplicity, each actor processes
only one message at a time; a processing-step is designated
by its entry-point in the actor's code; a processing-step
does not include any kind of WAIT operation. Parallelism, if
required, can be obtained by using several actors. Actors are
simply sequential message processors.
    A selection procedure associated with each actor permits
the kernel to determine which message, if any, is to be processed next. Parameters of the selection procedure can be
modified by the actor in order to influence dynamically the
selection policy, using the kernel service SELECT. The selection could for instance be restricted to a unique message
which the actor is waiting for, or to messages coming from a
given port, and so on .... The syntax of the call is:

                    SELECT (Port, condition);

where "condition" may be:

1) all; means that every message received on "Port" may be selected;
2) a list of ports; means that only a message sent from a port of the list onto "Port" may be selected.

When a message has been selected, a switch procedure permits the kernel to determine which entry-point must be entered to process the message. The SWITCH kernel service permits an actor to modify dynamically the switch parameters:

SWITCH (Port, entry-point);

means that messages received on "Port" have to be processed by the processing-step designated by "entry-point".

The end of a processing-step consists of calling the kernel by means of the primitive RETURN.

In order to decouple communication from processing, as said previously, messages sent by an actor are really emitted only at the end of the current processing-step.

In conclusion, invocation of kernel services (SELECT, SWITCH, TIME-OUT, SEND) are realized by the kernel in the RETURN primitive execution, in an indivisible way.

At the end of the processing-step, i.e. after completion of the kernel services calls, the actor is ready again for scheduling. That means that if a new message is present on one of its ports, and if the selection conditions fit, the actor is potentially schedulable.

At the time of its creation, every port is given a priority. After completion of the current processing-step, the kernel, which handles a table of all the ports present on the site, will select among them the one with the highest priority which has a message to process, according to its selection parameters. The actor owning this port is then started for the processing-step corresponding to the entry-point associated at this time to the selected port.

2.2.5. Objects. Objects exist independently of actors. However, objects are passive entities and nothing happens to objects unless acted upon by local actors.

In order to manipulate a local object, an actor must get a link to it. Establishment and release of links to local objects are performed as system services offered by the object management service

LINK (Object);
UNLINK (Object);

A linkage control procedure associated with the object permits the kernel to determine whether the actor is entitled to establish a link to the object (this is very similar to

linking a segment to a process with associated controls).
Once the link has been established, the kernel does not
necessarily control what the actor does on the object (in
contrast with capability-machines where each access is further
tightly controlled). The controls depend on the ability of the
machine. The actor as a whole is supposed to behave correctly,
i.e. possible errors in the manipulation of the object by the
actor are not controlled by the kernel; in other words, the
actor is the elementary protection domain.

CHORUS permits objects to be directly shared between actors
i.e. one object can be simultaneously linked to several actors
(if this is authorized by the link control procedure). The
main reason for making direct sharing possible is to reduce
overheads in actors switching by the kernel when the frequency
of access to a shared object is high. The alternative scheme
is to have one single actor responsible for all accesses to
the object and communicating with others by messages. One
advantage of this indirect sharing is that all actors need
not be on the same site.

2.2.6. Actor creation. Actors are created dynamically by
calling the actor management service implemented as a set of
system actors.

The effect of this system service is to create and to
initialize the new actor from what is called a model of actor.

A model of actor is constituted with:

1) the code that the actor will run,
2) the description of its execution structure,
3) the actor-creation control procedure,
4) the actor-destruction control procedure,
5) the interface procedures for the system service calls,
   etc. ...

From one given model of actor it is possible to create as
many actors as wanted. When an actor is created, the actor
management service loads it in memory, gives it a first port
called umbilical port and sends on this port an initial
message containing parameters for its initialization. This
message triggers the first processing step of the actor,
which performs its own initialization.

It is possible to create an actor either locally or re-
motely. The system service call has the following expression:

CREATE-ACTOR(MODEL OF ACTOR, SITE, INITIAL MESSAGE)

where "SITE" is the name of the site where the created actor
will be installed.

2.3. Structure of an Application Built on the CHORUS System

An application implemented with the CHORUS system is built as shown in Figure 3.

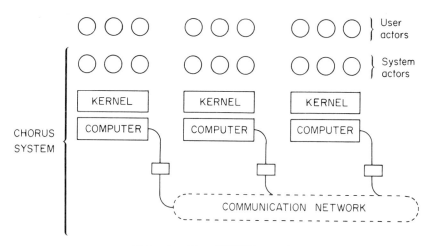

FIG. 3 *The CHORUS system.*

Application actors, or user actors, have the possibility to invoke CHORUS systems services. Services are implemented into system actors.

For example, there are management routines for port, actor, file, device, memory and object. Each of these services is implemented into one or several actors. Services implemented in system actors are called via system service calls which execute either asynchronously, or synchronously with the user actor.

The synchronous call is equivalent to a classical procedure call. In order to realize this mode of invocation, the kernel offers a second primitive, noted EP-CALL (for External Procedure Call). This primitive has the following syntax:

EP-CALL (P, Q, Message, Time).

An actor can invoke it in the course of a processing step. The effect of this invocation is to block the calling actor on this primitive, to send the Message from one of its ports (P) towards port Q, and to temporarily modify the selection parameters so that to select either the reply message (from Q to P) or a time-out message on this port (P). On reception of the reply, the previous selection parameters are restored and the current processing step can continue.

3. EXAMPLES OF SYSTEM SERVICES

3.1. Dynamic Actor Creation

One of the services provided by the CHORUS system is the
ability to create and destroy actors dynamically. This service
is realized by the "Actor Manager" actor (AM actor); this
actor is present on each site.

The assumption in the example (for the sake of simplicity)
is that the creation is requested on a site where the model
of actor is available. The creation is requested by a message
sent onto a port of the "AM actor". This message contains:

1) the name of the model of actor
2) the initial message (embedded in the creation message)
3) the name of a port on which the creation reply message
    is to be sent.

The reception of this message starts a sequence of processing
steps which is summarized below:

1) The actor AM sends a message to the "Memory Manager" (MM)
    actor to ask for some memory space.
2) The Memory Manager (MM) actor determines some place in
    the memory where the actor will be loaded depending on
    the memory policy. If no room is available, the memory
    request is rejected (and therefore forgotten); the actor
    is not created. MM sends to AM a reply message containing
    the location of the actor being created.
3) The AM actor sends a message to the "File Manager" actor
    to load the actor from the model of actor (which is on a
    file).
4) The File Manager actor is allowed to transfer data from
    secondary memory into main memory outside of its bounds;
    the model of actor is loaded directly in the location
    where the actor will reside.
5) The AM actor checks the validity of the creation with
    respect to the identity of the requesting actor and para-
    meters contained in the model of actor.
6) The AM actor sends a message to the "Name Manager" actor
    to ask for a name for the newly created actor.
7) After receiving the reply of Name Manager the AM actor
    sends a message to the "Port Manager" actor to ask it to
    create and open the umbilical port of the new actor. This
    request is reserved to the AM actor, as any other actor
    may open only its own ports.
8) After receiving the reply of Port Manager, the AM actor
    gives the kernel (by means of a special kernel service
    invocation) the definition of the actor in order to insert
    it in an entry of the actor table of the kernel.

9) The AM actor sends a "positive reply message" onto the appropriate port of the requesting actor. It also sends the initial message onto the umbilical port of the newly created actor.

Destruction of an actor triggers a similar, albeit simpler, sequence of processing steps.
   Some remarks about this description:

1) The specific role of the kernel is very reduced: it acquires information (existence and name of the actor, existence of a port, etc. ...) without any processing.
2) The whole creation is a complex operation but it involves several actors and the job of each actor is rather simple: the design of the system as a set of actors helps in gaining modularity and simplicity.
3) Several creations may be performed in parallel so long as the AM actor keeps a record of the current creations. The following mechanism helps in installing this: each message sent to request a system service contains a "user code"; this user code is provided by the sender of the message. The response message associated with the request message contains the same user code. Therefore, an actor may send several identical requests together with different "user codes" and distinguishes easily the corresponding answers.

3.2. The File Server Actor

In CHORUS, files are not directly accessed by user actors; they are managed by server actors called File Server Actors (FSA). For a user actor, accesses to files are performed through exchange of messages.
   This section describes the structure and interface of a simple FSA, i.e. an FSA which manages only local files, for local or remote actors. Access to a file is performed within a session. A user actor opens a session indicating its mode of access to the file: read only, read and write, rewrite, etc. ... Conflicts may arise between simultaneous sessions to the same file. The FSA applies some policy according to the application, in order to synchronize readers and writers and may reject or suspend the opening request. When an actor does not need a file any more, it closes its sessions. Time-outs may prevent deadlocks if an actor fails and never closes its session.
   Within a session, an actor may read and write a file. Information read or to be written is transferred in messages. The FSA has a public port on which the session opening messages are sent. And for each file, the FSA opens a new port on which all requests concerning the same file are sent.

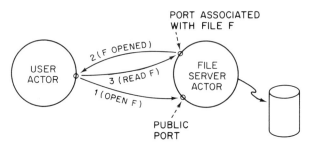

FIG. 4 *Local access to files.*

Conversely, each user actor must use the same port for sending
(and receiving) its request; this port is its identification.
Example of the first messages exchanged for the opening and
the first access to a file is given in Figure 4.

For the FSA, a file is a stream of bytes (as in UNIX).
Each user of a file is associated with a pointer on the file
which indicates the current byte in the file. Four elementary
operations are offered to access files:

READ(n)   : read n bytes starting from the pointer
WRITE(n) : write n bytes starting from the pointer
LOOK   : given the current position of the pointer
SEEK(p)   : set the pointer to a given value.

Using the simple FSA described above, more complex FSAs
may be built offering other services. For instance:

1) One FSA on each site. When a user needs to access a file,
    it sends an opening request message to its local FSA. If
    the file is local, the protocol is as above. If the file
    is remote, the local FSA, in co-operation with other re-
    mote FSAs finds which FSA handles the file and transmits
    the opening request to it. The rest of the session is as
    above. The schema in Figure 5 illustrates this situation.
2) Another construction of FSA may be to offer other services
    than only the access of files. Additional services may
    be: transfer of files, handling multiple copies of a
    file, hierarchical structure of files, protection of
    files, loading of actors in memory, etc.

4. CURRENT WORK AND CONCLUSION

A first version of the CHORUS system has been implemented on
a set of Intel 80/86 microcomputers interconnected through a
local broadcast network. A second implementation is now

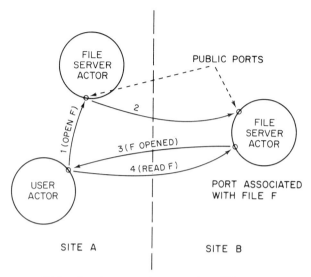

FIG. 5 *Access to remote files.*

started on a set of multi-microprocessors named SM90. This
very modular architecture has been designed by our colleagues
from CNET (National Research Centre for Telecommunications).
The machine can be composed of several (up to 8) computing
modules, each of them equipped with either a Motorola 68000,
or an NS 16000 or a 32-bit microprocessor. We are implementing
CHORUS on the 68000 version.

CHORUS will run in the machine in the same way as in a
network: each module will support an independent kernel and
a set of actors. This offers the advantage to get the same
degree of flexibility inside one machine as in the network
itself.

This implementation will reflect the results of our current research in the following main directions: fault-
tolerance, protection and security, specification and expression of distributed processing.

ACKNOWLEDGEMENT

This paper is the outcome of joint work by the research team
including A. Caristan, C. Gailliard, M. Guillemont, G.
Morisset and H. Zimmermann.

FURTHER READING

Banino, J.-S., Caristan, A., Guillemont, M., Morisset, G. and
Zimmermann, H. (1980). CHORUS: an architecture for distributed systems. *Rapport INRIA* 42, 68.
Banino, J.-S. and Fabré, J.C. (1982). Distributed coupled
actors: a CHORUS proposal for reliability. *In* "Proc. 3rd
Int. Conf. on Distributed Computing Systems", p.7. Ft
Lauderdale, Miami, Florida, USA.
Finger, U. and Médigue, G. (1981). Architectures multi-
microprocesseurs et disponibilité: la SM90. *L'écho des
recherches* 105, 15-21.
Guillemont, M. (1982). The CHORUS distributed operating
system: design and implementation. *In* "Proc. Int. Symposium
on Local Computer Networks", pp.207-223. Florence, Italy.
Zimmermann, H., Banino, J.-S., Caristan, A., Guillemont, M.
and Morisset, G. (1981). Basic concepts for the support of
distributed systems: the CHORUS approach. *In* "Proc. 2nd
Int. Conf. on Distributed Computing Systems", pp.60-66.
Versailles, France.

Local Area Networks for Distributed Process Control Systems

Michel Dang, Guy Mazaré and Gérard Michel

1. INTRODUCTION

Within the past decade we can observe the emergence of different classes of Local Area Networks, LAN [1]. The first one,
LAN1, aims at supporting a wide range of data processing
applications:

1) in a commercial environment, like ETHERNET for example
   [2] whose target is the office automation applications,
2) or in a scientific laboratory environment such as the
   NEWHALL loop [3], the CAMBRIDGE ring [4], the OHIO distributed loops [5].

The local networks of the second class, LAN2, are designed
to be used in an industrial environment for process control
and other real-time applications; they are, in most cases,
multi-access bus networks: serial bus as in the PROWAY project
[6], or parallel bus like IEEE 488 [7], CAMAC dataway [8].
    The last but not the least, the possible third class of
LAN, LAN3, is sandwiched between the two previous ones; it
aims at offering to users working in a factory or in an institution, the following services: telephone, "telematique"
(including videotext), office automation and data transfer
(for connecting peripheral devices to a central computer or
for accessing remote data bases); CARTHAGE [9] is a well-
known LAN of this class.
    Designers of these three classes of LAN are from different
origins:

1) In the first class, it is quite difficult to characterize
   the origins of LAN1 designers - perhaps it is due to the

Distributed Computing Systems
ISBN 0-12-543970-9

very wide range of applications supported by this class
of LAN - however we can note that among LAN1 designers,
many of them are working on general networks (such as
packet switching network, radio network), or more generally
on computer science.

2) In the second class, the electronic and electrotechnical
    origin of LAN2 designers is beyond contest.

3) In the last class, the LAN3 designers come from the tele-
    communication and telephony world, in most cases.

These designers have different targets. But the economic
constraints, the necessity to obey standards (to be conformed
to, to be adopted or to be defined), the existence of common
characteristics in their definitions and in their applications,
condemn them, sooner or later, to converge. We suppose this
convergence begins with LAN1 and LAN3.

First of all, we shall try to explain these convergent features and to describe the still divergent characteristics between the LAN2 class of local networks and the others. For this
purpose, we will compare standards to proposed-to-be-standards
in each group; this comparison will be made in relation with
the OSI (Open Systems Interconnection)[10] reference model.

These observations will be made up with a descriptive approach. They will intend to give an overview of the multiple
aspects of local networks, especially local networks for industrial process control. They will lead us to general considerations about major problems which need solutions or
further studies in real-time systems distributed on local
networks. Though these considerations will be given in a top-
down approach, we do not ignore that in this area, the main
and favourite approach of designers is bottom-up [11].

Anyway, solutions to each problem must be compared in
terms of effective realization cost. It appears then that the
temptation to solve some real-time problems at the upper
levels (OSI levels 7,6,5,4) is more expensive and less precise
than doing it at the lower levels (OSI levels 1,2). This
remark will be illustrated in the design of a VLSI communication circuit intended for industrial process control in
the CNET/CNS Laboratory of Meylan.

2. COMPARISON BETWEEN LOCAL AREA NETWORKS FOR INDUSTRIAL PURPOSES AND OTHER LOCAL AREA NETWORKS

2.1. Convergent Features

There are many common requirements between industrial and
other applications supported by local area networks:

1) length of the communication medium (1 to 2 km)*,
2) number of statically and/or dynamically connected
   stations (64 to 256),
3) packet length (128 to 256 bytes),
4) transmission rate (1 M bits to 10 M bits per second).

In addition to these quantified features, we can mention the common requirements of [12,13]:

1) heterogeneity to facilitate the connection of heterogene-
   ous devices and equipments,
2) ease to maintain,
3) data and/or address integrity,
4) possibility to connect and to disconnect stations when
   the system is running.

On the other hand several advantages given by the distri-buted characteristics of the system are identically perceived by the three communities such as modularity, versatility, parallelism, and better sharing of resources.

Of course, some constraints also appear such as the neces-sity of synchronization, of event ordering, and problem of allocation and re-allocation of resources.

As far as the communication medium is concerned, designers of all these local area networks have fairly often chosen the same solutions among the following ones:

1) as physical media:
   a) paired cable: LNA, EPI 2000,
   b) coaxial cable: ETHERNET, DANUBE,
   c) optical fibre: CARTHAGE, HITACHI DFW;

2) as transmission mode:
   a) base band: ETHERNET, EPI 2000 (let us notice that the
      Manchester code is very often chosen),
   b) wide band: CABLENET;

3) as architecture of the communication support:
   a) types of link: two-way-alternate, two-way-simultaneous,
   b) types of interconnection: point to point, or multi-
      point,
   c) topologies of the network:
      - simple loop, double loop: DCLN, DDCLN, HITACHI DFW,
        LNA, CARTHAGE,
      - totally or partially interconnected network: RHEA,
      - bus like: REBUS, EPI 2000, ETHERNET, CABLENET, CAMAC,
        IEEE 488, PROWAY;

4) as media access control algorithms [1,14,15]:

---

* The values given between brackets are average ones.

a) election algorithms:
   - by polling method,
   - by selection,
   - by "time slot" techniques,
b) competition or contention algorithms: ETHERNET, LISA,
   Note: under heavily loaded conditions [16], though the
         ETHERNET network remains stable (no congestion),
         the degradation of its utilization is a source
         of criticism by LAN2 designers.
c) token passing algorithms: NEWHALL LOOP, PRIMENET, LNA,
d) empty slot algorithms: PIERCE LOOP, CAMBRIDGE LOOP,
e) buffer insertion algorithms: DLCN, DDLCN.

Note: we must mention other mixed techniques where, for
      example, in CARTHAGE, an algorithm for media access
      control (token passing) and another one for media
      access (time devision multiplexing) are used.

2.2. Divergent Features

Unfortunately, several LAN features are defined or bounded
quite differently by the designers of LAN2 and the others. We
intend to present these characteristics in this paragraph as
well as to discuss the motivation for a need of resolution
and to propose solutions.

2.2.1. Response time.
The need of response time guarantee
for some information (which involves the security of the
distributed system) is well known for industrial applications.
Obviously, this time is defined between two points of the
same level of the decomposed network. This kind of feature is
less important in the design of LAN1 applications. For the
LAN3 applications which transport digital voice, for example
[9], the response time constraint does exist, even if it is
slightly less severe than in the LAN2 case.
     There are two parts in the measurement of response time.
The first one is involved with the communication support; for
instance, this measurement can be made between two data-link-
service-endpoints [10]. The second one is related to the
necessary time to go through the upper levels of the networks.
Note: listen to the controversy: "... control engineers have
      the complaint that the layering techniques remove con-
      trol possibilities by hiding control functions between
      application and control layers and at the same time con-
      trol functions are time-consuming by the obligation to
      navigate through the indispensable layers. Time con-
      straints are very important in real-time systems and
      they cannot be neglected for any reason, be it archi-
      tectural cleanness or other" [12].

2.2.2. Reliability. When designing a local area network for industrial real-time applications, one must be greatly concerned with the problem of physical failures of components (we deal with physical faults without ignoring design faults, and so on [17]). It is clear that unreliable communications may cause greater harm to an industrial real-time application than to a data processing application. Anyway, security measures against all possible failures require fault-tolerance techniques and solutions.

Let us give some examples of reliability requirements for LAN2 networks [17,18]:

The error rate is considered to be less than 1 message per 1000 years operation [19] in industrial applications, assuming a frame length of less than 100 bits and a data rate of 1 M bits per second. The specifications of IEEE 802 (LAN1) are less severe: at the link service interface, the undetected bit error rate is less than 1 link data unit per year (size: 200 bytes, rate: 5 M bits per second).

The failure probability of computers and local networks in an aircraft is defined to be 10^{-9} for a ten-hour flight.

The immunity from critical environmental conditions is an important requirement: operational reliability of LAN2 networks must be tested under constraints such as thermal shock, vibrations, electromagnetic interference, etc.

LAN2 designers are looking for an electrically continuous medium, i.e. the absence of active repeaters, amplifiers and electronic components in its construction [20].

2.2.3. Applications. Generally the LAN2 networks aim at supporting decentralized real-time systems for industrial process control and data acquisition, i.e. two sets of functions: (1) monitoring, dispatching, event logging, management of programmable or non-programmable apparatus, man-machine interfacing, data collecting, working tasks controlling, etc. and (2) data and program management, file transfer device to device communication and other data processing functions.

Though these industrial processes are continuous or discrete, they need to be synchronized and controlled. The industrial approach of the control problem is quite simple in fact. While maintaining the merits of distributed processing, LAN2 designers hardly have to choose a centralized form for control (one master, which can be switched or not, and slaves [20]), for maintenance [21,22], for optimization, even for storing data. The distributed control appears, little by little, when one is involved with the problems of accessing remote data bases of process synchronizing and so on.

Note: The application environment of LAN1 networks is intended

to be commercial and light industrial. They should support applications such as [23]: file transfer and access
protocols, graphical applications, word processing,
electronic mail, remote data bases access, digital voice,
etc.

2.2.4. Connected equipment and devices. The equipment and
devices connected to LAN1 networks are generally "intelligent"
such as [23]: computers, terminals, mass storage devices,
printers, plotters, photo- and tele-copiers, gateways to
other networks, etc.
  A proper characteristic of LAN2 networks is the ability
to connect devices with a very different degree of "intelligence" such as: computers and micro-computers, CRT/hard copy,
terminals and printers, programmable apparatus, numerical
control equipment, badges and magnetic strip readers, CAD,
alarm annunciators, etc. The presence of very low cost devices
must be taken into account while designing the coupler to the
communication support.

2.2.5. Other proper characteristics of LAN2 networks. Availability of the distributed system, especially of the communication support requirement is reiterated by the LAN2 designers
[24].
  Ease of installation and maintenance is required from the
commercial market point of view. The medium chosen to implement industrial real-time applications must be easy to obtain
at reasonable cost. The re-use of already installed cables in
a factory or an institution should be considered, such as
CATV or telephone cables for a few LAN2 and LAN3 networks.
  The interconnection of LAN2 networks via or to public
general network is neither a specific and real need of industrial applications, nor an extension tool. It is perceived as
a possible aid, for example, for product management. On the
contrary, in the case of LAN3 networks, this interconnecta-
bility appears as an important characteristic of their specifications.
  The transmission rate of industrial applications information flow may often be viewed as a regular one (with constant
load conditions), but in some cases it can become irregular
(with heavy load conditions, as in office automation applications).
  Perenniality of the installed network is an important
requirement and so is the necessity of conforming to the
legislation (often for security reasons).

TABLE 1.a

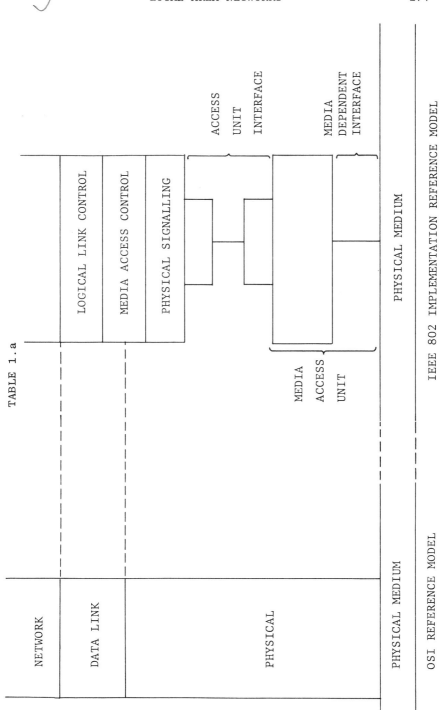

NETWORK				ACCESS UNIT INTERFACE	
DATA LINK	LOGICAL LINK CONTROL				
	MEDIA ACCESS CONTROL				MEDIA DEPENDENT INTERFACE
PHYSICAL	PHYSICAL SIGNALLING		MEDIA ACCESS UNIT		
PHYSICAL MEDIUM			PHYSICAL MEDIUM		
OSI REFERENCE MODEL	IEEE 802 IMPLEMENTATION REFERENCE MODEL				

TABLE 1.b

SIMPLIFIED PROWAY STRUCTURE

APPLICATION		NETWORK	HIGHWAY (BUS)	
APPLICATION FUNCTIONS	DATA INTERPRETATION			
APPLICATION COUPLER				
SERVICES			PATH	
MANAGEMENT			LINE	

PHYSICAL MEDIUM

OSI REFERENCE MODEL

APPLICATION
PRESENTATION
SESSION
TRANSPORT
NETWORK
DATA LINK
PHYSICAL

PHYSICAL MEDIUM

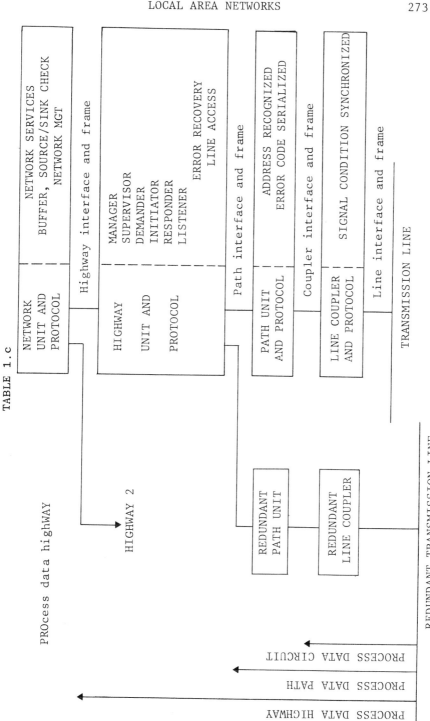

TABLE 1.c

2.3. Standards

These underlying convergent and divergent features are clearly readable in the various standards or proposed-to-be-standards of different committees or organizations. The International Standard Organization (ISO) (and its sub-committee SC16) has proposed the well-known reference model of Open Systems Interconnections. This reference is initially defined for general networks.

The International Electrotechnical Committee is now working on the PROWAY project intended for communication between devices and distributed process control systems.

The proposed IEEE 802 Local Network Standard is compatible with the ISO-OSI reference model. It intends to be used in commercial environment, but not at home or in heavy industrial environment.

Note: Let us mention that IEEE has defined and adopted within the past decade standards for industrial purposes, such as the GPIB (or IEEE 488), or CAMAC. In these two standards, one can find the past and present needs of the electronic and electrotechnic engineers, when interconnecting their devices to build up a process control system.

The European Computer Manufacturers Association has defined ISO-OSI compatible standards and is presently studying the problem of local area networks standards (which will be compatible with the IEEE 802). Some other international committee such as the CCITT, the NBS, the ANSI, the BNI, etc. are also concerned with local area networks standards.

Table 1.a, b and c is a brief overview of the PROWAY and the IEEE 802 standards. We cannot be more precise, since these future standards are not definitively adopted and may vary from their present form.

3. REAL-TIME SYSTEMS DISTRIBUTED ON LOCAL NETWORKS

3.1. General Architecture

Real-time industrial systems (process control, automated factories) have been existing for a long time in a centralized form. They are built from one (or several) CPUs, some exchange units (EU) dealing with disc drivers or magnetic tapes, and several data acquisition or command devices. These can be simple or complex, and are connected to the CPU via control units (Fig. 1).

Control or command software are designed as a set of independent processes, reacting to the events which arrive from the devices by performing a given task (data acquisition processing, calculation and feedback). The CPU is multiplexed

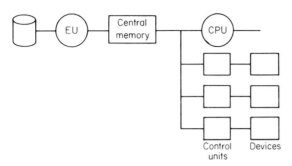

FIG. 1 *Real-time industrial systems.*

among the processes according to a priority scheme, allowing
fast execution of the processes associated to urgent events.
These processes communicate and synchronize by means of the
primitives offered by the nucleus and realized with the help
of the control memory (semaphores, mail boxes, shared memory
locations).

Such a system is a distributed one when the hardware is
geographically distributed in an industrial plant. When
dealing with a large process or factory, this distribution of
the devices may be necessary. The simplest architectures only
connect them to the central computer via low speed or tele-
communication lines (EPI 2000). Local networks do not only
allow the distribution of the devices, but also the distribution of processing units (PU) and exchange units (EU)
(Fig. 2).

Note: 1. Each PU includes local memory; the simplest configuration, with just one PU, is probably a very
common one.

2. The devices can be very complex stations, performing
calculations or local control functions; they can also
be very simple and the communication system protocols
must allow their connection.

The software architecture is closed to the centralized one:
there is a set of processes activated by the external events,
and processed by the PU. But some important differences still
remain:

1) Communication and synchronization primitives are no
longer realized via the central memory, but by using the
communication system (CS) compound of the media and the
communicators. This offers to each process some primitives
like "send message" or "receive message", realizing

M. DANG *et al.*

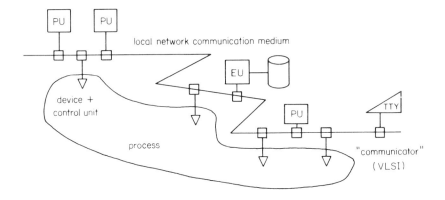

FIG. 2 *Local area network*

approximately the four lower levels of the OSI reference
model. On each station a local nucleus (part of the distributed nucleus) multiplexes the processing capability
among the processes.

2) The whole application is realized by distributing the
tasks or functions on the different stations. A way to do
it is to specialize the PU, in order to process the control algorithms close to the concerned devices, and to
let the global optimization be performed by one more
powerful computer station (hierarchical command). In the
same way, some operating system functions (as file management or file access methods) may be distributed, i.e.
performed by the PU connected to the given peripheral
equipment. But there is another interest in dealing with
several equivalent stations or PUs, in order to be able
to re-assign a given process from a PU which has failed
to another.

3) Distributed implementation of some complex functions often
needs new communication primitives, broadcast or multi-
cast, which did not exist in the centralized systems (or
were implemented via access to common memory)[25].

3.2. Response Time

Industrial systems have an important special constraint: they
need to guarantee that the reaction to an incoming event will
always take place before a given maximum delay.

To realize this, classical centralized systems use the
priority mechanism of process allocation based upon the knowledge of all the high priority processes, of their execution

delay and of their invocation frequency. One can then calculate a maximum boundary of the reaction delay [26].

When dealing with distributed systems, we need to take into account not only the waiting and processing time of the process itself, but also the waiting and processing time of all the messages that are needed, in order to calculate the worst case of reaction delay. Unfortunately, some well-known protocols of local networks (particularly CSMA) cannot give such a boundary, while other ones can. This is obviously the case of virtual ring and token-passing protocols. This is also the case of all the protocols allowing a priority-based message-sending (under the condition that the allocation medium needs no extra delay when several messages compete). The designer can calculate a maximum boundary to the reaction delay, by analysing not only the high priority process activations but also the high priority messages.

In some complex systems, a more "adaptive" approach can be used, when it is possible, to tolerate an unreasonably long message emission delay if the sender is advised and can take corrective decisions (as in fault tolerance techniques). Thus the communication system has to advise the sender process if a special emission delay could not have been respected.

3.3. Reliability

An apparent weakness of such a local network is the use of a single communication medium. For special (highly reliable) applications, we probably need to duplicate it. But in many cases, it should be possible to get a good reliability if the application can accept some kind of degraded functioning, and if the operating system and the communication system allow to bring such a mode into play (see Section 3.4.).

More frequent faults are transmission errors. The classical way to deal with them is to add redundant information to the message, to check it and to ask for retransmission if necessary. These operations have to be performed by the communication system.

3.4. Availability and Graceful Degradation

A well-known interesting feature of distributed systems is that they allow a degraded mode of functioning when some units have failed. But obviously the software has to be specially designed to make use of this possibility. When a given station is broken down, it may be possible to transfer its processes to another equivalent station. In some other cases, it may be possible to temporarily give up the processing of some tasks (as global optimization, or upper levels of hierarchical command) or it may be possible to change the

control or the command algorithm in order to perform the
task in spite of the unavailability of a given device. All
these possibilities have to be put into play by the application software, and this fact increases its complexity.

Another kind of failure is communication systems failure
(the most probable one will be cable cut). An interesting
feature of the communication system should be its availability
to go on functioning as distinct subsystems. The application
software could be built up to go on processing in a degraded
fashion. For example, all global optimizations could be suspended while local controls are still performing. But it is
necessary too that the network should be repaired, i.e. the
subnetworks merge into one.

Other expected reconfigurations are dynamic additions of
new stations. It should be possible to integrate them in the
system and to give them some functions without stopping the
whole operation. In particular, the system initialization
can use this possibility.

An important point in the communication and operating systems design can greatly facilitate the software implementation
of such dynamic reconfigurations: the naming and addressing of
communication processes. In the more rigid (but simple) system, every process knows all others by name and directly
addresses the destination process. In more complex systems,
one prefers to have the processes communicating via intermediate objects ("ports"). But in any case, a fundamental
choice is either to statically allocate the process or port
names to stations, or to accept possible changes of location.

In the first case, the name can be station number, process
or local port number. In the second one, process or ports can
dynamically migrate, and one has to perform the binding
between their absolute name and their physical address and
local number. Classical (addressed) communication systems can
make this painful if it is needed to consult and update re-
location dictionaries (partly duplicated). It should be very
interesting for the "communicator" VLSI circuits to directly
perform such a logical addressing. As each message emitted
on the medium is received by each communicator, the more
efficient method is to ask the communicator to store a table
of logical names of local receiver processes (or ports), and
when receiving every message, to check for delivering or re-
jecting it.

This logical addressing of communication systems can be
simple to implement and allows easy reconfiguration by mini-
mizing table management when processes (or ports) migrate.
Moreover, we only need a common name to be present in more
than one communicator to perform multi-cast or broadcast
communications.

3.5. Knowledge of the Network State

Nevertheless, a purely logical addressing is not enough and
we do need physical addressing too, to address each station.
For example, when reconfiguring (or initializing) the system,
it is necessary to know the exact configuration and the
physical address of each existing station. Consequently, the
communication system must be able to deliver this information.
  More information is needed to analyse the network state
and behaviour concerning the saturated instantaneous traffic
load as the possible saturated state of the communication
system. Extra features are needed in the communication system
to access this information.

3.6. Event Ordering

The design of several distributed applications has stressed
the necessity of ordering the events coming from different
stations, i.e. of getting the same order on each receiving
station.
  A classical solution based on timestamps has been proposed
[27]. In order to implement it, we need one local value of
the stamp in each station and to send the new value (local
value + 1) to each receiver with each message. Each receiver
must then update its local value by message value + 1. In
this way, one can guarantee that all the events are stamped
in the same way, and a unique order is maintained.
  A simple and efficient way to implement this mechanism is
to have it done by the communication system itself, which will
manage and transport the current value of stamps with every
message.

3.7. Event Dating

An industrial distributed system can need a more precise
dating of events than event ordering. It may be necessary to
associate to each event its occurrence time. For instance,
when two data acquisition devices are processing separately
and sending information, we need to date precisely each
information if we hope to perform compared analysis or cor-
relations between them.
  Such a dating is easy to perform in a centralized system
which has a unique clock. When waiting on different stations,
it is difficult to realize perfectly synchronous clocks. A
good solution is probably to ask the communication system to
re-synchronize them.
  These clocks are part of the communication system which
should allow to initialize or re-initialize them; moreover,
after a failure, it may occur that the communication

system becomes "non-synchronous". This state has to be known
by the upper (application) level in order for it to ask for a
re-synchronization procedure. Both advertisement and re-
synchronization procedures have to be offered by the communication system.

Another use of such clocks is to date every message when
it enters the communication system and asks for transmission.
Consequently a transmission waiting delay can be calculated
and the sender can be warned if the special maximum delay is
overcome (see Section 3.2.).

4. A PROPOSED SOLUTION: CICS 81, A VLSI-BASED LOCAL NETWORK FOR DISTRIBUTED PROCESS CONTROL

In order to give answers to all the above presented requirements, the CNET/CNS Laboratory in Meylan (Isère, France) has
designed a two-chip VLSI-LSI communicator [28,29]. We are
designing separately a VLSI chip to manage the data link
layer and network layer in reference to the ISO model, and a
LSI chip for the physical layer. With these two specialized
integrated circuits, it will be possible to build up a communication station. A communication system will include
several communication stations. The transformation between
these stations will be realized in a serial way, on a coaxial
cable.

The basic topology (bus, hairpin) is not unique. With
the VLSI chip managing the data link and network layers, it
is possible to provide several solutions. Obviously other
LSI chips are to be developed to manage the physical layer.

We discuss below the special features provided for these
chips to satisfy the given application class.

4.1. Real-Time Features

4.1.1. Response time. Let us examine the particular data flow
characteristics for the target application class. There are
two kinds of data: (1) the time function samples give a
regular traffic, with a non-variable load for the network,
and (2) the events result in bursty traffic, very urgent
messages can overload the network.

We then have retained the following features:

1) broadcast medium,
2) asynchronous transmission: we use packets,
3) a priority allocation technique: the priority is attached
   to each packet, it is a field in the packet,
4) the maximum length of the data field is 256 bytes,
5) the flow rate is 8 M bits/second,
6) an emergency value is attached to each packet to be

transmitted; with this number, the priority field is
regularly carried up, to avoid a packet staying in the
communication system,
7) a traffic analysis service allows the user to estimate
   a network load.

4.1.2. Events management. Two kinds of problems arise with
the events management: (1) the synchronization in a distributed system and (2) the physical time situation. The following services will allow to build at the upper communication
levels the needed primitives for the applications:

1) A stamp service provides a total ordering between packets
   so that each one is stamped by the communication system.
2) A time service allows to give to each packet the entry
   time value.
3) A watchdog-like service is provided to avoid a packet
   transmission after too long delay. In fact, the previously
   presented emergency value is used to get this property,
   i.e. when the maximum priority value is surpassed, the
   packet is not transmitted and the user is advised.

The stamp and the time are two global variables managed at
the network level. A copy of the current stamp value and of
the time, exists in each station. The coherence problem is
solved, but we will not discuss this point here.

4.1.3. Time function samples. The problem is a multi-observa-
tion of time functions and multi-correlations. We think that
the time service can also be used to solve this problem.

4.2. Reliability

4.2.1. Data integrity. Data integrity is classically provided
by a CRC mechanism, error messages and automatic retransmission. These are managed by the communication system. Using
the highest priority values, these packets follow immediately
the initial packet.

4.2.2. Transmission status. The transmission status indicates
to the users of the communication system (emitter and
receivers): time, stamp, a receiver number indication,
optionally a receiver name list, and whether problems have
occurred such as receiver buffer overflow, and persistent CRC
errors for other stations. A transmission status is delivered
to the emitter and to the receivers for which there are no
error and no buffer overflow.

4.2.3. Authentication. Authentication is an important problem in the target application class, essentially to avoid erroneous signature due to a failure in terminal equipment. We retain an encryption mechanism to solve this problem.

4.3. Naming and Addressing

A packet may be sent to a given station. Each station has a physical, unique name.

Logical naming is provided. In each communication station, there is a table of several addresses. The content of this table can be dynamically modified by the user of the communication system. When a packet is sent on the broadcast medium, each station looks at the address destination field included in the packet and compares the content of this field with the content of the table. If the comparisons in one or several stations hold, each of these stations gets a copy of the packet. Consequently, the broadcasting is also available at the upper communication level.

ACKNOWLEDGEMENT

We would like to thank Mr J.L. Mure for his very helpful advice.

REFERENCES

1. Shock, J.F. (1980), An Annotated Bibliography on Local Computer Networks. XEROX Palo Alto Research Center.
2. Metcalfe, R.M. and Boggs, D.R. (1976). ETHERNET: Distributed packet switching for local computer networks. *Comm. ACM* 19, No.17.
3. Newhall, E.E. and Venetsanopoulos, A.N. (1971). Computer communications representative systems. *In* "Proc. IFIP 71", Ljubljana, Yugoslavia.
4. Binns, S.E., Dallas, I.N. and Spratt, E.B. (1982). Further developments on the Cambridge Ring network at the University of Kent. *In* "Proc. Local Computer Networks Conference", Florence.
5. Liu, M.T., Pardo, R., Tsay, D., Wolf, J.J., Weide, B.W., and Chou, C. (1979). System design of the distributed double loop computer network (DDLCN). *In* "Proc. First Conference on Distributed Computing Systems, Huntsville, USA.
6. IEC, SC GSA, WG6 (1981). Draft on PROWAY, Process Data Highway for Distributed Process Control Systems. International Electrotechnical Commission.
7. IEEE Standards Board (1978). IEEE Standard Digital Interface for Programmable Instrumentation. IEEE STD 488.

8. ESONE Committee (1972). CAMAC, A Modular Instrument System for Data Handling, EUR 4100 e. Commission of European Communities.
9. Renoulin, R., Lefranc, J.P. and Takhedmit, M.J. (1982). Réalisation d'un système de communication par paquets à haut débit, destiné au réseau local en boucle du CCETT (projet CARTHAGE). In "Actes du Congrès AFCET Informatique".
10. ISO.TC 97.SC 16 (1979). Reference Model of Open Systems Interconnection. ISO.
11. Bey, Y. (1979). Computer aided control of industrial processes application, problems, standardization efforts. In "Proc. EURO-IFIP 79". London.
12. Malagardis, N. (1979). The standardization world and research and development in real-time. In "Proc. Real-Time Data Handling and Process Control". North Holland Publishing Company, Amsterdam, Netherlands.
13. Le Lann, G. (1981). Présentation du projet INRIA "SCORE" GAL.I.001.
14. Lettre d'information RESEAUX (1982). No.4.
15. Cornafion (1979). Systèmes informatiques répartis. DUNOD Editor.
16. Hupp, J.A. and Shock, J.F. (1980). Measured performance of an ETHERNET local network. Comm. ACM 22, No.5.
17. Avizienis, A. (1979). Toward a discipline of reliable computing. In "Proc. EURO-IFIP 79". London.
18. Goldberg, J. (1979). Advances in design, specification and validation of fault-tolerant computers. In "Proc. EURO-IFIP 79". London.
19. Ayache, J.M., Courtiat, J.P. and Diaz, M. (1982). REBUS, a fault-tolerant distributed system for industrial real-time control. IEEE Trans. on Computers C31, No.7.
20. SEMS (1982). EPI 2000: Equipement Périphérique Industriel, SEMS (France).
21. Takahashi, M. et al. (1981). DFW: optical fiber data freeway system: a loop network for distributed computer control. In "Proc. Spring COMPCON Conference". California.
22. Modicon Gould (1982). MODWAY: Communication Utility Multi-parallel Applications Industrial Standard. Internal Report.
23. IEEE Computer Standard Committee (1981). Draft of the Proposed IEEE 802 Local Network Standard. IEEE.
24. Dulac, G. and Peyrache, A. (1982). INCA: Projet d'Interconnexion de Matériels Informatiques et Automatiques Hétérogènes du Secteur Secondaire. APSIS. Internal Report.
25. Ricart, G. and Agrawala, A.K. (1981). An optimal algorithm for mutual exclusion in computer networks. Comm. ACM 24, No.1.

26. Kaiser, C. (1982). Mutual exclusion and priority
    scheduling. *Techniques et Sciences Informatiques* 1, No.1.
27. Lamport, L. (1978). Time, clocks and the ordering of
    events in a distributed system. *Comm. ACM* 21, No.7.
28. Michel, G. (1982). CICS 81: Communications integrated
    circuits. *In* "Proc. IFIP 7C6 International Symposium on
    Local Computer Networks". Florence, Italy.
29. Michel, G., Rouillard, J., Charles, G. and Tranvaux, D.
    (1982). CICS 81: a VLSI-based local network for distri-
    buted process control. *In* "Proc. Third International
    Conference on Distributed Computer Systems". Miami, USA.

MICROSS*: Graphics Aided Simulation of Distributed Computer Systems

Müslim Bozyigit, Harry English and Yakup Paker

1. INTRODUCTION

1.1. Modelling of Distributed Computer Systems (DCS)

There have been numerous studies towards modelling of DCS. A majority of these have been based on theoretical approaches, requiring mathematical understanding of the model related to a particular system under study. The designers of DCS as well as those in related fields are not necessarily in command of the mathematics involved. This gap can normally be filled by specialists who are able to formulate a particular model and present the results to others involved. This technique, apart from the cost and time factors, presents difficulties in practice as systems get more complex.

A considerable proportion of modelling studies is based on digital simulation techniques. Especially with high availability of computer power this has become a widespread practice. However, there is not any efficient formal approach despite the availability of some general purpose simulation languages or packages (GPSS, SIMULA, GASP, etc.). Here again, the practice has been the development of dedicated simulation systems for each application.

1.2. MICROSS Approach of Modelling of DCS

Development of MICROSS is based on an attempt to formally

---

* MICROSS' name was originally used as an abbreviation of Multi-Microprocessor based System Simulation

Distributed Computing Systems
ISBN 0-12-543970-9

286   M. BOZYIGIT *et al.*

express the interaction of basic components at functional
level.

The MICROSS approach is hoped to shorten the design cycle
by reducing the modelling effort involved in a distributed
computer system. The foreseen advantages of MICROSS are as
follows:

1) A designer can incorporate his system into MICROSS readily
   since the terminology used agrees with DCS terminology
   which he is also accustomed to.
2) MICROSS is interactive. The user is guided through the
   definition of his system components.
3) Interactive reporting facility provides easy examination
   and evaluation of a particular setup.
4) Imbedded optional standard networking alternatives such
   as protocols and routing provides alternative design
   studies.
5) The graphics aid is provided at three levels. Definition
   of the system can be aided graphically. State of simulation can be graphically displayed at predetermined
   points in time using incremental simulation times. The
   online graphical presentation of the results provides
   speedy decision making.
6) Adaptabilitiy of MICROSS regarding the computer installation, is high. Non-graphic MICROSS source package is
   coded in FORTRAN language which provides a broad implementation medium. The graphical MICROSS uses GINOF [1]
   graphics package. PLOT 10 version will soon be implemented
   which will broaden the implementation area further.
7) In view of contemporary widespread implementation and use
   of distributed computer systems, geographically dispersed
   as well as local computer networks, MICROSS can be used
   as an educational tool to create appreciation of DCS and
   also provide insight into them.

2. FUNCTIONAL COMPONENTS OF A DCS

2.1. What is a Function?

The context of a function depends on the level that function
is associated with. For example, at one extreme a DCS consists
of two main functional components (node) which undertake
application as well as switching tasks, and communication
lines which have certain capacity of transmission. At the
other extreme, there is circuit and/or instruction level of
functional decomposition which provides extensive details and
a number of options.

The highest level may be considered too crude, due to the
availability of various alternative arrangements of a node

Host side

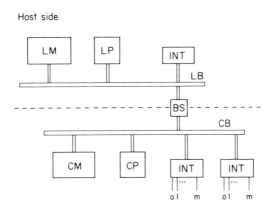

Communication side

FIG. 1 *A DCS node in MICROSS*

made possible with the advances of LSI technology. The lowest level, on the other hand, contains too many redundant details which can easily distract the purpose of simulation, may even render it unmanageable or impossible to implement.

This study towards generalization of DCS modelling, has assumed an intermediate level where redundant details are excluded but enough means of control can be given to the designer over the hardware and software arrangements of each node involved in this system.

2.2. MICROSS Functional Components and Specification Considerations [2,3]

A node in a DCS consists of two main components (Fig. 1):

1)   Host side
2)   Communication side.

The host side has functions associated to the application and communication side. The communication side on the other hand performs, basically, switching tasks by routing the transactions towards their ultimate destinations. Thus the basic hardware specifications that are related to the two components would be speed and memory size with which the host and the communication node perform their functions. The speed in MICROSS is given in terms of kilo (1000) instructions per second. This, in practice, is related to software size involved in carrying out specific tasks. The memory size is not a controlling factor of high importance but it should be of enough capacity for the allocation of real-time software and also the information in transit.

The local interface, between the host and the local communi
cation node, is specified by protocol employed and also transmission speed of the interface circuitry. The transmission
media in the communication subsystem is often connected to
the communication mechanism (or protocol) between the communication nodes.

The interface transmission timing is modelled as

$$t = a + \frac{1}{b}\ell$$

where a is a fixed value per unit transmission, b is a coefficient of transmission rate associated to a unit data and
ℓ is the number of units of data to be transmitted. The units
depend on interpretation. If, say ℓ is in bits and b is in
bits per microsecond, then a and t are in microseconds.

3. MICROSS SYSTEM OVERVIEW

3.1. Simulation Technique

The simulation of DCS, obviously involves concurrent execution
of various components on a single processor i.e. a mainframe
computer environment. It is therefore important how the
global time is advanced regarding discernible functional units
such as host, communication processors, input-output ports,
and communication links.

MICROSS employs event based discrete simulation technique.
This technique involves the ordering of the events, which
are referred to as transactions (TX in short), in time and in
precedence.

An event in the system can appear in one of the five
states:

1) scheduled: waiting to take place
2) active: taking place
3) suspended (or blocked): waiting for the requested
   facility to become free
4) pre-empted: pre-empted by a higher priority TX
5) dormant: TX completes its life through the system and
   terminates for good.

Figure 2 shows the transition of TX states. The states 1 and
2 have the common characteristics, scheduled to wait for a
certain duration of time before competing for the next
facility. The state 1 however, until the involved TX enters
the system for the first time, takes place outside the system with no effect on the system at all.

A TX enters the blocked state if the facility it is

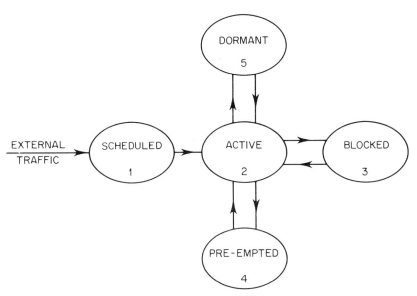

FIG. 2 *States of a DCS transaction*

competing for is busy. A blocked TX resumes requesting after
each time that it takes for a state transition. The state 4
has not yet been implemented in MICROSS, although provisions
are made to include it. The state 5 is obvious. The transactions, be it control or data, come to an end at a particular host or communication node. This state is referred to as
TX termination state later in the simulation and reporting
parts.

The facilities involved regarding the simulation model are
host computers, communication nodes and the transmission
medium with host-to-communication interface and communication
node-to-communication node connection.

3.2. Basic MICROSS Software System

In view of the general modelling aspects mentioned in the
previous parts the presentation in this part covers basic
descriptions of main components of the MICROSS software
system.

MICROSS is organized in the form of four loosely tied
submodels:

1) Definition
2) Simulation
3) Graphics

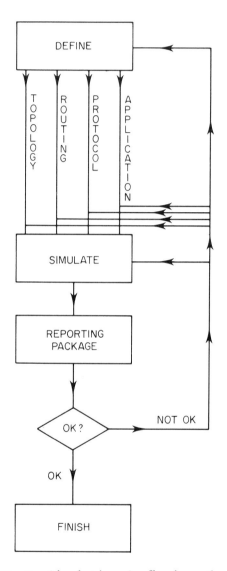

FIG. 3 *Simulation feedback cycle.*

4) Reporting

The interface between all four is monitored under the control of a small MONITOR. The graphics part is discussed mainly
in Section 4.

The user is aware of these main constructs while he is
guided interactively through the MICROSS system. He knows the

submodel in charge of the current action, by a prompt carrying
the first 3 or 4 characters of the name of the submodel.
Figure 3 shows the names of the submodels. Each model has
well-defined interface with the monitor. There is no control
from one to another unless it comes through the monitor. In
this section basic tasks undertaken by each submodel are
introduced.

3.2.1. Control of MICROSS submodels: MONITOR. The MONITOR
routine shows all the global data structures with control over
user and other submodels of MICROSS. Figure 3 shows the system
flowchart of MONITOR. With the interactive control the user
can switch between the submodels as many times as found necessary until a convincing architecture is achieved, judged by
the analysis of the performance results of each alternative.
    MONITOR satisfies the need of clear user interface with
MICROSS. The MONITOR is the only path to enter a subsystem
and also the only path to exit from the system properly.

3.2.2. System definition and initialization. This section
provides all the data necessary for the simulation regarding
the capabilities of the hardware components such as host computers and communication subsystem, and application such as
patterns of external message send requests generated at the
hosts. The upper limits are put both for modelling constructs
such as scheduling lists, and queuing buffers at host and
communication subsystem. The options regarding the communication protocols and routine techniques are also specified in
this section.
    The data structures used to implement simulation constructs
and also statistics on the facilities are initiated in this
system as well. The system data can be grouped into four
classes:

A) Topology Data
    – Number of nodes: each node consists of two parts: host
      and communication.
    – Maximum connectivity: for regular structures this can
      be equal to or greater than the connectivity, but for
      irregular structures it must be equal or greater than
      the maximum connectivity that exists.
    – Connection table: some well-known regular topologies are
      imbedded. Nothing much is required of the user except a
      code to indicate the topology of interest. For irregular
      structures, however, the connection data is presented in
      the form of a connection table which is created on node
      basis. Each row includes the list of neighbouring
      (adjacent) nodes directly connected.

292   M. BOZYIGIT *et al.*

B) Hardware Data
   - Speed of local processor: kilo instruction/sec.
   - Speed of communication processor: kilo instruction/sec.
   - Speed of local transmission medium: kilo bit/sec.
   - Speed of the lines between communication software only:
     kilo bytes.
   - Communication memory at the communication processor:
     kilo bytes.
   - Output queue lengths in terms of number of messages.

The processor speeds are used to simulate the seizure
duration of the processors given a task requiring a certain
number of instructions. Memory size, on the other hand, is
checked for the sufficient buffer space and is not a critical
factor with the low cost involved. The lines are assumed to
introduce delays proportional to size of data transmitted.

C) Routing Data
   - The routing technique: once decided upon, is applied
     system-wide. As far as a user is concerned, it can be
     parameterized for certain well-known routing techniques
     which will be imbedded. In the current MICROSS system,
     two variations of fixed routing have already been imple-
     mented. The flooding as well as an adaptive routing
     technique is being implemented.
   - Communication protocols: these are also parameterized.
     Each protocol is simulated by a fixed delay time de-
     pending on the complexity involved. The protocols
     covered are hop-to-hop HDLC protocol, BISYNCH, X25 and
     a simple handshake. User-defined protocols can be in-
     corporated with minor changes, as long as they are based
     on store-and-forward DCS.

D) Application Data
   - Application data is modelled in terms of the frequency
     of external message input at each node and a traffic
     matrix indicating the traffic flow requirements between
     node pairs. The former is presented in terms of message
     inter-arrival times and the probability distribution
     function. The latter is presented in terms of a proba-
     bility matrix. Optionally, actual traffic can be used
     to feed the simulated system. This approach is most
     helpful in testing the model against the existing
     counterpart.
       The traffic can also be grouped into a number of
     priority classes.

3.2.3. MICROSS simulation concept. The simulation subsystem
utilizes every structure defined and/or reset in the

definition subsystem. The software modularity is attempted by
functional partitioning so that easy access by the user is
possible. There are two disjoint but closely related sets of
functions at higher level. The event (TX) scheduling in time
and priority, activation of a particular TX at a point in
time (current time), advancement of global time as well as
updating the status of the facilities at that instant of
current time are all carried out in one of these disjoint set
of subroutines (using FORTRAN language terminology). The other
set of subroutines handles the facility seizure upon activation of a particular TX. The seizure can take place because
of one of the following functions:

1) Arrival of an external TX at the host computer.
2) Local transmission attempt between the host and the local
   communication node.
3) Receipt of local external messages at the communication
   node.
4) Receipt of remote traffic at the communication node.
5) Data transmission requests between two communication
   nodes.
6) Scheduling the amount of external traffic.

The model provides a degree of interaction between some of
the functions. For example, data transmission request at one
side of a pair triggers the other side for reception. The last
item, i.e. (6), does not involve seizure of a facility. The
pattern of scheduling at a node depends on the application
data parameters fed in during system initialization. Arrival
of a message is scheduled but is not guaranteed to be handled
at a host right away, unless the host is free.

The first five functions may require queuing at one facility
and dequeuing in the other depending on the success of action
that has taken place, and also the protocols involved. For
example if the protocol chosen is an HDLC utilizing hop-to-
hop with piggy-back acknowledgement then an arriving message
is queued as soon as transmission is complete. Its copy in
the sending node is not removed from the queue unless its
receipt is acknowledged. The acknowledgement, queuing and dequeuing operations are performed during the receive action of
the host and/or the communication node.

Timing of each operation is necessary to affect the seizure
duration of the facility in question. The smallest time increment corresponds to shortest independent process (function).
For example, an attempt to transmit at a sender may need to
be aborted because of the busy state of the receiver. However,
this attempt itself is an executable process and is timed
according to the number of instructions and speed of the processor performing it. Thus the attempted TX is rescheduled to

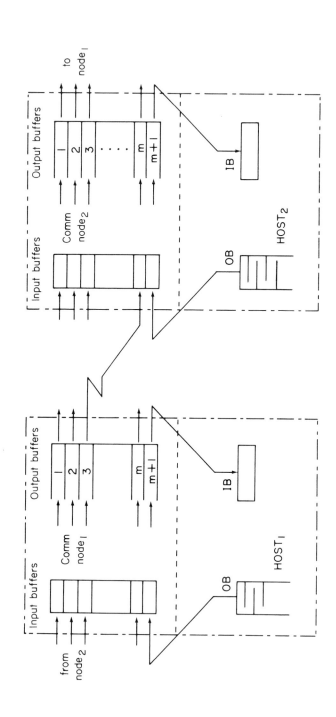

FIG. 4 *Two nodes of a DCS simulated in MICROSS*

be ready for re-attempt at a later time.
Figure 4 shows two nodes as they are simulated by MICROSS,
which appear as a network of queues. The host contains one
output queue leading to the local communication node via a
link. Communication node possesses m queues leading to the
local host part.
The details of the data structure used to represent the
facilities are summarized in the next section.

3.2.4. MICROSS basic data structure. The MICROSS data structure can be grouped into four main classes which are closely
interlinked:

1) Physical components.
2) Status of physical components.
3) Application traffic and routing.
4) Book-keeping constructs.

For all, except queues, the specification data and status
data are given in a simple array type data structure. Queue
representation requires higher sophistication. The representation of an output queue is a linked list structure. The
status data is kept in a separate array. For modularity reasons
each queue is also associated with a separate data area to
store the actual messages. The index of a message in the data
area is kept in the right queue. Therefore, no search is
necessary for the retrieval of a message.
Further data structures are added depending on the protocols employed. For example, for HDLC protocol utilizing
piggy-back window mechanism for acknowledgement, another
structure is employed to record the relevant data for each
queue.
The application data structures consists of an n × n
traffic matrix where each entry t_{ij} indicates the proportion
of the traffic at source i and destined for j. In case of
known probability distribution, this matrix is not used. A
parameter indicating distribution time is sufficient.
The routing constructs depend on the specific technique
implemented. For fixed routing technique an n × n routing
matrix (R) where r_{ij} indicates next node after i on the path
to j is the main structure. As support constructs, we have a
connection table where each row is a set of adjacent nodes of
the corresponding node, and weight table (W) where each W_{ij}
indicates the minimum distance between node i and j in terms
of weight associated to each link on the path i to j.
Two main book-keeping data constructs are employed to hold
the list of scheduled but inactive transactions, and corresponding active transactions. The TXs pingpong between these
two lists until terminated, after which they are removed from

either of the lists and also from the system altogether
("dormant" state).
    Both of these constructs are represented by linked lists
in which TXs are in time and priority order. The TX information carried in these lists is:

1) Source id of the TX.
2) Destination id.
3) TX id.
4) Time the TX is scheduled at.
5) The action to take place next.
6) Priority.
7) Link area.
8) Output queue id.
9) Current node id.

    The nodes are added or removed from the linked lists using
the avail (garbage collection) lists.
    The data structure allows the gathering of statistics on
the utilization of the system as well as the individual
physical and logical constructs.
    The aborted TXs are stored in a disk file during the course
of the simulation. This file is later used to provide further
data for the reporting subsystem.

3.2.5. Reporting subsystem. Reporting is naturally referred
to after the completion of a simulation run. Once it is
entered the level of reporting details is interactively chosen
by the user. A short report displays the main description data
as well as the results concerning the throughput and average
delay time experienced. One of the detailed reports is related
to the system throughput showing the cumulative distribution
of message delay time and the related histograms.
    The other reports are on nodal statistics such as:

1) current content, concerning hosts and communication nodes
2) nodal external traffic
3) throughput
4) unacknowledged external messages and unacknowledged
    successful deliveries
5) utilization of hosts, communication nodes, links and
    output queues.

    The graphical presentation of the results is separately
handled under the cursor control for clean screen starts. The
disjoint handling allows the non-graphical reporting to be
handled even if graphics facilities do not exist thus achieving higher adaptability.
    Figure 5 (a,b,c) shows frequency distributions and the
histogram of message delay time as shown in one screen page

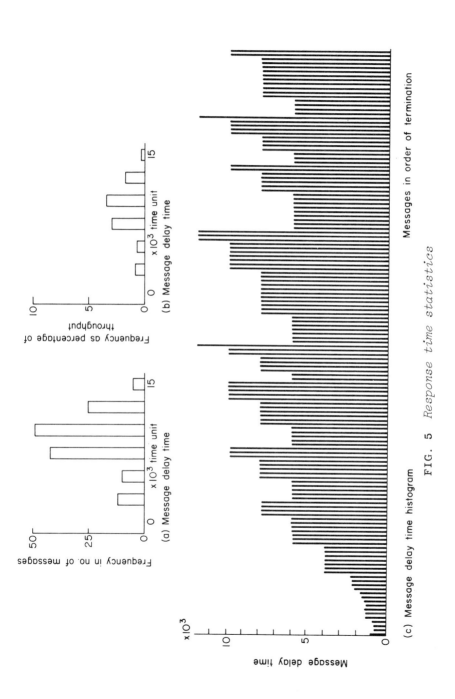

FIG. 5   *Response time statistics*

M. BOZYIGIT *et al.*

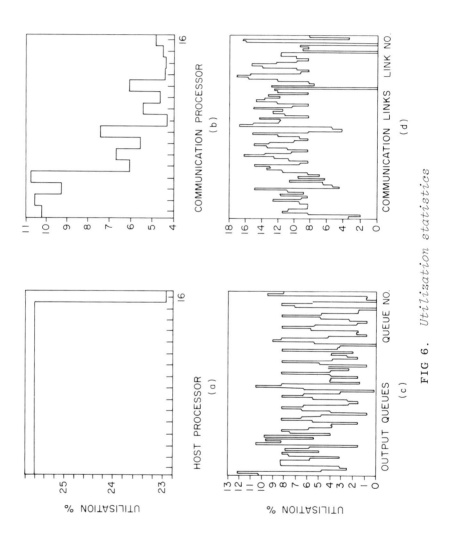

FIG 6. *Utilization statistics*

of a Tektronix 4014 graphics terminal. Similarly, nodal statistics such as external input, throughput, content, unacknowledged throughput can be displayed on a single screen. Figure
6 (a,b,c,d), on the other hand, shows the histograms of the
utilization data. The detailed non-graphical reports give a
comprehensive account of various features that characterize
the simulation run.

4. GRAPHICS AID

4.1. Graphics in Simulation of DCS

The graphics aids for reporting data processing applications
have, in general, proved very useful from a user point of
view. In fact, nowadays, a graphics facility has become an
integral part of a micro-computer even at the low end of the
market. At higher levels computer-aided design has been using
graphics for various applications.

Here we discuss the use of graphics in design and modelling
of distributed computer systems, mainly of store-and-forward
type. The implementation, as a whole, has revealed educational
value as well as easier grasp of a distributed system under
study.

The attempt initially focussed on defining certain
building blocks which can be integrated into a distributed
computer structure tied to the users' needs. The blocks that
are represented conceptually could thus be displayed graphically and also be related to each other according to the defined DCS architecture. The level of functionality and also
the level of integration, however, has been a matter of further investigations. There are two aspects of the problem.
The first is the conceptual representation of the DCS elements.
The second is matching a graphical representation onto the
conceptual one.

The preliminary study has shown that the conceptual representation can be implemented such that the user is given
flexibility over the definition of the target system. The
details of the representation level have been discussed in
previous sections. The graphical representation, on the other
hand, need not be even at the conceptual level as far as the
user (or designer) is concerned. Too many details can very
well distract a designer from the actual task of evaluating
the system level. It is found that a pragmatic approach, for
the system definition is to use graphics aid to model a node
and also concentrate on the presentation of performance at
this level.

The conceptual design setups concerning various regular
or irregular topological architectures with the communication

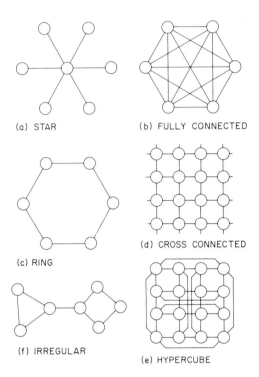

(a) STAR

(b) FULLY CONNECTED

(c) RING

(d) CROSS CONNECTED

(f) IRREGULAR

(e) HYPERCUBE

FIG. 7 *DCS topologies*

links in place, as shown in Figure 7, can consolidate a real
feeling about the distributed nature of the system. The system data accumulated over the simulation phase can also be
matched onto the topology.

For example, partial congestions involving a number of
links can spontaneously be seen on the system graphics. The
decision about the alternative networking technique(s) can
be taken online, towards the elimination of the unwanted behaviour. The online interactive actions may involve changes
in topology, routing, communication protocols and/or application traffic.

4.2. Graphics as Implemented in MICROSS

Graphics aid in MICROSS is utilized at 3 levels:

1) Definition
2) Simulation
3) Reporting

Graphics use in reporting is discussed in Section 3.2.4

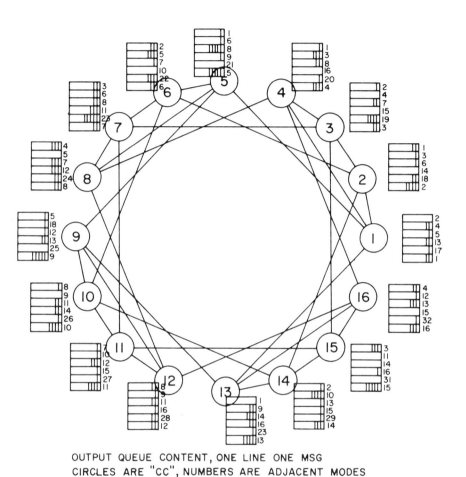

OUTPUT QUEUE CONTENT, ONE LINE ONE MSG
CIRCLES ARE "CC", NUMBERS ARE ADJACENT MODES

FIG. 8 *A snapshot of a DCS state during simulation.*

as a part of basic MICROSS system, and is used to display the
statistics in classical sense in the form of histograms,
curves, etc.

4.2.1. Graphics application to system definition. Graphics
aid in definition subsystem is limited to the node level topological layouts, although technically there is no restriction
on graphical details such as separation of local host from the
communication node and processor from the memory. These details, especially in a densely connected environment lose
their relevance and are therefore left out unless a multiprocessor structure is treated.

M. BOZYIGIT *et al.*

The topological patterns at a node level can be formed from the connection table, only if the physical co-ordinates of each node on the screen are also known. For regular patterns this data can be generated given the screen specifications and the connection table which can also be found under the program control triggered by a parameter indicating a specific pattern. For irregular structures, however, the co-ordinates may be specified interactively under the cursor and program control. In this case the co-ordinates need to be saved for regeneration and/or snapshot system state display purposes.

Under the program control the cursor input is parameterized to indicate a particular drawing function such as a circle to mean a node and a line in between the two circles to mean a link. The online deletions and additions can also take place. In all cases it is the topology information that is needed to be saved for simulation and for later display purposes.

4.2.2. Graphics aid at simulation level. At the simulation level graphics can be used to express the system state in a concise manner. In MICROSS this is applied to the current queue content at each node in the form of a network of queues as it is illustrated in Figure 8.

The simulation and the graphics are incorporated in MONITOR section where for each snapshot the incremental simulation time is added on to the global time. The simulation can then be stopped at a point in time after the exhaustion of the last time increment.

In Figure 8 the circles indicate the nodes with node id encircled. Each vertical short line across two horizontal lines indicates a message in the output queue leading to the node, id of which is indicated by an integer opposite to the queue. The first queue from the bottom indicates the output queue at host leading into the local communication node and the second from the bottom indicates the opposite. Note that host identifications differ from that of local communication nodes by a value of n, the total number of nodes in the system.

ACKNOWLEDGEMENT

This work has been supported by an SERC DCSP Grant.

REFERENCES

1. GINO-F. The General Purpose Graphics Package. Computer Aided Design Centre, Cambridge, UK.
2. Paker, Y. and Bozyigit, M. (1981). Computer Aided Multi-Microprocessor Systems Modelling, Simulation and Evaluation Final Report, Science Engineering and Research Council.
3. Bozyigit, M. (1979). A Dense Variable Topology Multicomputer System. PhD Thesis, The Polytechnic of Central London.

Subject Index

Abortion, 37-39
Abstract expression, 9,51
Acceptance thresholds, 69,71
Action invariants, 27
Actors, 253
Addressing, 282
Analysis of concurrent systems, 123
  adequate systems, 123
  deadlock free systems, 123
Archons computer, *see* decentralized computer
Atomic data sets, 27
Availability, 277

Basic COSY system, 115
  combined view, 117
  common view, 117
  concurrent operations, 122
  concurrent reachability in one step, 123
  concurrent system, 116
  cyclic histories, 119
  event, 115
  independent vector operations, 122
  individual subview, 117
  maximally concurrent reachability, 124
  potentially dangerous triples, 130
  sequential subsystem, 116
  traces, 115,116,119
  vector firing sequences, 116
  vector operations, 121-122
Buffer insertion, 268

CICS, 81,280
Centralized control, 10
Chorus, 251
Commit management, 34-35

Communicating concurrent software, 191
Communication assertions, 69,74
Communication protocols, 202
Communication support, 267
  architecture of, 267
Competition, 268
Concurrency, 4,197,202
Concurrent programming languages, 110
  evaluation, 110
Concurrent systems, 109-110,111, 124
  computer based environment analysis, 111,124
  program abstraction, 119
  simulation of, 124
  specification and analysis, 109,110
Concurrent updating, 31-35
Conformity, 27
Consistency, 8,14
Control algorithms, 267
Controller, 67,70
Co-operation, 4
  process, 155
  schemes, 149,150
Correctness, 209-217
  assertion, 69
Counters, 52

DCS, *see* Distributed Computer Systems
Data consistency, 28-30,31
  maintenance, 28-30
  sufficient condition, 30,31
Data encapsulation, 193
Data invariants, 26,27
Data objects, 26
Deadlock, 8,23,33-34,284-285
Decentralized computer, 23

Distributed Computer Systems, 299
  graphics in simulation of, 299
  modelling, 285
Distributed control, 10,51,54
  algorithms, 67
Distributed Path Pascal, 191
Distributed program, 203
Distributed systems, 3,54,67,192,
  201,251
  loosely-coupled, 163
  process control, 265,280
  real-time, 274
  synchronization, 3
Distribution, 10,77
  of an assertion, 77
  of synchronization variables, 10

Election, 268
Empty slot, 268
Event, 4,70,151,152
  dating, 279
  management, 281
  observable, 4
  ordering, 279
  perceiving, 6
  scheduling, 6
  total ordering, 15,17
  trace, 5
Extended Pascal Notation, 234-235

Fairness, 8
Formalism, 95-96
  role of, 95-96
  Mascot, see Mascot formalism

Graceful degradation, 44-46,277

IDA, see Intercommunication Data
  Area
Intercommunication Data Area, 230

Livelock, 184-185
Local Area networks, 265
Local assertion, 74
Local control, 56
Logical clocks, 19
Lower-upper bounds couple, 69

Mascot, 225-235,244-248
  ACP diagram, 229
  activities, 230
  channels, 230
  construction: templates,
    instances, 230
  formalism, 229-232
  interface, module and process
    examples, 244
  Kernel, 232-234
  Kernel in extended Pascal,
    245-248
  pools, 230
  synchronization, 233-234
MICROSS, 285
  application data, 292
  data structure, 295
  event states, 288
  graphics, 300
  graphics aid, 299
  hardware data, 292
  monitor, 291
  reporting subsystem, 296
  routing data, 292
  simulation, 292
  simulation technique, 288
  software system, 289
  topology data, 291
Multiprocessor systems, 225,236
  Mascot, see Mascot
Mutual exclusion, 10,81

Naming, 282
Network, 67,180-182,201
  diagrams, 226
  message-sending, 180
  n-node, 84
  2-node, 75
  truthful, 181-182
Node, 67

Object, 193,257
Operating system Kernel, 251

PALE, see extended Pascal Notation
Parallel programming, 149
Partial correctness, 67,68
Partial ordering, 69
Pascal-m, 163,165-170
  mailboxes, 167,169-174
  module, 169-170
  network protocol, 182-184

processes, 169-170,178-180
receive statement, 167-169
select statement, 167-169
send statement, 167-169
Path Pascal, 191-201
distributed, 191,192,201-209
encapsulated data type, 192,193,
202
language requirements, 192
network naming, 205-208
open Path expressions, 198,210-
211
Path expression invariants,
210-212
Path expressions, 197-199
remote objects, 202
syntax, 220
thread of control, 203
Ports, 254
Priority, 8
Process, 4,35-37,151-152,199-201,
208
co-operating, 35-37
instantiation, 200
interrupt, 200
lifetimes, 200
parameter restriction, 200
remote interruption, 37-39
time, delays and simulation,
200
Producer-consumer, 170-171
Protection, 193
Protocols, 67,70
Proving, of program termination,
157
Proximity relationship, 155

Relational model, 26
classification, 26
data consistency, 24,35
Reliability, 184-185,269,277,281
Remote procedure call, 38,202,
208,238-240
Resource allocation, 8
Response time, 268,276,280
Rollback avoidance, 33-34

Scheduling, 178
message passing, 178
process executions, 178
Serialization model, 24,25
database systems, 25
inadequacy of, 24,25

Shared resources, 192,197,201-202
Smoker's problem, 130
Specification, 93
constructive, 93
mathematical, 93
non-constructive, 93
Z language, 96
Standards, 274
Successive refinement, 191
Synchronization, 3,4,51,54,197
see also Distributed Systems
abstract expression, 9,51,52
circular buffer, 214-216
invariants, 209,210
Mascot, see Mascot synchronization
monitor, 4-5
points of, 4-5
specification, 197,209
verification of constraints,
191,210
Synchronization variables, 10,52
anticipatory updating, 12
approximate representations, 58
counters, 52
delayed updating, 11
distribution, 10
splitting of, 13,57
System dossier, 112,113
Systems of processes, 186
semi-extensible, 186
type extensible, 186

Telephone system, 94,95,96,98,99,
104,105
efficiency of service, 104,105
formally, 96,105
informally, 94,95
primitives, 96-97
system state, 98,99
Time stamp, 19
Token, 18,268
circulation, 18
passing, 268
Total correctness, 68
Truthfulness, 184-185
Type "any", 186-187
Type-security, 169

Virtual ring, 18

Way-station problem, 184